Blood on the Harp

Blood on the Harp

David Winston

BRANDYLANE PUBLISHERS, INC.
White Stone, Virginia

❋ Brandylane Publishers, Inc.

P.O. Box 261, White Stone, Virginia 22578
(804) 435-6900 or 1 800 553-6922; e-mail: brandy@crosslink.net

Cover art by Cynthia Dorman Bell

Library of Congress Cataloging-in-Publication Data

Winston, David, 1954–1990
    Blood on the harp/David Winston.
        p. cm.
    ISBN 1–883911–32–X (pbk.)
    1. Welsh—Ireland—History—To 1500—Fiction. 2. Ireland—
History—1172–1603—Fiction. I. Title.
PS3573.I5333B58   1999
813'.54—dc21   98–49273
                                                      CIP

This book is lovingly dedicated to our family members and especially to David's close friends in this country, in the United Kingdom, and in his beloved Ireland who have encouraged us to have David's manuscript published at last. This work of his, originally titled *Matty Groves,* was a consuming interest of his for several years, and he continually kept his friends apprised of the progress of his writing, rewriting, editing, etc. So much so, in fact, that upon his death one of the concerns expressed by his friends was what would then become of the book. It was their insistence that it must be published which culminated in this printed volume. Each of them can look upon this book with a sense of shared responsibility.

We are deeply indebted to Cynthia Dorman Bell for the cover design for this volume. Long before we had determined upon the course of publishing, she had sketched out her thoughts and presented us with what became the cover theme for the book. When we finally decided to publish, we knew exactly where to find the cover.

Pat and Ted Eggleston
Virginia Beach, Virginia

Prologue

Granada, Moorish Spain
July 1369

It was a clumsy ambush. That was the only thing that saved them. Hassan's men were spread out unevenly along the flat rooftops, armed with crossbows. The short horseman's bow would have been a better choice, faster to shoot, but that took skill and these were just thugs, not skilled archers.

Bran and Montargent were on their way home from the Catalan barracks after a hard night's dicing and wenching. Mostly dicing—the Catalans were particular about their women. Bran was content to watch them dance.

Montargent had invited four or five of the Catalan officers to come back with them—something about a barrel of Spanish wine one of the raiding parties had brought in. Everyone was a little drunk—but not too much—the Sultan didn't like that, and they had to be careful of him.

A crossbow bolt slammed into Montargent as he was lifting the wineskin to his mouth. He flung his arms out—the wineskin smacked into Bran's chest.

The bolts rained down on them, skittering across the cobblestones, chunking into plaster walls. One of the Catalans screamed and fell off his horse. Bran held Montargent against his shoulder as their horses ran side by side. The crossbows clicked and hissed after them.

The street narrowed, twisting sharply to the right. The Catalans were behind him, shouting. Montargent's horse split off at the turn, sliding on the slick cobbles. Bran hauled

3

Montargent across his saddlebow, arms and legs flopping, like a broken puppet. He knew that Montargent was dead.

There was a high arched gateway ahead, part of the city wall. Guards rushed forward to stop them. The Catalans swept them away with their swords. One of the Catalans leapt from his horse and threw down the heavy bar. They ran their horses at the gates, shouldering them open with desperate strength. The horses kicked free of each other, half stumbling into the open road.

A white-bearded Berber caught outside the gates by the night bell stared at them in slack-jawed wonder. He threw up his hands and turned to run. The last Catalan through the gate cut him down as he thundered past—a reflexive stroke, delivered without thinking. The old man floated to the ground.

Montargent started to slip down. Bran grabbed the dead man's belt, shouting at him wordlessly.

The Catalans were pulling ahead, fanned out on the wide road. Bran twisted his head back to look at the city. The sky was bright with moonlight ... the Sultan's palace glowed blood-red on its massive hill overlooking the city. He knew he could never go back.

Arrows rose in a high arc from the gatehouse roof. One of them struck his face. The heavy barbed head glanced from his cheekbone with stunning force, punching him out of the saddle. He hit hard and rolled. His head was full of noise. He tried to shout after the Catalans to come back and save him, but his mouth was clogged with dirt.

Bran jerked to his feet, spitting out curses and broken teeth, blinded, his face slippery with blood. He thought the arrow had taken his right eye. He screamed. An incredible torrent of pain washed over him. It seemed as if the arrow had spiked straight through his skull. Deep inside, a little part of him was cut off from the pain, calmly accepting, but the rest of him could not stop screaming.

Horses. There were horses around him, blowing nervously. He stumbled into a sweaty flank and clung to it, crying like a child. Strong hands gripped him painfully under the armpits and threw him over the back of the horse. He bumped down into the saddle; his feet strained hopelessly for the stirrups. He could not stop screaming.

Someone led the horse into a gallop. Wind ripped through his hair, drying the blood into a mask. Bran hooked his legs tightly under the horse's barrel, clutching the studded pommel until his fingernails split. The hole in his face felt enormous. He did not feel like himself at all, could not remember the man he had been. He could not stop screaming . . .

The First Month

Connacht, Western Ireland
November 1381

Rain poured down the curved brow of his helmet, splashing into his face. He cursed the rain mechanically; he had been cursing the rain for nearly a week. Godrotten place, Ireland.

Bran sneezed violently and wiped his nose on the back of his glove. God, I'm tired, he thought. His armour kept him braced upright in the saddle. But seeing the castle did not cheer him—he was beyond caring. He twisted in the saddle, armour creaking, and looked back on the mud-splattered troop he commanded. Rain slapped into his face.

He saw a score of men hunched over the high pommels of war saddles, profoundly miserable, their armour red with rust. He knew what they were thinking. They hated Arlen for bringing them out in such filthy weather, with little food, less wine—without baggage or servants. Bran didn't blame them. They had nothing to gain, no booty or ransoms—nothing. Lord Arlen had come to take a wife, that was all.

The marriage had been arranged three months before at the horse fair in Galway. The Burkes were in town selling horses, buying wine and spices, and had a marriageable daughter in tow. The landless knights and hedge barons followed her like hounds after a bitch in heat. Arlen saw her, decided it was time he had a wife, and somehow, all was arranged. He had paid the Bishop five marks in silver to waive the banns.

Bran tried to remember what the girl Alysoun looked like and couldn't. She was about half Arlen's age—maybe eighteen—

9

pretty enough, like most of the Norman-Irish wenches. Arlen mooned after her like a lovesick cowherd. Bran thought an alliance with the Burkes of Connacht might well be a good thing, but possibly very dangerous also. He thought that Arlen had acted too impulsively. Arlen had not asked his advice and he had not offered it.

Arlen rode as if in a dream, bareheaded in the pouring rain. He had lost his hat some miles back. His eyes were fixed blankly on the dark shape of the castle before him. Rain streamed from his hair in tiny rivulets. Bran snorted with disgust—Arlen was a fool.

Arnulf rode up to them, expecting orders.

"God's death!" Arnulf shouted; droplets of rain exploded from his mouth. "Another hour of this and I'll grow fins!" He waved his arm at the castle. "Is that really it, d'you think?"

Bran nodded. "I think so—that cur didn't have any reason to lie to us." He frowned. "It had better be."

He was beyond actual hunger, his stomach shrunken into a tight ball, still he knew from experience that it would be a good idea to eat. But fire was what he really craved, a good hot fire to warm his frozen, rain-soaked bones by. Thinking about it, he could almost feel the heat of the fire against his body, drying out the wetrot in his lungs. The thought of the fire kept him going.

"Well," Arnulf said, "what do you want to do about an honour guard?"

Bran shook his head. "Don't bring honour into this." He looked back at the troop. "There's no hope of cleaning them up."

"None," Arnulf agreed.

Bran sighed, leaning back into the cantle of the saddle. Water squelched under his riding leathers. "Who's got the banner?"

Arnulf grinned hugely, showing gapped teeth. "Bowyer. You

know how he revels in ceremony. Besides, he's pretty, the ladies will like that."

Bran laughed harshly. "If they can see him under the mud he's wearing. He's been riding in the back of the line for three days."

"You put him there, Captain," Arnulf said.

"I don't like him."

Arnulf laughed. "He's young, that's all."

"Hunh. Send him up."

Arnulf saluted, chuckling. "Aye, Captain." He wheeled his horse about and cantered through the mud to the end of the troop.

Bran reached over his saddlebow and pulled the slipknot free on the wineskin. His fingers were stiff inside the sodden gloves. He fumbled at the stopper without success. Finally he drew one glove off with his teeth and worked the stopper loose with his bare hand. He saw that his hand was corpse-pale; blue veins showed starkly under the deathly white skin. He cursed Arlen under his breath. It was madness to bring men out in this weather. Why couldn't he wait for spring, or better yet, summer? June was a merry month for weddings.

He held the wineskin close to his lips, kneading the stiff leather until the reluctant remnant of wine trickled out.

"Ahh." He smacked his lips. That was the last—no more until they got inside the castle. *If* they got inside.

Not wanting to take the trouble of refastening it to the saddlebow, he looped the wineskin's leather thong around his swordhilt. The empty skin flapped against his scabbard, forlornly flat.

Arnulf came riding back with Mark Bowyer. Bowyer saluted, wiping the mask of mud from his face. The skin showed through in brilliant white streaks. Bran laughed at him.

Turning to Arnulf he said: "If the banner is in the same condition, they'll think we're gypsies."

Arnulf laughed. He eyed the empty wineskin swinging from Bran's swordhilt. "Will they let us in? I wouldn't."

Bran snorted. "They'd better. I'm in no mood to go back the way we came." He slumped inside his rusted cuirass. God, for a gallon of something to drink and a soft place to fall down in afterward.

"You'd better talk sweetly to those MacSorleys then," Arnulf smirked. "They looked to be the sort who might . . . bear a grudge."

Bran scowled at him. "I didn't hit the poxy bastard that hard."

"Oh, no," said Arnulf. "Not so very hard. With a stool it was, I believe, but not hard. Lightly, in fact. They'll not hold such a trifle against you. Besides, he's probably recovered by now."

Bran flared at him, remembering. "Was I supposed to bear his insolence with Christian charity? I'd brain a dozen of the sheep-stealing bastards and not regret it!"

"I'm sure they'll be delighted to see you again, Captain." Arnulf grinned ruefully. "Probably lying in wait with a dagger for both of us."

A few torches sputtered on the wall above the gate. Bran could see men moving behind the ramparts—MacSorleys. A shiver rippled up into his neck; he shook it off. The MacSorleys were the greatest of the Scots mercenary clans, in service to barons and chieftains all over Ireland. Their ferocity was legendary. With their long coats of mail and two-handed swords, they seemed like warriors from an earlier age. Ghosts from the Norse Valhalla made whole again.

Bran pushed the sopping cloak back from his shoulders and thrust out his chest. He hated Scots. It was natural for a Welshman to hate Scots.

He watched as Bowyer uncased the banner and fixed it to a light lance. The banner was stiff and wrinkled with disuse. In a moment it would be a rain-sodden rag hanging from the end of a spear. Bran curled his lip in disgust. So much for pageantry.

Flanked on either side by Bran and young Bowyer, Arlen rode up to the gate and stopped. The men above the gate shouted down to them.

Arlen looked confused. Bran shouted back to them in Irish, "Open for Lord Arlen!"

The gate guards wore pointed helms with bars curving under their eyes like masks. Bran hated the sight of them. He could barely make out what they were yelling at him. He shut his eyes, shaking with the strain of trying to be strong. The men on the wall wanted proof of who they were.

"Open for Lord Arlen!" Bran shouted again. His throat was so dry it hurt. The men on the wall put their helmets together like ants debating over a piece of bread. One of them leaned over the edge and glared down at them. A huge red beard stuck out from under the chain mail. Bran thought he remembered him from Galway.

"Lord Arlen and five men only!" Redbeard shouted. "Leave the rest of your men outside!"

Bran exploded, "Open the goddamned gate, you whoreson!"

He shook his fist at them, swearing in three languages. So much for diplomacy. He did not like insolent Scots, and he especially did not like sitting his horse in the pelting rain with a castle full of hot food and brimming winecups within easy reach. Nor did he like sleeping, eating, and riding in sucking black mud for five straight days without once seeing the sun.

A wild, holy rage gripped him by the back of the neck and shook him hard. He thrilled with it. Thirst made him reckless.

The gate creaked open. Bran urged the black horse forward, pushing past Arlen. If there was a trap Arlen would only get himself killed. He was in no fit state to fight or even to think for himself. Disgusting, that love should do that to a man.

Bran ducked his head under the glistening stone arch and

rode into the mucky bawn. MacSorleys surrounded him, scowling behind lowered spears.

A boy ran forward to take his horse. Bran extracted his buttocks from the saddle and slid down the horse's flank, splashing ankle deep into a small lake. Cold water trickled through the hole in his boot—he'd meant to have it fixed.

Arlen followed him through. Bowyer was close behind, pitiful banner flopping at the end of his lowered lance. The troopers filed under the stone arch one at a time, nodding helms sunk into their shoulders, half expecting to be killed and not caring very much.

Arnulf yelled at them to dismount, which they did with some difficulty, leaving their horses to the shaggy-headed Irish grooms. Bran frowned. They'd grown as soft as pease porridge. Winter was a bad time for soldiers—he dreaded it. Nothing to do but sit close to the fire, tankard in hand, and listen to the rain on the roof. Bran hated the winter like an old enemy. He took off his gloves and folded them into his belt.

Reeking of wet metal and moldy leather, the men grouped together in front of the knock-away wooden steps to the keep entrance. Bran noticed that most of them had had the foresight to pluck a mace or an axe from their saddle rings. That might be taken unkindly by their hosts, but so far their reception had been less than hospitable.

Bran clanked heavily to the uppermost stair, broader than the rest, and pounded on the ironbound door with his fist.

Hinges creaked ominously; the iron-studded door swung inward.

So much light blinded him at first. There were figures moving in the light—women. Bran struggled to pull himself out of his numbing fatigue. A hand reached out of the wavering brilliance and touched his arm, gently drawing him across the threshold.

"You are welcome, my lord." A goblet was pressed into his

hand. Hot wine splashed over his fingers. He drank deeply, burning his lips, not caring, it was so good. Croaking his thanks, he cradled the warm cup in his palms, rocking slightly on his heels.

"You are weary, sir." A different voice this time. "Come, sit down."

Bran shook his head. "Nay, good lady. My thanks to you."

He realized he was speaking in Irish; he assumed that she had done the same. He knew that if he sat down now, he would not have the strength to get up again. That would not look good. He braced his armoured shoulder against the stone wall. That was better.

The men crowded around him, their rusted gear gritting and pinging together like a tinker mending pots. The light was not so bad now. He tried to focus his eyes—a woman's face swam into his vision. He thought it might be the one who had given him the mulled wine. She wore her red hair coiled over her ears in thick tight braids. He guessed she was at least eighteen, maybe older. She was not Arlen's intended, however; he was sure of that.

"Well met, lady," he said, raising his cup to her.

She smiled. "Lord Arlen?"

Bran laughed. "Nay, lass." He looked about for Arlen, who was standing in front of a drink-laden table opposite the door. Bran pointed him out. "That is Lord Arlen. With the fur on his cloak." And the look of a moon-struck sheep on his face, Bran thought.

"Ah," she said. She had not been at Galway, then. "And who are you?" she asked, looking back at him.

He made a little flourish and almost fell down. "Bran ap Howell, Lord Arlen's captain. And yourself?"

The girl took a flagon from the end of the table and poured more mulled wine into his goblet.

"Emer," she said.

It seemed to Bran that she was pure-bred Irish, but it was

so damnably hard to tell. God, let her be a servant. He did not want to trifle with one of Arlen's new in-laws.

As he stood talking and drinking with the girl, Bran noticed shadows moving behind the murder holes cut into the stone walls and ceiling. It was not difficult to imagine a broken-faced MacSorley with a spanned crossbow taking a bead on his throat. Unlikely though with so many women in the room. He was too tired to be nervous about it.

The girl was looking at him, silent. He realized that she had just spoken and was expecting an answer.

"Mmm. Yes." He nodded his head. "Excellent wine." It wasn't, but that was no matter.

She smiled. "The scar. How did you get it?"

Ah, the scar. He rubbed his fingers over the knotted skin under his right eye. Remembered the white-hot agony and his mindless, gibbering screams. The Catalans had wanted to knock him out, he screamed so much.

The truth didn't make a very good story, so he made up a grand fable about hand-to-hand combat with the Dauphin of France. That was good for another cup of wine. The girl seemed rapt with everything he said, and at one point reached over and took his hand. Bran embellished the tale as he went, adding new twists, half believing it himself.

"It looks like a claw," she said brightly when he'd finished. "A bird's claw."

"Talons," Bran said.

"Talons, then." She moved to refill his cup. "Oh. Will you have ale instead?"

"Gladly."

The mulled wine was making him thirsty. Too much clove. She filled a four-handled mether with foaming ale and gave it to him. He gulped it greedily.

"That's good," he said. Foam clung to his mustache. He blew it at her. The girl laughed.

When they'd drunk up most of the new ale and all of the mulled wine, a serving man brought a small keg of old ale from the cellar and they drank that. All of Bran's men were feeling merry. They didn't give a damn for the gallowglasses lurking behind the murder holes. The porridge-eaters were welcome to come out of their hidey-holes and face true men if they dared.

Bran said something to make the red-haired girl laugh— that seemed easy enough to do—and suddenly they were all laughing, clunking the heavy methers together like weapons, spilling ale over their boots and the women's dresses. Nothing mattered.

It seemed to Bran that his mether had a hole in it—each time he looked it was empty. Arnulf tilted the keg over the edge of the sideboard and tipped it so that the ale spurted up from the bung like a fountain. Bran had his mether there with the rest, jostling young Bowyer aside, all cups competing for the dark jet of ale streaming from the keg. He filled his mether to overflowing and drank off the excess, wiping his mouth on the back of his hand. He looked around and saw Arlen in a corner with his intended, murmuring over her delicate white hand, which she had graciously allowed him to hold.

Suddenly the red-haired girl made a curtsey. Bran caught movement out of the corner of his eye.

"My lord Captain."

He turned his head. A handsome black-haired matron stood close by him.

"You are welcome here, sir."

Except for the fine wrinkles around her eyes and mouth, she could have been Alysoun Burke's twin sister.

"Lady Burke," he said. "Thank you for your fine hospitality. Lord Arlen is a very fortunate man."

"Yes, I think so," she said, smiling. "I'm sure my daughter will make your lord very happy."

She stood up on tiptoes and gave him the kiss of peace. He

returned it hungrily, relishing the opportunity. A fine, handsome woman, he thought. But the daughter . . . well, the daughter meant trouble. He didn't have much to base that on, but he was sure of it, somehow.

Lady Burke enjoyed the kiss. She rewarded him with another of her charming smiles. "Are you hungry, sir?"

"Famished."

"A feast is being prepared for you upstairs. We had word of your coming."

She was pleased with herself for that. So, the little churl they'd pulled from his hut for directions to the castle had outrun them to bring in the news. Bran nodded, impressed.

"My thanks, lady. Good health to you." He raised the heavy mether.

Lady Burke lifted her delicate silver cup in a salute. "*Slainte.* Emer will see to your needs."

A servant, then. Bran was relieved. He half-bowed to Lady Burke as she walked away. If it weren't for the MacSorleys behind the murder holes, he could really enjoy this.

The red-haired girl and several feral-looking grooms led Bran and Arlen through a low stone corridor into the wooden bathhouse built onto the side of the keep. Bran realized that what had seemed to be a passageway was actually the thickness of the wall. Old Norman work.

His scabbard chape clacked against the flagstones as he walked, half stumbled, into the steamy bathhouse. The weight of the armour dragged him down. He had worn it for most of the journey. If the cotter pins had rusted shut . . . He had a sudden vision of the shaggy grooms having to cut him out with snips and chisels. Bran laughed.

"My lord?" said the red-haired girl, anxious to please.

"Nothing." He waved his hand. "Got to get out of this harness."

One of the grooms bent down and started to work the straps

loose on his leg armour. Bran lifted his leaden arms as high as he could, and the other two grooms unfastened the buckles and pins holding the breast and back plates together. They lifted the hinged plates over his head and set them carefully on a wooden bench along the wall.

"I want that cleaned," Bran said, swaying with the sudden lightness. The other groom was still struggling with the straps on his leg armour. Bran pushed him away and bent over to do it himself.

He browned out completely, pitching headfirst into the wall. The bench broke his fall. He slumped over it, ears ringing. The red-haired girl shook his shoulder.

"I'm all right," he said, feeling sick.

Someone picked him up and moved him so that he was sitting on the bench, back braced against the wall. It was Arlen.

"You're bleeding," Arlen said. He had taken off his riding robe, but he was still wearing the mail shirt. It was well oiled and had not rusted much.

Bran put his hand to his forehead and felt the bump there. His fingers came away bloody. He could not remember hitting the wall.

"Sweet Jesus," Bran muttered.

Arlen straightened Bran's legs—as if laying out a corpse, Bran thought—and removed the rusted poleyns and greaves as nimbly as a squire.

"God you stink!" Arlen exclaimed, wrinkling his nose in disgust.

The rotting leather arming-doublet and breeks were foul with mildew. The violent stench clogged Bran's nostrils.

"Well and truly spoken, my good lord," he said, trying to rise.

"Stay there," Arlen said, grinning.

"As you command, my lord."

Arlen laughed at him. "Impudent man!"

He's merry enough now, Bran thought. God keep him that way.

When they had stripped him of his ruined leathers, peeled away like leprous skin, Bran was made to sit in a scalding tub of water while buckets of equally hot water were poured over his head. He was too weak to protest.

In the next tub—a bronze-banded masterpiece of the cooper's art—Lord Arlen was being treated in a similar fashion. A glum-faced lackey, his fat jowls running with sweat, dutifully scrubbed Arlen's back with a long-handled brush.

Bran relaxed his head against the side of the tub, letting his arms float out in front of him. He had not had a bath like this since Granada. Water lapped against his mustache.

The red-haired girl sat on the edge of the tub watching him. He bubbled air through his lips like a playful child. The girl laughed. He spat a little jet of water at her. She jumped up, shrieking delightedly.

"You're a pretty thing," Bran said. What was her name? The edges of the bath water were rimed with gray scum. It felt good to be clean again. The girl leaned over and scrubbed his chest with a rough cloth.

"Mmm," Bran murmured. "That's good."

After the bath, he and Arlen put on fresh clothes provided by the Burkes. All the gear in their saddlebags was soaked, they were told. Bran pulled on a loose blue tunic with red and green interlace stitched around the collar and sleeves. It was better than anything he owned.

For a moment he was angry. Arlen owed him four months' back wages, and here he was getting married, playing the great lord. They'd trailed a packhorse behind them the whole way, bearing gifts for the bride's family.

He slipped his feet into the soft leather shoes the Burkes had given him. God, but bathing was thirsty work! He took the cup the girl held out. It was Spanish wine, from Rioja in the north. The wine was nearly always good, not like the cat's piss shipped over from Calais. He drained the cup.

"Careful, my lord," clucked the red-haired girl. "Leave room for the fine feast you'll be getting."

"Bugger the feast," Bran said. "Get more wine, I'm thirsty."

Alysoun was only just beginning to realize how desperately unhappy she was. She sat at the high table with her hand trapped inside Arlen's tight grip. Arlen's palm was sweaty. Alysoun managed to slip her fingers free and pointed him toward a fresh flagon, discreetly wiping her hand in the folds of her gown as he turned away. Already she was beginning to loathe him. It was not so bad in Galway with the excitement of the town and the young men around her, eager to please. But now it was more serious, he was really going to marry her. In Galway she'd barely noticed him—a face in the crowd, a polite introduction. One of the many worshipers. Now he was to be her husband.

The hall was filling up with her relatives. Most of them were drunk and their laughter echoed off the vaulted ceiling. She drank her wine too quickly and choked, sputtering fine droplets over the front of her gown. Arlen turned back to her and presented a sickening smile. Alysoun returned the smile, wanting to dagger him under the table . . . then slip out while he slumped slowly, slowly to the cloth. . . and ride with Matty on her father's fastest horses—to the coast—to freedom. To anywhere.

An imperfect plan, she realized, grinning a little at her foolishness. It would not be so bad living with Arlen. *Lord* Arlen, at least. She would have her own castle and servants. And he would take her to England—she would make damn sure of that. To court, even. Arlen had many important friends from his years in France. The Black Prince had been his friend too, but he was dead. Still . . .

So many things to do, so many plans to make. It was not so bad, really. Her mother had organized a very lovely trousseau for her, and her father had given her a lot of furniture and other useful things . . . She felt tears coming on and clenched her eyes shut, trying to hold them back. They spilled over onto her cheeks. Arlen's face blurred. He was looking at her.

"Are you happy?" he asked gently.

She smiled and reached shakily for the winecup he'd filled. "Yes. Very happy, my good lord."

Bran was drunk before the feast started, but that didn't bother him. He wasn't hungry anyway. He rested his elbows on the table and leaned over the silver winecup cradled in his hands. Italian. Probably from a church—it had that look about it. Booty from the wars travelled far and wide, even to Ireland. He'd stuffed many a cup like this into his haversack in France and Burgundy. Sometimes—very rarely—the cups were made of gold. They had mashed the gold vessels with hammers and used the broken pieces to gamble with. He sipped daintily at the wine, pretending that it was a gold cup.

The hall took up the third and fourth stories of the keep. Soot-encrusted banners hovered over him like old ghosts, stirring in the draft. There was a man-high fireplace at each end of the hall piled high with blazing sea-coals. The heat was intense. Sweat trickled down his face, dropping in little pats on the linen tablecloth. The cut in his forehead was still bleeding. He dabbed at it with the large napkin he'd been provided with.

Arlen was up at the high table of course. There were a lot of Burkes and MacWilliams in for the wedding, so Bran didn't rate a place there. He was seated across from the MacSorley commander, the redbeard who'd shouted at him from the wall. When introduced they had shaken hands, but after that did their best to ignore each other.

Bran's men were down at the far end of the table. They hadn't taken baths yet, and sat stinking in their riding leathers. No one sat near them. Most of them were drunk, a few already slumped over their trenchers, snoring soundly. The MacSorleys who were not on duty sat at a table across the way, staring daggers at them. None of the MacSorleys were drunk. Bran knew that sooner or later there would be a fight—there was no getting around it. He hoped the weather would improve. There was nothing worse than a bad-tempered group of fighting men cooped up in a castle together because of bad weather. He still hadn't seen the man he'd clobbered in Galway. They were probably keeping him out of sight.

Lord Burke was dressed as an Irish chieftain—a dazzle of bright colours and decorated leather. His heavy black beard spread over his chest like a stained-glass prophet's. Under the flaring brows, Burke's eyes—Norman eyes—were cunning and hard. Bran thought that he would make a formidable father-in-law.

Lord Burke had given him the silver cup. That was well done. Bran ran his thumb along the edge, revelling in the fine workmanship, automatically computing its value. The Italians made good armour too—light, good for raiding, not like the German stuff you could get a heart attack just walking around in.

The finest helm he had ever owned had been an Italian bascinet. God help you if anything solid hit squarely, but it was a pretty thing, and more than adequate for his purpose at the time, which was to ride around and look formidable on behalf of the Sultan's tax collectors.

He'd left the Italian bascinet behind in his house in the Albaicin, along with the slave girls, his houseboy, and the little crocks of gold buried in the garden walls—the fortune he'd set out to make. He fingered the talon-shaped scar on his face. Everything left behind; his whole life gone. I should have died there, he thought, remembering . . .

"Sir Bran?"

He started out of his reverie, spilling wine on the tablecloth. The red-haired girl was beside him offering a plate of stewed meat. Bran fingered a few chunks into his mouth. He needed something solid to keep the wine from roiling in his belly.

"You look troubled, my lord," she said.

"Ah, no," Bran said. "Never as troubled as I look."

She smiled. "That's well, then." She filled his cup from the swan-necked flagon.

He decided that he would make an effort to be cordial.

"Your lord has a fine hall," he lied. "I've only seen one better in Ireland—the King's hall in Dublin castle."

"You've been to Dublin, then?" She asked this as if he'd said Byzantium or Cathay. A servant. This would be easy.

"Oh, aye," he said. "I'm a well-travelled man."

"Where do you come from?" she asked. "You're not English, are you?"

Bran smiled into his cup. "Not English at all. I'm from Wales—"

"Holy Mother!" she exclaimed, her eyes brightening. "Matty Groves comes from Wales!"

Bran laughed, taken off guard. "And who is this Matty Groves?" Welshmen were not rare in Ireland, but he could not help but be interested.

"Matty Groves is Lord Burke's harper. He plays for us every night." She shook her head, looking at him. "You've heard of him surely?"

"Never," Bran told her, relishing his role. "I've never heard of Matty Groves." If he had, he couldn't remember. "He's a minstrel, you say?"

"Not at all," she said emphatically. "He's a great man. He plays before princes. A fine man altogether."

Bran sucked the remaining wine from his cup. "He'll play for us tonight? I'd like to meet him."

"A fine man," the girl repeated. "A fine man altogether."

Two kitchen-jacks staggered past, carrying a gigantic roasted boar on a platter. Bran's mouth watered; suddenly he was very hungry. Roast boar was his favorite. He wished that he had a squire to go and cut a choice piece off the boar for him.

The kitchen-jacks held the boar up in front of Lords Burke and Arlen for their admiration. Arlen's mouth moved; he was saying something complimentary to his host.

Bran could not hear what he was saying because of the noise. He finished his wine and held out his cup for more.

"There he is," said the red-haired girl.

Bran turned to look at her. "Who?"

"Matty Groves." She breathed his name as if he were the greatest man on earth.

Bran scowled into his empty cup. He slammed it down, scanning the confusion of scurrying servants and boisterous guests for sight of this Matty Groves.

The harper took up a position on the cushioned stool set in front of the high table. He was small and lightly built, with a close-cropped beard and curly yellow hair. Bran was surprised. Most Welshmen had dark hair. A touch of the Dane in him, then. Or Norman.

The little man slid the soft leather case from his instrument and rested the harp against his shoulder. It was the small kind used by travellers, richly ornamented with interlacing dragons and bright enamels. He took a T-shaped key from around his neck and began to tune the harp. The hall fell silent

25

immediately; the revellers leaned forward against the tables, straining to hear.

Bran helped himself to the wine in the swan-necked flagon. His bad eye was getting cloudy. He had to squint through his left to see the harper clearly. The little bastard was wearing a fortune on his back—a gold-buttoned tunic of red Burgundian velvet, the finest red and yellow parti-coloured hose, boots of Spanish leather. Ah well, but can he play? Bran propped a leg up onto the bench and tried to look bored.

The harper's long knobby fingers trilled over the strings, making sudden gentle music in the dead quiet of the hall, like running water in a shallow stream.

Bran relaxed, hanging over the winecup, hypnotized by the rhythmic interweaving of the harper's hands over the strings. The subtle music seeped into his fatigue-numbed brain . . . balm poured into an open wound. He lifted the silver cup slowly to his lips. So much wine, so little time . . . he could not remember the Latin for it.

He felt the girl's cool fingers touching his hand. That's better, he thought. He was starting to feel very good. He deserved to feel good, he'd been through a lot. The girl's impossibly light fingertips played with the hairs on the back of his hand. Bran purred. He nuzzled her neck, the fine hair tickling his nose. She smelled good. He would hammer enough sperm into her to fill a jug. He closed his fingers over her hand, trapping it.

The music changed. The harper's playing became more furious, the dramatic bell-like chords filled the hall with sound. Bran dropped his casual leg off the bench and sat up, straightening his shoulders. The girl's hand slipped through his fingers.

Matty Groves began to sing. Songs of a dead king . . . of fateful lovers . . . of good men drowned at sea. All of the songs were sad. Tears fell from the harper's eyes. Everyone in the hall was crying. Bran touched the wetness of his own cheek. The man was a devil, he decided.

The music changed again. Matty Groves rocked joyfully over his harp, plucking strong, exuberant, wildly happy notes from its blurring strings. A MacSorley gallowglass leapt onto a table and began to jig, kicking over flagons and bowls. There was wild hand clapping and cheering from the Burke relations. Even Arlen was clapping his hands, looking like a delighted schoolboy. Lady Alysoun sat beside him, nostrils flaring, watching Matty Groves as a cat eyes a bowl of milk.

Bran did not care for those eyes at all. If she and Matty Groves had not yet played the two-backed beast—well, it was only a matter of time, given the opportunity.

He was comforted by the fact that in a few more days there wouldn't be any opportunities. Arlen was anxious to get back to his business. Ballinasloe was a new fief, only about ten years old, and the Irish churls there were not used to working for Normans. They would take some watching. Arlen's steward, Sad Hugh, was dour and stiff-necked, but soft. Arlen's affairs could not go long unattended.

Three days was not a long time, Bran told himself. He would have a word with the harper and that would be that. He poured himself another drink. There was a hard core of worry still inside him, unblurred by the wine. He would do what he could, he owed Arlen that much. No—he owed himself. Arlen would rise, and Bran ap Howell would rise with him. Arlen's interests were his interests. Damn those eyes of hers . . .

The music took hold of him again. He surrendered to it a little, laughing and shouting with the rest, pounding his dagger hilt on the table. During the wildest of the glad songs the harper laughed out loud, and everyone laughed with him, until it seemed that the world was a merry place and plagues and famines and ruinous wars were things in a dream.

Bran took the girl's hand and pressed it to his lips. She

smiled a little smile, pleased at the gesture. Like a lord to his lady. He knew she'd like that. I'll lord you, he thought. I'll swive you till your teeth rattle. The girl turned her face away, pretending shyness. Such a young girl.

Something inside him made him wince. I was never young, he told himself. Liar. Liar. He did not care to remember. Young men were so foolish. It pained him to think that he had once been so foolish.

The girl looked so trusting, so eager, as if he were some jongleur's fable of a knight who would bear her away on his white horse into a world full of adventures—away from the sewing room and the chirping gossip, the thousand little pettinesses that made up her life . . .

Matty Groves laid his hands flat on the strings and the music stopped. He stood up and bowed to the high table, the harp tucked under his arm. Everyone cheered. Arlen made a great show of handing him a purse filled with silver. About three marks' worth, Bran calculated sourly.

Lord Burke offered the harper a drink from his own cup and made a place for him at the table. Not much chance of getting to him now . . . Still, he had to piss like everyone else. Bran could wait.

A server set down a bowl of mushrooms beside him. The red-haired girl picked one out and fed it to him. It was fresh. They must grow them in the dungeon. He wondered if the Burkes had any prisoners in their dungeons. Could they hear the feasting and music going on above them? His mind was filled with such idle speculations. When had it started to do that? He could not remember thinking this way when he was young. He could not remember thinking at all.

He speared a mushroom with the point of his dagger and plopped it into his mouth. The stewed meat was cold; he'd forgotten to eat while the harper was playing. Matty Groves. That didn't sound like a Welsh name. Probably Madoc, originally. Ah well, he'd find that out too, and a lot of other things besides.

The piper was playing again, whistling and wheezing for all he was worth. The reedy music grated on Bran's ears after the smooth mellow tunes of Matty Groves' harp. Bran stood up and filled his cup from the swan-necked flagon. The flagon was heavy and hard to control. He spilled some wine on the tablecloth. The girl smiled at him. Bran laughed, tilting the cup up until wine ran down his chin. It was good wine. His ears were numb. A steaming joint of roast boar had appeared magically by his side. He picked it up, hot grease burning his fingers, and saluted the MacSorley commander across the room. Redbeard nodded gravely and lifted his goblet. Bran laughed at him. Silly sod. Honour among fighting men and all that. The Scots captain coughed and looked away. A pleasant tension gripped the back of Bran's neck. I could eat you all for dinner, Bran thought. He grinned at the red-haired girl. He felt very powerful. Thank God for good wine.

The harper got up and left the hall. Bran set down his cup and eased out from between the bench and table. He mumbled something to the red-haired girl. She smiled and nodded.

Bran followed the harper through a low door and down a narrow, winding stairwell. Rush lamps gave off a dim, red glow. Bran's legs were wobbly. He clung to the cold stones, going down one step at a time.

The sword scabbard caught between his legs, half tripping him. He pressed his hand hard over his face, trying to shake off the drunkenness. The stone steps were badly worn, set there by the Devil to kill drunken men. His heart pounded with the exertion of trying not to be drunk. He heard the harper's soft boots padding below, just out of sight.

Well, at least he's taking his sweet time, Bran thought. Doesn't have it running down his leg or anything. The pipe music from the hall grew fainter, like ghost music from the fairy mounds.

The steps widened into a little landing. A garderobe was cut into the wall, dark and full of smells. Bran stepped inside.

Matty Groves was unlacing his hose, preparing to piss. Bran stood next to him over the squarish hole and fumbled the laces loose on his new trews.

The harper turned his head slightly. "Well met," he said politely.

"Well met yourself," Bran grunted, letting go. It burned a little. Their two bright streams of piss wavered and hissed together the length of the long chute.

"Ahhh," Matty groaned. "That's good." He shook off the last drops and deftly relaced his hose. "Do my ears deceive me, or are you a Gwynedd man?"

"Your ears serve you well enough," Bran said, making the best of his own unfamiliar lacing. "Would that your eyes would serve you better."

"What do you mean?" the harper asked suspiciously, stepping prudently out of dagger range.

Bran laughed harshly. "I mean that any fool can see that Lady Alysoun and Lord Arlen are to be wed."

The harper stood in the shadows, holding his hands carefully away from his sides. "I know that," he said quietly. "Everyone knows that. I don't understand what you're saying."

"You understand well enough," Bran said in Welsh. "Look you, Minstrel, and look well. You cannot afford the kind of trouble that lady is prepared to give you. Being dead will afford you no great pleasure, I think. No wench is worth eating that much dirt over."

The harper moved back as if he'd been struck.

"You're mad," he said stiffly through clenched teeth. "Go out and howl at the moon."

Possibilities clicked quickly through Bran's mind. Draw and straight thrust through the heart . . . Or, a boot to the ballocks followed by smashing his sword pommel into the harper's face. The first fatal, the second nearly so. The harper had only a small court dagger to defend himself with. He didn't look like much of a fighter.

Suddenly Bran remembered the MacSorley he'd nearly killed in Galway. Another incident would not be politic. Arlen would be very angry. Bran backed through the doorway, dropping his hand away from his swordhilt.

"Take your life back, Minstrel," he said. "I'm a guest here. I won't shed blood my first night under this roof."

Matty Groves smiled grimly from the shadows. "Very noble of you."

"Keep away from my lord's lady," Bran told him.

Bran turned and went back up the steps. He was not so drunk now, trembling a little, his blood quickened by the prospect of a fight. His teeth were on edge. He wanted to kill something—a MacSorley, young Bowyer—it didn't matter. His chest made little wheezing noises. He was breathing too hard. Sweat rolled down his face like rain.

The girl welcomed him back with a freshly poured cup of wine. She offered it to him with both hands. He felt like a king. The wine was different—a cool white Rhenish. He held the wine in the back of his mouth, enjoying the bittersweet prickle of it on his tongue.

Bran looked into the grinning, distorted image of his face reflected from the inside of the empty cup. The face did not seem to belong to him; the eyes wild and staring—a madman's eyes.

"Perhaps I will go howl at the moon," he said.

"My lord?" The red-haired girl poured Rhenish into his cup from a stone bottle. She smiled uncertainly.

"Nothing, sweet lady." Bran patted her hand. "The ravings of a madman."

She laughed. "My lord! Certainly not that."

"Oh, indeed," he said. "Mad for the pleasure of your sweet company. I've been out of it far too long—I resolve never to piss again, as long as I may live—"

"My lord!" she squealed, covering her mouth. Her cheeks coloured as if suddenly slapped.

"Well . . . perhaps not so long as that."

Bran picked up a barrel-shriveled apple from the tray and bit into it suggestively, holding the girl's eyes. She looked away, lashes fluttering, nostrils flaring. Oh, aye, pretty maid, he thought. You know what is in my mind and what is expected of you. God love Lady Burke, and God love her lord for this good wine.

Bran ate the apple down to the core and spat the seeds onto the floor. Sweet Jesus, I feel good.

He put his arm around her shoulders and pulled her close, biting her lightly on the neck.

"I'm weary," he said, stroking her rounded belly through the smock. "Show me where I'm to sleep."

The skirmish with the red-haired girl was rough, awkward, and quickly over. He had a fleeting after-image of white thighs spread wide over his hips and the girl's jerks and smothered cries as he swived her. In his impatience and wine-numbness he'd hurt her, then fallen asleep, crushing her under his spent body, his face pressed against her soft neck.

He dreamed about Granada. He was walking through the Silk Market, past the bright crowded stalls of the merchants, protected from the hot sun by awnings stretched from rooftop to rooftop over the narrow alleyways. Jostled by whores and slaves, Syrian emirs, Jewish scholars, a few black-skinned horse traders from the Sudan, infidels like himself. One of the

Catalans waved to him from a wine shop. Bran bought a basket of pomegranates and a paper twist of fine white almonds.

Montargent was there at the gate of the carmen, welcoming him with an icy silver cup of wine from a stone jar packed with mountain snow. In the patio of the carmen they would sit for hours drinking wine with the other *renegados,* snapping almonds between their proud, strong teeth while they watched the evening sun turn the fortress stones blood-red as the sun sank slowly behind the Sierras.

The fair-skinned Spanish women they'd bought or stolen moved silently among them, birdlike, filling winecups, playing strange, sensual music with flutes and *guitaras,* lulling them into a trance . . . Peace and delight without end.

The little crocks of Moorish gold—buried under bushes in the garden, plastered into walls—were like all-encompassing plates of proof, unbreachable armour against the worst the world had to offer. Bran felt so lazy, so wonderfully secure. It was true that he was a renegade, probably excommunicate. But the Saracens paid well—on time and in gold—and he could not imagine that it would ever end.

When he woke the girl was gone. His head hurt so much that he could not see straight. It was hard to decide which was worse, the pain in his head or the sorrow of losing the dream.

The light coming through the arrow slits in the wall was mercifully dim, a lighter gray than the stones. It was early yet. The pain had waked him. His lips were cracked and rimed with dried wine. The need to move his bowels fought a vicious but undetermined battle with his heartfelt desire to vomit. He lay with his head lolling over the low frame of the bed, retching weakly. Eventually he gathered enough strength to crawl on his knees a little way across the cold stone floor and dropped his head into a bucket of icy water, left there no doubt for the convenience of guests.

The spike-like pain in his temples numbed gradually into a general miserableness. He arose from the depths, water streaming from his hair. Stumbling over the blanketed, snoring demons he recognized vaguely as his men, Bran lurched toward the mild comfort of a dying hearth-fire. He slumped carelessly onto the stone bench built inside the fireplace, cracking his head against the mantel. He vowed as he had vowed a thousand times before—never to drink wine again. Even as he spewed his guts out into the sizzling white ash, he knew he would be forsworn by noon.

With the kind help of a pot-boy and a sleepy serving maid, he put on the clothes he'd left scattered by his bed and sat back while they did up the laces on his new boots. The pot-boy offered him a dram of aqua-vitae, watching him furtively as if he were some half-tamed, meat-eating beast. The boy's legs were slightly bent—ready to spring out of range if Bran should strike.

Bran drank the whiskey down in a shuddering gulp. After a few moments he found he could hold his razor steady enough to shave, although it was the last thing he wanted to do. Summoning his courage—a hung-over man hasn't much—he peered into the little ivory-framed lady's mirror he'd gotten at the sack of Harfleur . . . Saw a face that was older than he remembered, with a sharply creased forehead, sunken cheeks, a limp mustache drooping nearly to the edge of his jawbone. His hair, once as black as a raven's wing, was now dull and streaked with gray. And yet five or six years ago he'd had some thin claim to being young.

The wind blew up again, sending a spray of rain through the open arrow slits. The soft yellow flames of the oil lamps fluttered in their sconces. It was a gray, bleak, miserable day and he wanted no part of it. The serving maid nervously held out a steaming bowl of water, probably the only hot water in the castle at that moment. The anxious pot-boy stood by with a long towel, ready to bolt if Bran's humour got any blacker.

Bran dashed some of the scalding water onto his face and scraped gingerly at five days' growth. The girl held the mirror as steady as she could, and Bran held the razor as steady as he could, but between them they managed to inflict a nasty cut just under his chin. Bran roared, the girl screamed—but didn't drop the mirror, it was worth her life to do that—and the pot-boy bolted, kicking over the bowl of water. Bran snatched the mirror away from the terrified girl, dismissed her with a scowl, and determined to shave later when his planets might be more favorably conjoined. A fat drop of blood fell onto the front of his new tunic. Bran sought out the wooden bottle of aqua-vitae the pot-boy had left and sat down again with his boots in the fireplace.

The pain in his head was overwhelming. Bran hunched over his knees, massaging his temples, restraining an urge to whimper.

The men snored more loudly than before, mumbling nonsense in several languages. Bran rocked back and forth, moaning softly. He wasn't aware of the harper's approach until he felt the daggerpoint prick his neck.

"Good morrow, gallowglass," said Matty Groves.

Bran spat into the ashes. "Kill me and be done, you pox-ridden bastard."

"Such a sweet reply," the harper said. He sheathed his dagger and hunkered down beside Bran, well in range of the mercenary's crushing fist. "Bacchus's gentle disciple." The harper laughed musically, pleased with his joke.

Bran stared hard into the ashes.

"Devil's whoreson," he said flatly. "I'm in no mood for your pandering insults."

The harper shifted on his hams, squatting like a toad. He stole a drink from the wooden bottle. Bran ignored him.

"Ahh. The good stuff." Matty wiped his mouth on the back of his hand. "You're the saint's own jest-wit on Sunday morning," he said. "How come you by your wry tongue and artful gesture?"

"Travel and the conversation of harpers have made me what I am," Bran said. "Is it really Sunday?"

"Aye, Sir Gallowglass. And soon all good knights will be on their pious knees in Burke's chapel, praying forgiveness for their wicked deeds."

"That won't be necessary," Bran said. "My heart is as pure as yours, Sir Minstrel . . . singer of priestly rimes, bard of Bible lore."

Matty laughed. "Aye, sir, you speak sooth. My knowledge of the Holy Writ nearly rivals your own." The harper took a long pull on the bottle, tilting it up like a trumpet, his throat working mightily.

"And the practice too?" Bran took the bottle from him and shook it.

"And the practice too," Matty agreed.

Bran held the bottle to his chest, trying to keep back a rasping chuckle.

"You've drunk all my fucking whiskey," he said.

Two hours later Bran was clean-shaven and sober upon his aching knees on the cold stone floor of the chapel. The quality folk had embroidered prie-dieus to pad their more fortunate knees.

Matty had one, and he perched upon it like a lustful cherub, with the future Lady Arlen fixed firmly in the corner of his eye. The way they traded ardent glances back and forth across Arlen's shoulder made Bran blush.

The hawk-nosed French priest enjoined the congregation not to fornicate or take strong drink or otherwise enjoy themselves.

Bran's attention wandered to the rather dingy stained-glass windows. The scenes in the windows showed Christ scourged, Simon flayed, Sebastian shot full of bolts, John the Baptist beheaded, and other right edifying examples of true justice. He did not appreciate having his knees mortified into frozen lumps of callus on their behalf. He had never cared much for saints, except when their particular Days gave rise to riotous excess and debaucheries, fueled by the lordly distribution of free wine and ale.

Then at last the choirboys were led in a song—the impudent pot-boy among them, amazingly—and they had the Mass. The thin brittle wafer on his tongue chased by a teasing taste of the Communion wine. Not bad, he thought. A little sweet.

The choirboys—all apparently recruited from the kitchen and stables—scratched their arses and bumped restlessly against one another, looking for the bad-tempered priest's next command. When it came—a slow solemn peck of his vulture's beak—they blasted into song, a little hoarsely, but well enough for a backwater chapel and dunghill aristocrats.

After the service Bran hustled his men into a common room just off of the kitchen, where Arnulf could keep an eye on them. He didn't want any trouble now that it was nearly done with. After seeing them settled with a cask of ale, he went out to the stable and looked over his horse.

The black horse did not seem particularly interested to see him. Bran gave him one of the shriveled apples. The horse chomped it mechanically, slobbering over Bran's hand. Bran wiped his hand on the hem of his tunic and sat on a bale of hay near the stall.

Two of the young stable boys approached cautiously. Bran gave them each a penny to look after his horse. It was always a good policy to bribe stable boys. They took a greater interest in the horses than the older grooms and would sometimes report to the owner if his horse was being neglected or ill treated. Bran spoke with them in Irish for a while and left.

When it was time for the main meal of the day, Bran looked around for the red-haired girl. No one had seen her. He got drunk with Arnulf and listened to Matty Groves play the harp. Matty had written a special song in honour of Lord Arlen. Bran recognized it as a standard Welsh piece with the words reworked a little. He laughed loudly. Arnulf looked at him as if he were mad, grinning uncertainly. Bran did not tell him why he was laughing.

Arlen looked happy enough to shit a goose. He gave Bran a bone-handled flesh-hook and half of the back pay he owed him. Bran accepted the fist-sized sack of coins with considerably more grace than he felt, and made a low bow to the soon-to-be Lady Arlen. She smiled absently but would not meet his eyes.

She knows I know, he thought. He went back to his place and started a fresh flagon with Arnulf. The MacSorley commander stood by, watching him. Bran felt expansive.

"Join us, won't you? You look like a drinking man."

Redbeard moved in closer and hung over Bran's shoulder.

"I willna drink with you," he said in a thick Scots burr.

An alarum bell rang in Bran's head. He forced himself to smile. It was a great disadvantage to be sitting like this with his sword wedged the wrong way under the table.

"Why not?" Bran asked. He knew that Arnulf's dagger was already out and ready, hidden between his thigh and the bench.

Redbeard's face was hard. "Because you killed one of my men," he said simply.

"Ah," Bran said. "Well."

"I wanted you to know that," Redbeard said. Bran did not think he was going to draw on him.

"Thank you," Bran told him. "I'm sorry you won't drink

with me." He winked at Arnulf. Arnulf grinned back at him.

The MacSorley commander walked away. When he had left the hall, Bran poured more wine for himself and Arnulf.

"He doesn't like you," Arnulf said.

As his heartbeat returned to normal, Bran pretended that it was a great joke. "No, he didna," he said, imitating the Scot's broad accent. Arnulf laughed too loudly. They were both very relieved.

Bran went to bed drunk and alone. He did not dream. In the morning he was in better shape than he expected. He lay in the bed listening to the snoring of his men. He knew the different sounds that each of them made. Arnulf whistled as he snored. The Gascons grunted like pigs—Armand was the worst of them. Young Bowyer did not snore at all, but sometimes he would mumble to himself in English. Bran did not know enough English to understand what he said.

At precise intervals a racking, wet cough would fill the room. The Old German had caught a cold. Johann. The men never called him by his name. They always called him the Old German. He was the only German in Bran's company. Bran thought that the Old German must be lonely. It was a hard thing not to have someone to talk to in your own tongue.

Little boys with white linen smocks over their tunics carried wrist-thick candles before them into the chapel. The dull drizzling day outside failed to light up the stained-glass windows. They looked gray and colourless, like the shadowy walls of the chapel itself. Alysoun shivered. She had never liked this place, never liked coming here.

The candles the boys were holding flickered in the draft, making the shadows dance. Alysoun's hands were clammy. Her feet, in the too-thin kidskin shoes, were like two lumps of ice. She was frightened and hungry and sick at heart. She could hardly believe that she would walk out of this chapel with Arlen and be his wife. For the rest of her life. Her mother smiled at her and she smiled back, forcing the stiff muscles of her face to do their work. This was the way of it. Her mother had not married for love, and she could not hope to either. And in truth, she had never expected otherwise. Except ... Except Matty changed everything. But he had no lands, no retainers, not even a house to call his own. He was well respected and known throughout the Christian world for his beautiful music and magical voice—but it was not enough. If only she did not love him. He always had as much money as he could spend, but never enough to be truly rich. Land meant nothing to him. He was content to roam the world. That was romantic and exciting for a man, but she needed more. Much more.

She looked around for him. The hawk-nosed priest seemed to scowl at her. She had never liked him. He was French, and that was his only saving grace. So she had learned good French from him, but little else.

Suddenly Matty's face stood out from the blurred crowd standing behind the rail. She held the image of it tight in her mind and turned away to look at nothing. She felt the hard eyes of the priest upon her.

The Mass was said. She barely listened, mumbling the responses when required, amazed that she could actually remember what she was supposed to say. The priest led them through it in a droning monotone, saying horrible things about the sanctity of marriage and alluding to the repulsive but necessary act of procreation. Her face twisted for a moment, imagining Arlen on top of her in the bridal bed, grunting and moaning.

They exchanged rings. Arlen slid the cold band onto her finger, smiling shyly. He was almost afraid of her, she thought. Good, she could use that, if she was careful. The priest tied their hands together with a long embroidered cloth, and they turned to face the chilled, hungry throng of relatives, servants, and mercenaries jammed shoulder to shoulder.

Then it was over. The little boys sang sweetly, holding their heavy candles with strained looks on their less than angelic faces. Most of the candles had blown out with the draft.

Arlen led her from the chapel, followed by the singing boys. A path cleared for them almost magically, people backing away earnestly as if the married couple were holy saints—or plague-struck. Alysoun spied the Welsh captain out of the corner of her eye. He stared at her. His eyes were like stones. Why did he hate her so? She swallowed dryly. His eyes made her afraid. He was as old as Arlen, but much harder. The scars on his face made him look crueler than he probably was. Still, she would be very careful of this one. Sometimes she felt that he knew what she was thinking. But that was just nerves. When she was settled into Arlen's castle, there would be plenty of time to sort him out. After all, she was Arlen's wife, and Arlen paid his wages.

The sounds of the feast hall merged into a steady roar in her ears. Some great beast snarling and roaring its displeasure. Alysoun wished that they would all go away—except then she would be alone with Arlen in his lawful bed. That did not bear thinking about. She would have to pretend to be a virgin, of course. That might not be too difficult if he was drunk enough. She signaled one of the pages and had Arlen's cup refilled. Arlen was talking to her father about money. A drop of hot wax fell from the chain-slung chandelier above and stung the back of her hand. She was too miserable to care. The page leaned over and filled her winecup from his swan-necked flagon. Alysoun rewarded him with a slight smile—she knew that he was in love with her. The silver rim of the cup was cold against her lips. She tipped it up until the wine touched her tongue. Arlen was still talking to her father. No doubt he would pay closer attention to her later . . .

There he was again—staring at her! The sour-faced Welsh captain with his stony eyes. Sweet Mary, but the cold bastard made her nervous! She forced herself to stare back and smile, except the smile wouldn't come. The force of his basilisk gaze made her look away quickly. Where was Matty? Probably teasing the serving maids on their way to and from the kitchen. He would come in soon to play. Then she could drink in the sight of him as much as she liked, without fear of being noticed.

Alysoun finished the wine in her cup. It was thin stuff, almost tasteless. She realized that it had been watered. That would never do.

"Dickon!" she snapped at the page. "Bring my lord some of our best wine."

His face coloured instantly. "B-but, my l-lady," he stammered, "this is the . . . "

"Then stop watering it, you little fool," she told him.

He gaped at her, then nodded and backed away to the sideboard where the good wine was kept. She knew that her father had ordered it watered down, either for economy's sake or to save his little girl from the drunken ravages of her new-made husband. She doubted that Arlen was the ravaging type anyway, drunk or otherwise.

Arlen turned and took her hand. "My dearest lady," he said in flawless French. "You are so beautiful. No woman on this island can compare with your beauty."

And what about *off* this island, she thought pointedly. That wasn't fair. She knew he meant well.

"Thank you, my good lord," she said demurely, half under

her breath, eyes downcast. The perfect virginal bride. The little dab of wax had hardened on the back of her hand. She peeled it off and crumbled it between her finger and thumb. Arlen grinned, and brought her hand up to his lips for a chaste kiss.

"Poor little dove," he murmured, "did it burn?"

"No, I don't think so," Alysoun told him. "I don't feel anything."

Alysoun sat stiffly in the massive bridal bed, her back propped against the too-hard bolster. The freshly starched sheets made her skin itch. Around her, women giggled and made rude jokes under their breath. Her mother patted her bare shoulder and smiled. Alysoun turned her face up, not really looking at her, and smiled back. Her nipples showed through the thin sheet they had so carefully arranged over her. She was cold and tired of waiting for Arlen. He was still carousing in the hall below. Even in the wavering candlelight, her pink body was clearly visible through the sheet. They would not let her have a blanket until Arlen had come to her.

"Bring me some wine . . . please," she asked no one in particular. Her mouth was dried up like old leather.

"Now, now, my sweet," her mother said soothingly, "you want to keep your breath sweet for your lord."

Alysoun wanted to do nothing of the sort. "I'm thirsty," she said, a deliberate edge in her voice.

Someone handed her a cold silver goblet. She gulped the contents—water. Ah well. It made her feel a little better. Out of the corner of her eye she caught her Aunt Maire speculating with her hands about the size of Arlen's cock. Maire held her hands wider and wider apart—the women around her tittered nervously, eyeing Alysoun.

"Don't listen to her. It'll be all right," her mother told her. "Something every woman has to go through."

Maire laughed. "You'll want to go through it again and again."

Alysoun's mother shot her sister a hard look. Maire shook her head, clucking merrily.

"You'll like it, my girl. See if I'm wrong." The other women laughed and told Maire how awful she was.

Alysoun grinned inwardly. They thought they knew so much. Well, she *had* kept her maidenhead intact until Matty came along. It had been easy enough to resist her shag-haired cousins, with their foolish boasting and rough ways. Besides, they had sport enough with the hired girls. But Matty had taken her within his first week at the castle. She had wanted him so much. She thought of him downstairs with the other men, drinking the bridegroom's health. It must gall him. She prayed that it did.

The room was dark, but she could still make out the painted designs on the roof of the bed. She concentrated on their interlacing swirls and flourishes. The thick posts at each corner of the bed seemed to support an invisible wall, holding her in. She doubted that she could leave the bed now. Arlen would be coming for her soon. She stared hard at the painting until it blurred. All feeling had left her, she felt hollow, a dried-out husk of a corpse.

Voices rose in the stairwell. The men were coming up the winding steps and Arlen with them, all singing and shouting to burst their lungs. Alysoun felt a hand squeezing her shoulder. She forced her eyes down and tried to look meek and pleasant. Her mouth was dry again.

The beaming faces of the women gave way and suddenly Arlen was standing there, looking down at her.

"My sweet lady," he slurred, wobbling a little. "Sweet, sweet lady."

One of his soldiers slapped him on the back and roared his approval. The Welsh captain was not there, for a mercy. Arlen staggered forward and half fell onto the bed. Several of his hearty companions—her father among them—stripped him clean and slid him between the sheets. His thigh brushed against her, burning hot. There was a concerted effort by too many people to close the curtains. Laughter echoed off the high ceiling. Someone thrust a slopping cup of wine into Arlen's hands. The last curtain was pulled shut, closing them in. She was alone with him.

It was cold enough that morning as they prepared to leave, but it did not rain. Bran accepted a boost up into the saddle from one of the stable boys. The hard ridge of the saddle felt strange to him after so many days of luxurious drinking and no work. The armour pinched him a little too, as if he'd put on an extra pound or two. They'd done a marvelous job of scouring the rust off the plates, but these were still badly pitted and stained almost black. Ah well, he thought—the fortunes of peace.

Arnulf marshaled the men together in the bawn and filed them out through the gate, followed by the two creaking carts. Lord Burke had given them the carts and a string of packhorses to take Alysoun's gifts and household goods. Arlen had grumbled about the carts, which would almost double the time it would take to get back to Ballinasloe, but his new lady had smiled a most winsome, pouty little smile and overcame all objection.

Arlen tarried by the keep entrance with his lady, taking leave of Lord and Lady Burke. Bran squirmed in the saddle, looking up at the bleak sunless sky. The sharp morning air made a fog of his breath. He was ready to go. The strain of waiting for the MacSorley attack which never came had worn down his nerves. Good discipline. The MacSorleys had good discipline. He had almost told their commander that. Bran grinned behind his half-mask of chain mail.

"Welshman."

Bran looked behind him. Matty Groves was leading a well-fed courser harnessed with tassels and tooled leather. The small harp hung in its bag behind the saddle.

"Go back," Bran said quietly.

Matty shook his head, smiling. "Not possible. Your lord has offered me his hospitality and—" Matty winked, "his generosity, for the rest of the winter."

He put a boot into the stirrup and sprang lightly into the saddle.

"You could have refused," Bran said.

"I didn't want to," Matty replied. "Look you . . . I'll be gone by the spring. I spend every spring with the Earl of Thomond. You worry too much."

Bran puffed air through his mustache. "Just enough, I think. You're wanting in caution . . . Welshman."

Matty laughed. "All right. Watch over me with your eagle eye if you will. Steer me from the path of wickedness."

"We'll see," Bran told him.

Matty nodded. "So we shall."

The Second Month

Ballinasloe
December 1381

The wind ripped loose a row of tiles and sent them clattering
into the courtyard below. The deep-rooted tower stood firm
against the onslaught, but the bitter wind shrilled through every
chink and rattling shutter, making a sound like a hundred
banshees wailing.

Sitting in his corner in the common room, Bran shrugged
the cloak closer around his shoulders. Even he was frightened
by the sound the wind made. He shuddered. Damn this country
anyway, with its fairies and elves—and banshees. The air was
so cold that a man had to climb into the fire to get away from it.
He had been drinking whiskey since the early afternoon. There
was a warm spot in his chest, but all the rest of him was cold,
icy cold, like the fingers of dead men clawing at his flesh. His
teeth chattered uncontrollably. He clenched them together,
trying to wedge them shut with his tongue. It was tiring, holding
his tongue like that, but he could not stand the sound of them
clicking together inside his head.

The shutter nearest him blew open—the candles flickered
wildly. He jumped up to close it. His legs were heavy and stiff
from sitting so long; he felt like a cripple. The catch in the shutter
was loose. He took a wood chip from the floor and wedged it tight.

Some of his men huddled in front of the fire, forming a wall
to hold in the heat, their faces shiny with sweat. They smelled
of horses and damp leather. No one spoke. They were too intent
on drawing heat from the fire.

Bran sat down again, half afraid his bones would snap under him, and carefully curled his fingers around the little knaggin of whiskey. Across the table from him, Arnulf sat bowed in silent misery. His wife was dying in one of the chambers above. The kitchen knaves were heating stones to lay against her feet. Bran thought that it might almost be worth dying to have hot stones laid against his poor frozen feet.

He rubbed the little knaggin between his palms, trying to work some heat into the cold whiskey. Arnulf was so far gone that he wasn't even drinking. If I were in his shoes, I would be railing, pissing drunk, Bran thought. So drunk they'd have to kill me.

He could not bear a sadness like that. It had never occurred to him that Arnulf loved his wife. It was obvious now. Bran had never really thought of her as a real person, just a smiling round face, good for sewing new tunics and patching up his old trews. She made good pies too. She was a maker. He didn't pay much attention to those kinds of people, the makers. They just existed, and made whatever they made. Very useful, but individually of little consequence.

He looked at Arnulf's tight expressionless face. He had always thought of Arnulf as just Arnulf, without considering his wife at all. He sipped the whiskey, cherishing the sting on his lips. Aaah. The glow spread in his chest. Arnulf should drink whiskey. It made you think, but the thoughts didn't seem to matter very much. Bran rolled the whiskey around in his mouth before swallowing it. The wind howled louder than before. He tried not to care. Not to be frightened by the banshees.

The Old German opened his pale watery eyes when Bran came into the room. Bran could see that even with his eyes open, the Old German was not really awake. He looked terrible.

Except for the liquid rattling in his lungs, the Old German might have easily passed for a corpse in urgent need of burial. The translucent yellow skin of his face was stretched tightly over the bone. His withered lips were pulled back from his teeth in a perfect imitation of the death rictus. He smelled bad too. Yet he lived.

Bran moved closer, reluctantly, wanting to turn back before the sick man awoke and saw him. He did not want to be here, but he felt it was his duty because the Old German was one of his men and he was dying. He had been a long time dying, and Bran was angry with him for that. But he was a tough old bastard and couldn't help it.

Bran forced himself to sit on the edge of the sick man's bed. It creaked under his weight. The Old German's eyelids fluttered.

"Johann?" Bran said softly. He gingerly touched the sick man's shoulder. "Johann . . ." he said again, more loudly.

The Old German's feverish, glistening eyes rolled toward him. His crusted tongue moved over his lips in a vain effort to moisten them. He made a croaking noise. Bran thought that he was trying to smile. There was a jug of water lying on the floor next to the bed. Bran poured some into a cracked cup and held it to the sick man's lips.

"There," Bran said. "That's better, isn't it?"

The Old German coughed wetly, clearing his throat. Bran bunched up part of the sheet and used it to wipe mottled phlegm from the corner of the sick man's mouth.

"Cap . . . tain. Cap . . . tain," the Old German gasped.

Bran patted his shoulder. "You're looking better, Johann," he lied. "Is there anything I can get for you?"

"Nein, danke," the Old German replied. The wisps of white hair remaining on the top of his skull stirred in the draft. The cramped stone chamber was bitter cold. As cold as the grave, Bran thought. He pulled the blankets up around the Old German's neck, aware of the futility of it.

"There's nothing at all?" Bran felt compelled to ask. "Some wine, perhaps? I'll have them mull a nice cup of wine for you."

The Old German grinned weakly, shaking his death's head slowly, so slowly. It was incredible that he was still alive. *"Nein, nein,"* he repeated. "It . . . is . . . good of you . . . to see me."

Bran's face flushed hotly. Sick old men made him uncomfortable, and this was the first time that he had looked in on the Old German.

"I'll come again," Bran told him, knowing that it was a lie. Fiercely wishing that the sick man would die before it became a lie—why did he cling to life so stubbornly? Suffering like this was useless. The Old German was all used up. Surely he must know that.

"Are you getting enough to eat?" Bran asked, straining for something to say.

"Ja . . . ja . . . but I am not so hungry." The Old German closed his eyes.

"Well, I'll let you go back to sleep. Get a good rest, Johann. You'll feel better tomorrow." Bran rose from the bed. He could see that the Old German was already asleep.

Standing outside the sick man's room, Bran was angry with himself. He had meant to say something of comfort, but there was nothing left to say. It was a bad death the Old German was dying, and Bran wanted no part of it. He knew that it was not the Old German's fault. Even so, he could not help feeling that the old mercenary had made a mistake somehow, to warrant such a death. It was better to be hacked apart on a battlefield than live a few more empty years and die by inches in a cold, lonely room, far from home. Bran had promised himself that he would not drink very much wine today, but that was before he went to see the Old German. So now he would unpromise it, of necessity. He would drink a lot of wine and do his best to forget the Old German and everything else that was bad to remember.

The weather broke a week before the start of Christmas. Bran set Arnulf to drilling the men in the flat unplowed field between the village and the castle bawn. He had decided to ride out to the tavern on the river road to Limerick. He had not been to the Bird In Hand since before MacTieg died, and that was a long time now, five or six months at least. MacTieg was a Scotsman. He and Bran had fought to a bloody draw outside the tavern one Saint Andrew's Day a few years back, and they had almost liked each other after that.

Bran normally preferred to do his drinking close at hand, in the common room of the tower, or at the cramped little alehouse at the north end of the village. Lately though, the castle stock had run pretty low. Arlen was saving the last two tuns of good wine for the Yule feasts. They had taken to drinking the siege wine, which would rot your guts out, and had to be well-watered to be drunk at all.

The little village brewer's sour ale had made him pretty weary too. Arnulf had said that MacTieg's widow kept a respectable store of wine, and wasn't afraid to charge good money for it either. There wouldn't have been many travellers in the past few months, so Bran thought there was likely to be a taste of it left.

Bran had a holy passion for some good Bordeaux. He'd picked up a taste for it in France years ago. King Edward had taken Bordeaux in the sixties, which Bran thought the wisest move he ever made. The tavern was an hour and a half away on horseback—two if the road was muddy, which it was likely to be. Still, he could almost feel the rich, blood-dark wine rolling over his back teeth. He needed to get out of the castle anyway; he hadn't been farther than the end of the village since bringing Arlen's wife back a month ago. The black horse was badly in need of exercise. A ride in the cold clean air would do them both some good.

Before he left, Bran went looking for Matty Groves. He liked drinking with Matty and hearing the old stories in Welsh. Sometimes Bran tried not to like him, but that didn't work for very long. Matty had a way about him. Everyone liked him. In the winter-bound, suffocated world of the castle, Matty Groves had no enemies. That was very strange.

Each night Matty played for them in the hall, and no one ever got tired of listening to him. Arlen seemed in awe of him. He felt like a great lord, having a famous harper in his household.

Bran liked having someone to talk to after so many years. He recognized that this had its dangers, but speaking Welsh again made him feel like a different man. The man he had been before coming to Ireland. He shrugged off the thought and checked the kitchen. None of the sculls working there had seen the harper.

Bran watched Matty and Alysoun carefully, but he could see nothing amiss. Matty played for Alysoun in the drab sewing room she called her bower, but there were always two or three of her maids about. Sometimes Arlen was there too. Bran did not think Matty would dare anything with Arlen so close by.

That would soon change. Now that the weather had lifted, Arlen would take eight or ten of the men and hunt every day to bring in game for the Christmas feasting. Bran did not think Matty would let every opportunity go by untried.

Finally, one of Alysoun's wenches told Bran that Matty was playing chess with Lord and Lady Arlen in their chamber on the top floor of the tower. That seemed safe enough. Arlen would hunt tomorrow though, if the weather held.

Bran saddled the black horse and led him out into the bawn. The black horse had bitten one of the Irish grooms the day before. Bran was secretly pleased. He liked his horses full of spirit. The black horse chewed the bit impatiently. Bran stuck his boot through the stirrup and hoisted himself into the saddle. The horse reared and jerked, trying to throw him. The men on the wall laughed. Bran clamped his heels under the horse's barrel and tightened up on the reins. The horse twisted and bucked from side to side in a vain effort to shake him off. Bran leaned over the pommel of the saddle and pounded on the horse's head with his fist. The horse bent his head back and tried to bite Bran's leg. Bran lifted his boot out of the stirrup and pushed the horse's head away, laughing. He waved to the men on the wall. They waved back. The black horse trembled under him. It would be all right now. Bran touched him gently with the rowel spurs, steering him toward the gate.

He rode through the village and followed the river east. The sky was almost blue. It was a fine day. The watery sun dazzled his eyes. He couldn't help singing.

"She took my horse by the bridle and the bit and she led him to the stable—" The cold air made him cough.

"She said there's plenty of oats for a soldier's horse, to eat 'em if he's able—"

The black horse grunted.

"With a tur-ril-lie, fala-diddle-da, tur-ra-fala-diddle-derry-o." Bran laughed, petting the horse's neck. "What's the matter? You don't like my singing?"

Later on, he watched a hare jump out of the hedge and run across the road. A fox chasing it, perhaps. The fox would not dare to cross the road while Bran's horse was there. Bran rode the black horse close to the hedge, leaning over it to look for the fox. He couldn't see anything. Perhaps the hare was just running for the hell of it. They did that. *He* did too. He had been running since he was fifteen. Running from Howell had started it. Bran felt a heaviness settling in his chest. He tried to shake it off—felt the rare happy feeling slip away like water through his fingers.

The castle was dead asleep. Warped floorboards creaked under the weight of each step. Bran hugged the wall, keeping to the darkest part of the shadows. He had to remind himself to breathe. His heart pounded like a war drum. He was sure everyone could hear. Only one more floor to go, then he'd be down in the byre and through the door. He hoped the beasts penned there would not make too much noise. If Howell caught him . . .

If Howell caught him, then he would be soundly whipped, and Bran would have to kill him for that, somehow. Kill his own father.

Huddled shapes lay massed on the floor all around him. One of them stirred, shrugging the blanket from his face. Bran froze. The sleeper turned on his side and began to snore. His neighbor took it up, and then there were three or four of them snoring together.

Bran edged toward the ladder. The man nearest the ladder coughed. Bran prayed for him not to wake. He stepped over the sleeping man—and accidentally kicked over a metal cup. He froze. The rattling of the cup sounded like an alarum bell. His throat tightened, he could hardly breathe. The snoring continued undisturbed. After what seemed like an hour he moved again, straining his eyes against the dark. He found the ladder and carefully started down. The man coughed again. Bran gripped the ladder so hard he thought he might break it. He let himself down one foot at a time. His soft leather buskins made no sound on the rungs.

The air in the byre was thick and hot. The milch cows rubbed against each other, chewing twists of hay. Their brown eyes rolled toward him, regarding him with calm indifference. A pregnant sow squealed at him from the pen in the corner. He shut his eyes tightly, listening for any sounds from above. There was nothing, only the shuffling of the animals around him. The stench made him gag. He made his way cautiously among the beasts, praying that he would not alarm them. A heifer stepped on his foot—he jerked it back, swearing under his breath. She twisted her head around to look at him. Bran patted her rough flank.

"There now," he whispered sweetly. "It's all right, you great stupid beast."

His foot ached. Plodding through dung-filled straw up to his ankles, he reached the door. The iron-shod bar was heavier than he'd imagined. He'd never had to lift it before. He held it against his chest, grunting with the strain, and leaned it carefully against the stone wall. The door swung open on rusty hinges.

The cold, stinging air seemed to him like a wind from Paradise. Bran stepped outside and shut the door. The curtain wall rose up all around him, a rough timber palisade. He sprinted across the yard toward the gate, running low to the ground, like a fox.

The sentry was asleep in his little wooden tower. Bran grinned, smelling the mead on the man's breath. Howell's men were pretty useless in peacetime. They hadn't even raided for two years. Useless. He edged past the sentry and opened the wicket in the gate, ducked through, and closed it gently behind him.

The path was steep and rough, but he knew it so well that he never stumbled once. Where the hill flattened out, men had farmed the terraces in Arthur's time. The whole hill was a fort then. Howell had told Bran that his grandfather had built the stone tower in the middle of the stone fort, but the Normans had built it. They built well.

The rickety wooden stable lay on the end of the widest ledge. His grandfather *had* built that. The stable was framed with living trees, gnarled and black, with boards nailed over them.

Bran called out like an owl.

Rhodri stuck his head out of the stable door. He was five years younger than Bran, but they were friends. Bran let Rhodri follow him around and do things for him. Now Rhodri was helping him escape.

"I've been waiting," Rhodri said. He had fallen on a rock last month, and there was a gap between his teeth.

"I know," Bran replied. "Have you got her saddled?"

Rhodri shook his head in annoyance. "Yes, look you, hours ago. Are you really going?"

Bran's heart jumped. "Yes." He was really going.

Rhodri led out the old dun horse. "She's a nag," he said. "Why don't you take one of your father's?" He gestured at the back of the stable where Howell's horses were kept. "How about the gray gelding? That's a good horse."

Bran shrugged. "He'd come after me for sure." He patted the dun mare. "I'll take this one."

Rhodri tied a leather sack onto the saddle. "Food," he explained, looking over his shoulder at Bran. "Not much. All I could get without being noticed."

"All right. Thanks."

Bran went to the back of the stable and dug into the straw for the sword and bundle hidden there—his only possessions— wrapped in the red cloak Howell had given him last Christmas. Inside the bundle there was a dented cup that his brother Tristan had given him the night he left seven years before, and a wooden bowl and spoon that Bran had carved himself.

He tied the sword onto his belt. The sword had belonged to Rhodri's father, killed on the raid two years ago. The leather-covered scabbard was worn through in places, exposing the dark wood underneath. Bran cupped his palm over the heavy wheel pommel. It was loose; he'd have to get it fixed somewhere.

Rhodri had given him the sword. Bran fastened his cloak over his shoulders and walked back to where Rhodri stood holding the horse. Bran stuffed the bowl and spoon into the leather bag. He weighed the cool pewter cup in one hand, holding onto the saddle with the other. Tristan had given him the cup. It was the only thing that he loved. He felt Rhodri watching him.

"Here." Bran thrust the cup into the boy's hands. Rhodri stepped back, cradling the cup against his chest.

"You're going then?" the younger boy said. His eyes looked away.

"Yes." Bran's heart beat wildly. He felt like weeping.

"Take me with you," Rhodri said.

Bran swung up into the saddle; his head scraped against the roof. "No," he said. "You're too young." He gathered up the reins, wrapping the supple leather around his fingers.

Rhodri pulled the door back all the way. Moonlight showed through cracks in the walls. The gray gelding whinnied from the back stall.

"It's too late," Bran told the gelding.

Rhodri grinned. "Farewell, then. Godspeed."

Bran forced down the lump in his throat. "Thanks." He urged the mare through the opening, ducking his head under the low lintel.

The sky was bright, but it was very dark in the trees all around him. He looked back and saw Rhodri framed in the doorway, waving. Bran waved. He kicked his heels into the mare's flanks and started down the trail through the trees, to the open fields beyond.

The black horse stumbled, jerking Bran into the present. It had been a long while since he had thought of that morning at Dinas Emrys and the look on Rhodri's face. It surprised him that he still remembered what Rhodri looked like after all these years. It was better not to think about it. He was very thirsty.

The black horse wanted to run, to stretch his stable-cramped legs, but it was too muddy for that. Bran did not want to arrive at the tavern looking like some mud-splattered churl of a friar. He tried to remember what MacTieg's widow looked like. She must not be too handsome or too ugly, he thought, because he could not think of her face at all. He didn't look at other men's women anyway—that was almost a law with him. But after all, MacTieg was safely dead, and she might be worth taking a look at. He hadn't had a woman since the red-haired girl at the Burke castle.

The rest of the ride was uneventful. Bran drifted off into reveries about Granada, and about the early days in France when he was so impossibly young. Sometimes he would dream whole days away like this, especially in winter. Especially in winter—but more and more all the time. Spring, summer, fall . . . all he did was dream. He was like an old man, dozing and dreaming by the fire, listening to the wind whistle in the rafters, mistaking the sounds of gulls screaming and wheeling overhead for battle cries. To be old without money or position was undignified.

Until coming to Ireland this had never troubled him. Bran had always imagined that he would make his fortune, somehow, at some point in the not too distant future—three or four years away from where he happened to be at the time. He could not remember exactly when he stopped thinking that way, but it was after coming to Ireland.

When Arlen had asked Bran to go to Ireland with him to claim his dead brother's lands and title, Bran had made up his mind to go at once. Still, he had waited two days before giving Arlen his acceptance—it looked better that way. Arlen needed a seasoned man to recruit and maintain his troops, and Bran was the first man that he asked. Bran had known Arlen since the mid-sixties, when Arlen was a young knight, one of the many landless hangers-on that the Black Prince surrounded himself with.

When Arlen had made his offer, in a crowded tavern in Calais, Bran hadn't been surprised at all. Bran was a man of some reputation then. A lot of wild stories had come out about his days as a renegade in the south of Spain—none of which he denied. He was ready for a change. He had been in the King's army of course, and been a *routier* too, and done his share of extortion and unauthorized looting. It was good money, but he could never seem to keep any. He owned a full suit of plate and two good horses, but that was all he had to show for nearly twenty years of soldiering. Garrison duty in a castle or town was dull and unprofitable, and the out-and-out brigandage of the Free Companies was getting too dangerous.

It had been much better in the sixties. In those days the great Free Companies were often larger than the regular armies that were called out to fight them—but rarely did. In Bordeaux he'd met a Welsh man-at-arms who told him that Tristan had gone over the Alps into Italy with Hawkwood's branch of the White Company. From what Bran had heard, the White Company had done great things there. Many of the knights and even some of the common soldiers had married into the Italian nobility and become lords themselves, with palaces and hundreds of servants to wait on them. Bran didn't believe all the stories, but he hoped that his brother had done well.

Bran sighed and patted the black horse's mane. Tristan was probably dead by now.

Many of the old soldiers in Calais had thought him crazy to go to a boggy, inhospitable frontier like Ireland, where it rained too much and all the wine had to be imported. Where excellent opportunities for a man to get himself killed lay behind every tree. But they were thinking about the Ireland of ten or twenty years ago.

The wars in France had drunk the royal treasury to the lees, and Parliament would no longer send money and troops to be wasted in the Irish wars—so the wars had stopped, more or less, with only the usual ceaseless raiding. Steadily, inevitably, the borders of the Pale had shrunk, and many of the settlers had gone back to England. The ones who remained came to terms with the Irish chieftains or holed up behind the walls of great towns like Galway and Limerick. Only a few years ago, Art MacMurrough had taken back the whole of Leinster and made himself king there.

Bran rode through a steep little ravine made before the river had changed its course. Trees ran along the top of both sides of the ravine, crowded close together like black skeletons, rubbing their bones against each other in the wind. When spring came the trees would have leaves again, and a man would not be able to see anyone hiding there. Good place for an ambush, Bran thought. A strange chill ran through him, raising the hairs on the back of his neck. Perhaps the place was haunted. He laughed out loud—mostly to hear the sound, it was so quiet.

"Now I'm afraid of ghosties," he said to the black horse.

He needed a drink badly. They were almost at the tavern— only a short distance to go. The old song came into his head again . . .

"And I got up and I made the bed, and I made it nice and easy . . ." He sang loudly to armour himself against the fear he still felt.

"Then I picked her up and I laid her down, saying 'Lassie, are ye ready?' With a tur-ril-lie, fala-diddle-da, tur-ra-fala-diddle-derry-o!"

White hearth smoke hung over the trees where the road bent. Bran spurred up the black horse. His belly growled resentfully; he could almost taste one of those hot, flaky meat pies dissolving in his mouth. The horse must be hungry too, he thought. It probably hadn't been fed since biting the stable boy.

"Pray God she's got some good wine," Bran yelled into the horse's ear.

The Bird In Hand hadn't changed any—a long, low, rambling

structure of timber and wattle, with little sheds and outbuildings tacked onto it. A covey of peahens and chicks scattered before his horse's hooves; and a chained dog which appeared to be part wolfhound barked out a greeting—or warning—Bran couldn't decide which. His horse shied, and started walking sideways toward the hollowed-out log that served as a watering trough.

Bran dismounted and wrapped the reins around a handy post near the trough. He stood in front of the main entrance, hands on hips, and gave the place a good looking over. The timber was freshly chinked, and the wattle newly limed; the place in general had a healthy, well-kept look. MacTieg's widow seemed to be doing all right for herself.

He straightened his swordbelt, shaking out the long cloak as he walked toward the open doorway. The door beam was set low enough to stove in a tall man's head, but he managed to avoid it, stepping into cool darkness. He blinked, seeing nothing, not wanting to go much farther until his eyes adjusted. Gradually he could see. Fragrant smoke hung below the rooftrees, partially obscuring bundles of herbs and smoked meat. Clay bottles and leather pitchers vied for the remaining space, and those that could found places on shelves that stuck out handily from the walls, or in dark, carved-out recesses. Dismantled trestle tables leaned against one wall, benches lay stacked against another. The hard-packed earth floor had been freshly swept, waiting now for another coat of rushes. He heard the scratchy rustle of a willow broom farther back in the shadows.

"Hallo," Bran called, resting his hand casually on his dagger hilt.

"God be with you," the woman answered. She stepped closer, holding the broom in both hands.

"God be with you, Mistress." Bran let his dagger hand dangle free and tried to soften his eyes.

As his eyes adjusted, he saw her more clearly. She had a

thin, delicate-looking nose which MacTieg had apparently neglected to break, with a spray of light freckles on her cheeks and forehead. The faintest of lines were making an appearance on her face, but there was something of the girl in her yet, he thought.

"You look thirsty, sir," she said, peering up at him.

Bran smiled. "I am thirsty, Mistress. Thirst is my constant companion."

She relaxed a little. "You and your friend are most welcome. You're the captain at Ballinasloe, aren't you?"

"Yes." Bran plucked a three-legged stool from a peg on the wall and set it down by the open hearth in the middle of the room.

"What shall you drink, sir?"

"A quart of good ale to wash the road out of my throat, and a flagon of Bordeaux thereafter." Bran plopped down onto the stool and stretched his legs across the floor. The left boot was wearing through at the toe.

Mistress MacTieg put her hands on her hips and looked down at him, shaking her head. "Will you be requiring food with that ocean of drink you've ordered?"

Bran nestled his shoulders into the smooth warm stones of the hearth wall and yawned mightily in her direction. The place felt good to him.

"By all means, Mistress. I've heard that the Pope himself can't go to sleep without a bite of your pork and mushroom pie."

Her eyebrows rose. "Now where would you have heard that? The Holy Father was here only once, and he ate roast mutton!"

They laughed together at that, and she went off to get the ale. Bran leaned back and let his thoughts float up into the sooty rafters and swirling smoke. He dug a tiny trench in the dirt floor with one of his spurs. A fleabite in the small of his back started to itch abominably, but he was too lazy to do anything about it. He closed his eyes, hearing the faint clattering of pots in the kitchen, the clucking of the peahens and chickens outside ... the discontented stamping of his unfed horse. Bran rose groaning from the stool and went out to have a look.

A boy came out of the stable and moved to take the black horse's bridle.

"Careful, he's a devil," Bran said.

The boy took hold of the bridle and patted the black horse's neck.

"Oh no, sir, he's just a horse. He'll be all right."

Laughing, Bran said, "He'll eat you if you let him. Give him a bucket of oats and comb him down."

The boy grinned. "Yes, Sir Knight." He had flame-red hair like his mother, the same freckles too.

Bran's vanity was touched. He threw the boy a penny— knightly largess—and went back inside to drink his ale.

Mistress MacTieg was waiting with the quart jack of frothy brown ale and a round loaf of bread. She set the loaf on the hearth beside him.

"This will tide you until I get the pie heated up. I've some cold beef and mustard if you're really hungry."

Bran gulped back a third of the ale. It was cool, and he quickly realized—potent. Wiping his mustache on his sleeve, he said, "No, I'll wait for that pie. Nothing else in the world will suit me."

She liked that. "Did you meet my son?" she asked.

"Yes, a fine lad. Looks every bit like his father."

She laughed. "He does not! He looks like me!"

"My God, so he does!" Bran guzzled down the remainder of the quart. Her eyes crinkled around the edges when she laughed. He liked that. "Is there no one to help you with this place?"

She stuck out her lip and fiddled with her apron. "Well,"

she said slowly, "there's old Hobb, who comes in every day to cut the firewood. Sean looks after the horses, and I cook and clean and brew the ale. There's really no need for anyone else."

Indeed, Bran thought. Indeed. "You're close to the road here," he said.

"Yes, yes," she said, brightening. "A lot of travellers stop here. There isn't another inn for twenty miles."

"I'm sure there isn't a finer one either."

"You've been in Ireland a long time," she said, smiling.

"Not so long," he said. "Three years."

"You've picked up a fine flattering tongue," she said.

"Ah no, I've always had it. The Irish don't have a monopoly on pretty speech." He looked meaningfully at the empty jack.

"I think you'll be having some more," she said.

"That is well thought, Mistress," Bran said, patting the hard leather jack. She picked it up and carried it out of the room.

A spark flew out of the fire and landed on Bran's shoulder. He brushed it off, swearing mildly. He felt very happy. I suppose I should ask her Christian name, he thought. To his knowledge he had never heard it spoken. Even if he had, he wouldn't have remembered. The boy did look a lot like her. Bran guessed that he was about ten years old. Seemed like a nice lad.

He really was very hungry. The ale had piqued his appetite. It was good ale, not like the dog's piss they made in the village. He would be coming here more often. It seemed silly that he had not come sooner, weather or no. Arnulf had said that it was a good place, even without old MacTieg to knock a few heads together. It was odd that he had never noticed the woman before. He didn't suppose that she was any different now. Running the place all by herself, that took guts. A fine strong woman.

She returned with the steaming pie on a board and a brimming jack of ale. Bran took the board out of her hands and set it on his lap.

"That looks grand," he said. He crumbled the pie apart with

his fingers. It was very hot. He took out his dagger and speared a chunk of meat out of the ruined shell.

"I hope you like it," she said, holding her hands behind her apron.

Bran blew on the chunk of meat and put it in his mouth.

"*Mmm.* Good. Very good. The Pope was right."

She filled a pewter cup from the jack and handed it to him. He drank deeply. The ale tasted better than it had before—the pie had improved it somehow.

She was looking at him. Bran raised his head, dagger poised midway to his mouth. "Yes?" he asked.

"Don't mind me. I like watching a man eat."

"You must get a lot of opportunities for that," Bran said, putting the morsel in his mouth.

"Not really," she replied, all innocence. "I'm usually too busy in the kitchen or taking other orders. I get most of my business all at once, when I get it. Most people don't travel alone."

Bran picked up a dripping broken section of the pie in his fingers and popped it into his mouth.

"True," he mumbled, chewing his way through the mouthful of food. "I imagine you get some pretty rough . . ." he searched for the right word, "patrons, as well."

She kneaded the apron with her hands. "Ah. Well, the soldiers would be the roughest, I suppose."

Bran looked hard at her. "Do my men give you any trouble?"

Mistress MacTieg shook her head. "They're not so bad. The gallowglasses from Kilconnell are the worst, but I know how to handle them—" She picked up a heavy flagon and held it up high, like a weapon. "We speak the same language."

"You brain your patrons when they get too much of your hospitality?"

"Ach, no," she said, laughing. "But they think there's a chance I might."

"Well, that's good enough, then."

"I hope so." She pulled up a stool and sat down next to him. "Most of them knew Ronan, you see. We were at Kilconnell before setting up here."

Bran frowned. "Ronan? Ah—MacTieg, you mean. Yes, I knew that. For a Scotchman he wasn't half bad— Jesus! I'm sorry. Your fine ale has addled my wits, such as they are. You're a Scot too, aren't you?"

Mistress MacTieg poured herself a cup from the jack. "I'm afraid so," she said, humour sparkling in her eyes. "I hope you won't have to wrestle me outside of my own door on Saint Andrew's Day . . ."

"You remember, then?"

"How could I forget? He talked about you for days afterwards—he liked you, you know."

No, I didn't know, Bran thought. "He was a good man." He couldn't think of anything else to say.

"He was a man," she said quietly. "Both good and bad in him."

"How about that wine?" Bran asked. "You'll take a drop yourself?"

"Oh, more than a drop, Captain, and at your expense."

Bran laughed. "Good. Good." God, but she was a fine-looking woman. Even the freckles were starting to look good to him.

They sat there drinking wine until it got dark. She talked about her village in Scotland, high in the mountains, and the people in her clan. All of the men were bred to war, she said. Her father had been a soldier too, and gone to France with a Scottish knight. The Scots always fought for the French king. They hated the English even more than the Welsh did. Bran had to admire them for that. Still, he didn't think that was reason enough for liking them. He had admired the Moors too, but he didn't particularly like them. He was starting to like this woman though. Her name was Fionna, he eventually discovered. A good name. The boy's name was Sean. Sean came in at intervals and sat down on the floor near them, watching. After a while he would get up and leave again. When they ran out of wine, they sent Sean back to the kitchen for more.

Some of the Kilconnell men came in. Fionna was more than a little drunk, but she got up and greeted them merrily enough and attended briskly to business. Bran approved. The Kilconnell men nodded gravely in his direction and sat on the other side of the hearth, talking together in guarded voices. They were speaking Scots-Gaelic, which Bran didn't understand. Even through the drink he began to feel the weight of their eyes upon him. He didn't like Scots; they didn't like him. Fair enough.

He stood up and stretched ostentatiously. "Well," he said to Fionna, "I'll be taking my leave of you. Miles to ride before I sleep. You serve excellent wine here." He bowed slightly, the cloak trailing away from his swordhilt.

She nodded, smiling with her eyes. "Come again, Captain. A safe road back."

"Thank you, Mistress." With his hand resting casually on his swordhilt, Bran turned and walked slowly to the door. The hostile stares of the Kilconnell men seemed to push him across the threshold.

Sean was suddenly beside him in the dark.

"I'll get your horse, Captain." Before Bran could say anything, the boy had disappeared into the stable. Bran relaxed his fingers from the leather-wrapped grip of the sword. He thrust his thumbs through the belt, whistling the tune of the song he had sung earlier in the day.

Sean brought out the black horse. Bran kneed the horse hard under the barrel and tightened the cinch.

"When you saddle him, he pushes his belly out," Bran explained. "He'll throw you if the cinch is loose."

"Oh," Sean said, looking confused.

"I told you he was a devil," Bran said.

Bran rode back to the castle in a pleasant alcoholic haze; the cold didn't bother him much. There wasn't much of a moon to light his way. He slumped back in the saddle and let the black horse follow the road as he pleased. Going through the steep black ravine troubled him, and seemed to affect the horse too, which picked up his pace and quickly put the place behind them.

Torches burned for him above the gate. They opened the wicket for him, and he dismounted and led the horse through.

Bran found one of the grooms under a heap of straw in the stable and kicked him awake.

"Take off his saddle and rub him down," he ordered. "I'm going to bed."

He went into the tower and found a rushlight. As he climbed the winding stairs, rushlight flickering weakly, the curving wall seemed to reach out suddenly and strike him on the shoulder.

"I'm drunk," he told the wall.

As clumsy as a blind man, he felt his way along the corridor until he found the narrow icy chamber that was his privilege to occupy alone. He set the rushlight down on the chest and stripped his clothes off quickly, before the cold air could sober him up too much. The freezing wool blankets felt as stiff as a corpse's shroud.

Ah, God, he thought, I'll bet she's warm enough right now. He imagined her lying next to him in the bed, her smooth buttocks pressed against his belly. Bran rolled over, rubbing his stiffening cock against the hard mattress. I'll have that woman, he thought lazily, then he was asleep.

The next day, Bran was dicing with Arnulf and Mark Bowyer in the hall. Matty came up to them, obviously pleased with himself, and wished them all a cheerful "good day!" He was dressed in his riding clothes.

Bran looked up. "If you're going hunting with Arlen, he left over three hours ago, before dawn." Bran and Arnulf were both losing to Mark Bowyer.

"I know," Matty said brightly. "Just thought I'd go out for a ride."

"Where are you off to?" Bran asked. He had eleven pence left in his purse that he was going to lose if he kept playing.

Matty grinned and hopped lightly into a quick little jig. "Nowhere in particular. I thought a bit of fresh air would do me good. Want to come along?"

"Fresh is right," Arnulf grumped. "It's going to pour down rain in an hour or two. You'll think God is pissing on you— For all I know He should be." He pointed an accusing finger at Mark. "On you, anyway!"

Mark leaned back on his stool, chuckling quietly.

"Yes, I'll come," Bran said. "Anything to get away from these two."

Mark laughed. "You just hate to lose, Captain."

"Who doesn't?" Arnulf snorted. He took out his dagger and started slicing strips off the edge of the table, looking meaningfully at Bowyer. Mark leaned forward and rattled the dice cup in Arnulf's face.

"Another cast?"

Arnulf spat and got up and left.

"Well, you've certainly made him happy," Matty said.

"Will you play, sir?" Bowyer asked. "You only need a penny to play—"

"To start, maybe," Bran interrupted gruffly. Mark pretended to cower. Insolent bastard, Bran thought.

Matty watched them both, eyes sparkling. Bran felt like he was studying them.

"Well, why don't you try a cast?" Bran asked, feeling devilish.

Maybe Matty would lose. The great Matty Groves, losing at dice like other men.

"No," Matty said, holding up his hands. "I never gamble."

"That's why you're so rich," said Bran, annoyed.

Matty laughed. "I never get rich either." They all laughed at that.

"Let me get my cloak," said Bran.

Arnulf was right, it was going to rain. Bran eased back into the saddle, slipping his feet out of the stirrups. His right leg was starting to cramp. He massaged it, wincing with relief. "Ahhh."

Matty turned. "Hmm? Did you say something?" He looked as if he'd been off in a dream. Probably thinking about that damned Alysoun.

Bran shook his head. "I said your mother was a whore and your father fucked little boys."

"Ah, nothing of importance, then."

Bran wiggled his toes inside his boots. "Arnulf was right."

"Hunh?" Matty turned to look at him.

"About the rain," Bran said irritably.

Matty looked up, sniffing the air. "Yes. Yes, he was. Do you think God will piss on us?"

"Hunh? If He's not pissing on someone else already. I wonder if Arlen will get any deer. Did you bring some wine?"

"No. I didn't think about it. Sorry."

Bran put his feet back into the stirrups. "That's all right. I'll live." He doubted that he would.

The black horse shuddered, throwing back his head. It looked as if a gnat was bothering him, but there weren't any gnats in this weather. Perhaps it was the coming storm. "Easy, boy." Bran patted the horse's neck. He had never given the horse a name.

"Look at that," said Matty, pointing at the mountainous black thunderheads. "It's going to hit us all right."

"This was your idea," Bran hissed through his teeth. God, he thought, not even a swallow of wine.

The first spattering of rain hit their faces. They spotted a turf hut growing out of the hillside just before the storm broke loose over them. The rain fell on them like a wave, soaking them to the skin instantly.

"I must have forgotten my prayers this morning," Matty said.

"Aye," said Bran, "and the morning before that, and the mor— Christ!" A wind rose up from nowhere, lashing the rain into their faces, blinding them.

Matty yelled to him through the rain, "We'll have to leave the horses outside!"

"Too bad for them!" Bran yelled back, wiping the water out of his eyes.

The little hut hardly looked big enough for the two of them, much less the family he supposed was inside. A white curl of smoke tried to rise out of a hole in the domed roof, quickly cut to pieces by the wind and rain. A rickety pen farther up the hillside held chickens, but his forager's eye didn't see any signs of other livestock. The pig was probably inside with the family— if they had a pig.

They leapt down from their horses and tied the reins to a stunted tree that seemed to be growing out of the hut itself. Bran pounded on the crude hatch-like door, made from rope-bound slabs of bog oak.

"Open up!" he shouted, pounding the rough wood. The little door shook too much; someone was holding it on the inside. "Open up, damn you!"

Matty had unfastened the cased harp from his saddle. He cradled it under his cloak like an infant. "Here . . ." he said, kneeling in front of the door, "let me talk to them."

"Talk away," Bran said. "It's a fine day for wasting breath on serfs. Tell them their chickens are drowning; that'll bring them out."

"Shut your great ugly mouth," Matty said. He murmured something in Irish through the gap in the door.

The door was pulled back and laid aside. Matty crawled headfirst through the hole, cradling the harp against his chest. Bran stuck his dagger into his boot where it would be handy and crawled in after him.

Thick smoke from the dampened turf fire blinded them at once. The acrid reek of it turned their lungs inside out with coughing. Several tense minutes passed before they could see anything at all. The churls could stick us with a pitchfork or something, Bran thought, his hand gripped tight around the dagger hilt.

"I think we were better off outside," he said.

"Jesus wept!" Matty said disgustedly. "I'll grant you it's not as grand as your Sultan's palace, but it's dry enough."

"My throat is dry enough for both of us," Bran replied. He switched to Irish, "Do you have any water?"

A hand came out of the smoke and dropped a leather bottle into Bran's lap. He jerked out the plug and gulped the cold water greedily.

"Let me have some of that," Matty said, reaching for the bottle.

"Take it," said Bran. "When it's empty we can set it outside for a moment and fill it up again."

Matty shook his head. "You clever man."

When enough of the smoke had cleared out, someone got up and replaced the door. Bran couldn't tell if it was a boy or a girl. There were at least six other people in the hut. He heard a baby crying somewhere in the back. Seven. Bran looked at the dagger hilt jutting out of his boot and felt embarrassed. Ah well, he thought, better safe than sorry. Matty handed him the bottle. It was almost empty. Bran tilted it straight up and finished it.

"Ahhh, water," Bran sighed. "Nothing like it. The Irish are noted for their hospitality to strangers."

"Mind your manners," said Matty.

Bran laughed. "They can't understand Welsh."

"Mind them anyway." Matty smiled at the people in the hut. The woman nodded and smiled back uncertainly. The man stared at them with dead, stony eyes. Matty handed the bottle across to him. The man took it and shoved it into a narrow shelf cut into the wall. Smoke started building up again. The baby squalled. Rain poured steadily through the hole in the roof, drowning the fire. It wasn't much needed anyway. Eight people packed together like cod in a barrel made enough heat to drive Satan out of Hell. Stinging sweat rolled into Bran's eyes, already scratchy from the turf smoke. Sweet Jesus, he thought, I'd be better off outside with the horses.

Matty took the harp out of its padded leather bag and set it against his shoulder.

"God's death, Matty!" Bran exclaimed. "You're not going to play for them?" Hopeless, the man was hopeless.

Matty plucked out a few notes with his tough, overgrown fingernails, frowned, and adjusted the strings with the T-shaped key that hung from his neck.

Bran leaned back against the wall and shut his eyes. The low, curving wall made a kink between his shoulder blades; he felt like a hunchback. An hour of this, he thought, and I can charge people a penny to rub my hump for luck. His throat ached for wine.

Matty finished his adjustments and began to play. He started with a slow piece, to suit the melancholy of the moment. The woman and children watched him, rapt, drawn into the music like sailors to a siren's song. Bran smiled. Matty was a siren of sorts, then. Bran could not decide exactly why he liked him. It wasn't because he was Welsh—there were a lot of Welshmen in Ireland; Bran didn't feel it necessary to go around making friends with all of them.

There was the music of course. Bran respected that as much as anyone else, but he'd never felt particularly drawn to minstrels. Most of them were pampered, tale-telling parasites, no matter how well they could play. Always getting the choicest food, drinking wine from the honour cups of kings and dukes, swiving the wives of honest knights right under their noses . . . He couldn't see that Matty was any different, but somehow he was. He had a way about him. Bran was damned if he knew what it could be.

The crusted sweat under Bran's armpits started to chafe him abominably. Sweet Jesus, what a hole this is, he thought. How can people live here? The mellow strains of the harp filled up the little hut. Bran cracked open his eyes. The mother rocked her baby in her lap; several of the younger children hung about her legs, swaying gently to the unaccustomed sounds. The expression on the young-old mother's face was almost beatific, like a painted Madonna in a church.

Even these filthy, half-starved peasants are starting to love him, Bran thought. Their stiff, fierce-eyed churl of a host was softening a little; Matty's music had taken hold of him too. He hunkered forward, arms hugging his bony knees, his sooty face streaked white by runnels of sweat. The faint glow of the fire made his face look like old, cracked leather. The man was probably not even thirty. He'll be dead before he's my age, Bran thought, trying to derive some comfort from it.

If the man died, the woman and her children would die soon after. In a few years even the miserable hut would crumble back into the hillside, worn down by wind and rain. They had nothing, not even a pig. Bran sucked in a long breath and let it out again, slowly. He had the power to terrify and destroy, nothing else. It was a power, an ability, that had contented him for years; he had never questioned it before and felt foolish for doing so now.

The soft, dreamy harp music wove a web of memory in his

brain. He relaxed, resting his cheek against his knees, slipping back to the comfortable world of Granada, the warm, spice-scented bath water lapping about his neck, the taste . . . of oranges . . .

The music had stopped. For one murderous moment Bran considered wringing Matty's neck. What gave him the right to play so lightly with people's dreams?

Matty watched him, a puzzled grin on his face. "Where've you been?" he asked. "No, don't tell me," he said, raising his hand. He sat still for a moment, listening. "I think the rain is letting up."

Bran looked up at the smoke hole. Only a little water was coming in now, mostly drip from the edges. A few spots of rain hissed into the low mound of fine yellow ash, all that remained of the turf fire.

"All right," Bran said. "Let's go."

He pulled on the rude door. It was tightly wedged. Bran pulled again and it fell back against his shoulder. "Come on," he said, irritated.

Matty was taking courteous leave of the family. Bran saw him press a silver groat into the woman's hand. Her husband stared at the wall, pretending not to see.

"Come on, let's go!" Bran hissed urgently. He pulled himself out of the hut, angrily brushing the mud from his knees.

When they returned to the castle, they found that despite the rain, Arlen had managed to bring in a stag and a doe. The meat was butchered and hung up in the smokehouse. With Christmas so close, Arlen was determined to hunt whatever the weather might be. He felt strongly that he should be a good provider for his castle folk.

Over a cup of wine before going to bed, Arlen asked Bran if he would hunt with him in the morning.

"By your leave, my lord," Bran said, "I will not. This

morning's adventure with the harper put a grippe in my throat. I think I'll spend the day by the fire pondering my sins." He ladled another cup of mulled wine for himself out of the bowl. "Why don't you ask the harper to go with you? Do him good—he seems to enjoy bad weather."

Arlen shook his head. "No. He won't go. Says he's not much of a hunter. Ah well . . . " Arlen slapped his hands on his thighs, "seems to be a gentleman's sport after all."

You bastard, Bran thought. Bran already knew that Matty had refused the hunt; that's why he'd planned to stay in the castle, to keep an eye on Matty. Bran coughed.

Arlen cocked an eye at him. "Grippe, hunh? You don't get sick, Welshman." Arlen sipped slowly from his cup, waiting for a reaction.

Bran's anger flared, bright and quick as a shooting star. He fought it down. Arlen was just playing with him.

"We do sometimes— Englishman," Bran said coolly.

Arlen laughed. "Hunt with me tomorrow."

Bran grinned wryly. "All right. As my good lord wishes."

"But my lady . . . "

"Enough! Leave me!" Alysoun snapped. "Find something else to do besides pester me!" Really, it was too much, the simpering ninny . . .

The maid withdrew in a fluster of tears, and Alysoun was finally alone in the solar. The continual lack of privacy had been her lot since birth, but it had never ceased to bother her. It might be better, she thought, to be a shepherd's wife, all alone in a stone hut high in the hills; just the fire and the bleating of little lambs and sweet, quiet solitude. No. That would be too much of a good thing. Besides, shepherd's wives were common, common as dirt. She could not imagine Matty, with his fine clothes and the sword given him by the Duke of Navarre . . . she could not imagine him in a patched up leather jerkin, tending sheep. She could not love someone like that anyway. But Matty . . . with his curly golden hair . . . the gallant minstrel-lover every girl of noble blood dreamed about . . . well, a man like that was worth loving. And she did— God! She loved him so much.

Arlen was so boring, and he loved his little sweeting Alys so much . . . that made it all the worse. Not because she felt sorry for him, but because he was such a fool. Next to Matty Groves he could hardly survive the comparison.

Matty . . . his face swam into her mind, there was a gentle nagging stirring in her groin. Soon, she knew, to be an aching, ravening hole that only he could fill best. Damn Arlen! Damn, damn, damndamndamndamndamn . . . Where was Matty? He'd promised to be here—she'd been waiting all day. Arlen would be back tomorrow from his hunting—God love him for his hunting. And that weasel-eyed guard captain gone with him.

She could not bear it if Matty did not come. Could not bear it . . . ah, my love, hurry! Godspeed and hurry!

There was a scratching at the door. He was here! She ran across the chamber and threw open the door.

Matty looked back over his shoulder, stepped nimbly inside and embraced her, hooking the door shut with his boot. Alysoun felt deliciously crushed in his embrace, breathing in the horse sweat and leather man-smell of him. He was so small—she barely had to look up to him—and yet he was so much greater than Arlen or his tall mercenary captain, or any of the roughneck swordsmen in their employ. With his gentle ways and sweet, lilting voice, he was yet more man than any of them.

"Matty . . . " His lips closed over hers, preventing further speech. There was no need for speech; they shared a secret language all their own . . . She thrust her thighs against him, feeling the hardness straining against his breeks. She stole one of her hands away and slyly cupped him there, kneading the ballocks with her practiced fingers . . . like a harlot. The thought inflamed and emboldened her. Matty groaned like a dying man; she felt his weight leaning on her.

"Come, my love," she whispered, drawing him to the cushioned window seat. They shuffled across the stone floor, locked together in lust. He lifted her by the buttocks and braced her against the edge of the seat.

"Ah, God," she breathed into his ear, the fine golden hair tickling her nose.

Matty lifted up her dress, crumpling it in a bunch in front of her bodice. Fumbled one-handed with his trews—the other held her steady. Alysoun groaned with impatience.

"Fuck me, love . . . please God fuck me . . . "

His straining prick held in one hand, he thrust into her, right to the hilt. "Yes-s-s-s . . . " she hissed, "my sweet love . . ."

Rolling his hips, he stretched her all around. Her fingers gripped his back like claws. Matty thrust with long, gliding strokes, harder and faster. She felt as if he would split her in half. Alysoun stretched her thighs out wider and shifted her hands to hold them up. His prick swelled inside her—he was near the end, she knew, his breath coming in sobs now. She reached her hand way down under her buttocks and squeezed his tightening cods—

"Sweet Jesu!" Matty groaned. "Sweet fucking angel . . . "

She gripped him tightly, revelling in the seed spurting inside her—his gift to her.

They hung together like exhausted children, murmuring nonsense to each other. Presently her legs started to ache, and she gently pushed him away, sliding down from the window seat.

Matty slumped against the wall, his trews opened up like a little boy who'd forgotten how to tie his points. Giggling to herself, Alysoun adjusted her smock as best she could. Semen slid down her thighs unseen, all that was left of their secret sin.

"Matty . . . " She nudged him. "Someone might come in!"

He stirred, looking at her with faraway eyes; he seemed to look through her.

"Matty!"

He blinked twice, shaking his head dazedly. "What, my pet?"

Alysoun tittered nervously, "Your clothes, my love! Put them to rights . . . "

He nodded, at last comprehending. "Yes, of course. Yes."

Matty fumbled with the points, drunk with the fuck. She bent down to assist him. Someone might come in. She was beginning to worry now. Before their mating, during, she never worried. Nothing else mattered. But after, ah, there was so much that mattered. So briefly sensible, but then it would begin again. And again. They were like moths fluttering around a flame, heedless to the peril. Surely they must be burnt . . . she drove the thought from her mind. She kissed him, gently urging him toward the door.

"My love," he murmured, kissing her. His lips sucked upon hers greedily.

Alysoun pushed him away, reluctantly, almost willing to gamble. "Another . . . " she whispered, "there will be . . . "

Matty kissed her fiercely, unwilling to break free. She reached behind him for the latch, the door swung inward. Matty roused himself, thrust his head carefully through the opening, checking to see if the passage was clear.

Outside in the hallway, he turned. "My love," he said, shaking his head. His mouth twisted wryly. Then he was gone, lost in shadow.

Alysoun shut the door. Her heart fluttered like a little bird. Little bird. He called her that sometimes. So did Arlen. All men must be fond of that expression. It meant nothing, but she liked it when Matty said it.

Alysoun sat down in the wicker chair where she did her sewing, resting her head on her shoulder. Now that he was truly gone she could hardly bear it. If he scratched on the door again, right now, she would let him in, heedless of the consequences. Why wasn't he at the door right now? Couldn't he hear her thoughts screaming through the passage after him? What kind of a lover was he, this Welshman?

The best. The sweetest, most dear lover that ever breathed.

"I love Matty Groves," she said to herself.

The window, Arlen's solar window, stared at her disapprovingly. She looked about the room. Everything in it, Arlen's.

"I love Matty Groves," she said, louder this time, a little afraid. "And I don't care who knows it," she whispered.

Late the following afternoon, just before sunset, Matty met Bran in the bawn with a cup of wine.

"Well," said Matty, "I see that you managed to bring back a bit of meat."

Bran took the cup and drained it. He wiped his mouth on his sleeve. "Ahhh. Kind of you to notice. We did all right. Two stags, five does, and a few hares that just happened along."

Matty pointed to a crudely butchered cow that was being dragged in on a skid. "What's that?"

"Bowyer shot it," Bran said. "Through a hedge."

"Through a hedge?"

"Well, it was dark," Bran answered. They laughed.

Matty took his arm and they started walking toward the tower. The rest of the huntsmen crowded into the bawn and called to the grooms to help unload the meat. The stags were carried in slung under poles, eyes staring widely at nothing, mouths crusted with dried blood.

"Where is Arlen?" Matty asked.

Bran shook his head disgustedly. "He went after a hare

just before we got to the village. A hare. The hunting has loosened his brains—"

"A fine, noble sport," said Matty. "And a useful one, as it happens."

"Oh, aye," Bran said. "Convenient enough, no doubt."

"I meant that we need the food," Matty said hastily.

Bran looked at him. "And you know what I mean, harper. Have you managed to keep yourself to yourself while the lord and master was away? Or could you not resist the cruel temptation? It's a hard thing, isn't it, keeping faith with a man who gives you money and honour, food in your belly, and all the wine you can swill?"

Matty looked straight ahead. They were almost at the steps leading into the tower. He looked at Bran, a grim smile playing on his lips.

"You need a drink," he said.

Bran frowned. "You're a fool. A goddamned fool."

"I love her."

"And that makes everything wonderful, doesn't it?" Bran's face hardened. "She's got to be married to that man for the rest of her life. You can pack up and leave any time you feel like it. And I wish to God you'd feel like it!"

Matty put his hands on his hips and looked down at the ground. "You said April. We agreed."

Bran glared at him. "I said nothing. I agreed to nothing. I did not say that you had the right to come in here and swive my lord's whore of a wife under his very nose."

"All right, all right. Keep your voice down—"

Bran stepped in close. "By God, Matty," he growled through his teeth, "if I was any kind of loyal man, I'd kill you now and save everyone a lot of trouble."

Matty stared back into his eyes, standing very still.

"Why don't you then?" he asked quietly.

Bran stepped back. "You bastard." He turned on his heel

and walked quickly around the corner toward the stables.

Matty stared after him. Shrugging, he started up the steps into the tower.

When Christmas started, they feasted every night and drank too much of the bad wine. Arlen still went hunting nearly every day, often camping out overnight. Bran stayed close to the castle.

One day he took Matty with him to the Bird In Hand. They were still uneasy with each other, but Bran did not want to leave Matty in the castle with Alysoun while Arlen was away. Also, Bran wanted to see Fionna. It surprised him how much he wanted to see her. He was not in love with her; he was lonely, that was all. She had good wine.

They arrived at the tavern at midday. Matty had not spoken much during the ride. The sun was out with barely a cloud in the sky. The air was cold, with the feel of snow about it. Tomorrow perhaps, Bran thought. He did not think it would snow very much. Being snowbound depressed him immensely.

They got down from their horses and tied them by the trough. Matty stood in front of the door and looked all around the tavern and yard. He nodded.

"I like this place," he said. A peahen edged around his feet, eyeing him suspiciously.

"I'm sure Fionna will be relieved to hear it," Bran said dryly. He pushed open the door and went inside.

The inside of the common room was more lit up than Bran was used to seeing it. Cold, sharp sunlight streamed through the open shutters, broken into angles and black patches of shadow by the support crucks and long tables.

Bran pulled a deep breath into his lungs and yelled in the

direction of the kitchen. "Mistress MacTieg! Succor for dying men if you please!"

Fionna came running out of the kitchen, hastily fastening her apron. She took in the two men and shook her head.

"Dying men, indeed," she said. "I was taking a nap, you nearly stopped my heart with your yelling— I suppose you'll want wine?"

"A tun at least," Bran answered. "My throat is as tight as a virgin's arsehole."

"Forgive him, lady," said Matty, making a courtly bow.

Fionna smiled. "You've brought a gentleman with you, I see. What is your pleasure, sir?"

Matty sat down at a small table near the hearth. "The best wine in the house, Mistress, though it be wasted on the likes of us."

"Oh, sir," she clucked, "you do yourself great wrong, but you're halfway to the mark at least."

Bran pulled up a stool and sat down across from Matty.

"I'll not be insulted and buy the wine too," he said.

"Very well," Matty said, laying his clinking purse on the table. "Three cups please—you'll join us of course."

"Of course," Fionna replied. She went into the kitchen to get the wine.

Bran leaned across the table. "Can you manage not to be so charming?"

Matty's eyebrows rose. "So? You fancy her, don't you?"

Bran made a face. "I wouldn't say that exactly."

"Oh, what would you say?"

"I'd say you'd better tend to your own affairs—" Bran punched himself in the thigh. "God in heaven!"

Matty laughed. "Stop worrying. For a fighting man, you worry a hell of a lot. As handsome as this alewife of yours is, you have nothing to fear from me."

"I'm not worried about that."

Matty leaned back against the hearth. "Well then, don't worry about anything else either. It's Christmas, for God's sake. Peace on earth, that kind of thing."

"Don't mock me," Bran said.

Matty snorted. "God! You take offense better than any man I know. The wine will mellow you though."

Bran sighed, looking up at the arched beams holding up the roof. "Oh, aye. It has that effect."

"Thank God for it. Here she comes."

Fionna brought in a tall leather jack of wine and set it on the table. Bran stood up and helped himself to a cup. He held the cup under his nose. "Spanish. What happened to the Bordeaux?"

Fionna shrugged. "It went off. Over a year old, what did you expect?"

"Ah well," Matty said, "this is good enough." He poured a cup for Fionna and one for himself. "Your health, Mistress." He raised the cup and drank.

Fionna drank. "And yours, sir. Captain," she said, glancing at Bran, "you haven't told me this worthy gentleman's name."

Bran grimaced into his cup of wine. "A thousand pardons, gentle lady. This is the famous arch-priest of minstrels, Sir Matty Groves. He's staying at Ballinasloe for the winter, if he lives long enough."

Fionna sat down. "With such cutthroats as you keep there, I doubt he stands much of a chance. Matty Groves? The harper?"

Matty nodded, smiling softly. "Have you heard of me, lady?"

"Yes." Wrinkles appeared in her forehead. She frowned, remembering. "Yes. There was a man here about a week ago. Five days ago, I think. He would not say what his name was. He said that if I saw you I was to give you his regards, and tell you that he would stand as your friend if you were ever in need."

"A strong friend there, Matty," Bran said. He looked at

Fionna. "He wouldn't say his name? That's strange."

Matty set down his cup. "Did he have a scar here?" He traced a line under his lower lip.

Fionna shook her head excitedly. "Yes! Yes, he did. He's Irish, isn't he?"

"Aye." Matty picked up his cup and drank.

Bran leaned forward on his elbows, pushing the leather jack away with his forearms. "Well? Who is this mysterious friend?"

Matty looked uncomfortable. He set the cup down, playing with the edge. "Just a friend. Leave it be."

Bran filled his cup from the jack. "I suppose you have a lot of Irish friends—"

"Leave him alone," Fionna interrupted.

Matty put up his hand. "It's all right." He looked coldly at Bran. "I have some. I'm welcome in any house in Ireland—"

"And I can't say the same," Bran said. "All right, what of it? I don't like them either. They are our enemies—you seem to have forgotten it."

"Your enemies!" Matty cried angrily. "Not mine!"

Bran glared at him. "Enemies of the King, harper!"

Fionna stood up. "Please . . . "

"Your king, gallowglass," Matty sneered. "I'm a true Welshman, not some—"

Fionna knocked over the tall jack; wine fountained over the edges of the table. Bran and Matty leapt up instantly, jumping back from the splash.

"God's blood!" Bran shouted. "What a foul waste. You must be mad, Mistress MacTieg!"

"I think not," Matty said, smiling slightly. He grabbed a rag from the wall and helped Fionna mop up the mess.

Bran leaned against the hearth, watching them. "Perhaps not," he murmured.

When the table had been wiped off, Fionna went to refill the jack. Bran and Matty sat on the edges of their stools, watching each other out of the corner of their eyes. Bran was the first to speak.

"Well," he said quietly, "who is this friend that you're willing to get yourself killed over?"

"Leave it be, Bran. Just let it lie."

Bran screwed up his mouth, gnawing on the ends of his mustache. "You'd better be careful having Irish friends. Especially inside the Pale."

"We're not inside the Pale," Matty said.

"Close enough. You know what I mean."

Matty sighed. "Only too well. Look, it's just someone I helped once. He's grateful, it's not that he's such a great friend."

Bran put his hand over his eyes. "God's death, Matty . . A scar on his chin—"

Fionna came in with the wine and a round loaf. Bran gestured to her.

"Was he wearing a shirt of mail?" he asked.

She set the flagon down, cradling the loaf against her breast. "Yes, I think so. Yes."

"Were there men with him?"

Fionna, uncomprehending, "Two or three. Is that—"

"And more outside," Bran said, rolling his eyes. "God's Holy Splendour." He looked at Matty. "You're more of a fool than I thought."

"All right," Matty said softly. "Just leave it alone." He picked up the flagon and poured wine into all the cups.

Bran laughed in his face. "The most notorious rebel in the west of Ireland, and he's your cherished friend. Like brothers you must be. God's death, Matty!"

"What are you talking about?" Fionna asked, annoyed and scared. She started breaking up the loaf to have something to do with her hands.

"Conor-In-Iron," Bran said, smiling beatifically. He drank

off the entire cup. "Ahhh." He looked intently at Fionna. "You mustn't mention this to anyone."

Fionna knew who Conor-In-Iron was. "Yes. All right." She got up and went into the kitchen.

"Now you see what you've done," said Matty.

Bran stood up halfway and refilled both their cups. "Sweet Jesus," he said, chuckling to himself. "Is it true that he never takes it off—the mail?"

Matty set his teeth and reached for the cup. "I never saw him take it off. I wasn't with him long."

"He's sworn to wear it until the Normans are driven from Ireland, is that right?" Bran laughed. "He must be popular with the wenches."

"Until the shangoll are driven from Ireland."

"Ah," Bran said. "Shangoll. The strangers. He'll be wearing that mail a long time, I think."

The Third Month

Ballinasloe
January 1382

It snowed just after Twelfth Night, and kept snowing for three days. On the third day, the Old German died, a late victim of Arlen's miserable trek into Burke-land to get his bride. The Old German was not greatly missed—his hacking cough had worn the nerves of his barracks-mates to a fine edge. Although he had no friends, he had no enemies either—none of the men was actually pleased that he was dead, just glad to be rid of the irritation.

Bran took to pacing the wallwalk, stopping occasionally to rest his palms on the cold stones and stare blankly into the swirling fog of snowflakes. He could not even see the village from where he stood on the wall. The snow bound him inside the castle as effectively as the rain had, more so, and he grew to hate it. He thought of Fionna trapped comfortably inside the Bird In Hand, and gritted his teeth. He prayed for an end to the snow.

On the fourth day it rained, melting the oppressive white ocean of snow into ragged drifts. It was hardly an improvement. Bran exercised his horse in the slushy bawn, heedless of the cold water seeping through his boots. The crushing inactivity had drained most of his spirit. He would think of the hot Andalusian sun on his bare shoulders and feel like weeping.

Hold on till spring, he told himself. Things will be better then. The black horse raised his head, showing his huge white teeth. Bran stroked the horse's neck. Spring. It was not so far away, really. He went through this every winter. I should be used to it by now, he thought. But it was harder and harder with each passing year. Time moved so quickly, too quickly—except for the winters. The winters in Ireland were the hardest he had ever known.

Arlen stayed in his bower with his lady, fretting, making everyone nervous. Everyone except Matty. The minstrel sat on a fur-covered chest and sang gaily of love. He looked straight at Alysoun when he sang his love songs—Bran could hardly believe it—but Arlen never seemed to notice. Arlen was upset that he had not been a better provider for the Yuletide feasting. Coming late to his position as lord-of-the-manor, he took his responsibilities far too nearly to heart, Bran thought. Arlen was fiercely determined to hunt, hating the bad weather even more than Bran did. All the while, Matty smiled, singing sweetly, plucking out hopeful chords on his harp—biding his time.

Alysoun picked up the little ivory-framed mirror and stared intently into it. She tried a little smile. The skin crinkled around her eyes. She frowned.

Matty was watching her. "What's the matter, my pet?" There was no one else in the room.

She sighed and set the mirror down, carefully. It was too valuable to risk in a snit. "I'm getting old," she said. "Can't you see it? Old and . . . ugly," she lied.

Matty laughed. "Old and ugly, is it?" He picked up his harp and set it against his shoulder. "I wish more women were as old and ugly as you."

"Do you really?" she asked, frowning more deeply.

He squinted one eye and cocked his head. "Do I what?"

"Wish more women were like me?"

He shook his head, smiling at her. "Now why would I need any more like you. I've got you, don't I?"

She turned away and picked up the mirror again. "I'm . . . not . . . convenient for you."

"Gentle Mary," he sighed. "What will you worry yourself with next?" He lowered his voice. "You know I love you. I'll always love you."

"Always?" she breathed in a little voice.

"Always," he said more loudly, stroking the strings of the harp. The music trilled into the room like a soft breeze, caressing her. She set the mirror down and smiled at him.

"I believe you," she said.

"Thank God for that." He took out his key and adjusted one of the strings. Tried it again. "That's right," he murmured to himself, satisfied. Matty began to sing an Italian love song, her favorite. Arlen did not know any Italian. Neither did she, but Matty had explained all the words to her.

I love you, she mouthed at him. He nodded, striking the chords more vibrantly, making love to her through the harp. She felt wet. Wanted him.

Bridget came in with a fresh flagon of wine. She set it on the cupboard within easy reach.

"Will there be anything else, my lady?" she asked in Irish.

Alysoun shook her head, vaguely irritated. "No. No, nothing else."

Bridget made a curtsey. "Yes, my lady."

When Bridget had left the room, Matty stopped playing and leaned back on the stool, laughing at her with his eyes.

"Stop it," Alysoun said peevishly. "Stop, now."

"You are beautiful," Matty said. "Not old and ugly at all."

"You are . . . beautiful," she told him.

He grinned. "Now we can't have that. Men should be handsome, not beautiful. You'll turn the world upside down if you keep on with that. Frogs will sprout wings and poor men will wear golden crowns."

"You are beautiful," she said firmly.

When they could chop a short trench through the frost line, they brought the Old German up from the cellar wrapped in sacking and laid him in the crude grave, just outside the north end of the bawn wall. The Gascon crossbowman, Planchard, would keep him company. He was out there somewhere, although the marker had disappeared, probably stolen by one of the villagers for firewood.

Planchard had come across with them from France, but died the first year. He told the filthiest jokes Bran had ever heard. Bran liked drinking with him. He was so merry. One morning, Planchard was dead, his eyes closed, not a mark on him.

Arlen's scrawny clerk of a priest intoned a few words over the open grave, and hastily signed for it to be filled in. Death made him uncomfortable, which was an odd thing in a priest. The old soldiers, Arnulf and Armand, shoveled expertly— gravedigging is a part of the soldier's trade. They left the face for last, as men always do, and then that was covered up too. Everyone went inside for a hot drink.

After the main meal Bran put the Old German's things up for auction. Bowyer bought the dagger, a fine weapon, and Sad Hugh outbid Arnulf for the gilt chalice the Old German claimed to have taken at the sack of Limoges. Lord Arlen bought the horse himself to add to his remounts, and paid a fair price for it. No one wanted the old-fashioned sword or the much-mended leather and steel harness, so Bran had these placed in the armoury. The money was set aside to buy wine for the troopers' mess.

Bran ap Howell sat on a rough bench in the Bird In Hand, watching the other patrons through barely parted eyelids. He was getting drunk, feeling no pain, and most of the others were doing the same. The wine in his cup kept getting drunk up, practically every time he looked it was empty. Fionna's boy, Sean . . . or was it Seamus? Sean. Sean kept his cup full, attending him more faithfully than any of the others; most of the time Bran didn't even have to shout for him. Which was a pity in a way; Bran liked to shout when he was drunk. Sometimes he felt like roaring for a week. He drained off the sandy dregs in his cup and turned to open his mouth, but Sean was there with the flagon, smiling shyly. On impulse he stroked the boy's hair, feeling awkward, and hid his embarrassment in the fresh cup of wine. Looking up again, Bran saw that Sean was gone, and he was angry with himself. The wine pooled in his belly like blood in a beating heart. Bran felt like seizing the table and hurling it through the air, like picking a fight with the sour-looking kerne with the black beard, killing him, killing everything in the world. He drank more wine.

The sun was almost gone now, glowing red through the oiled cloth windows. The black horse would be hungry, feeling the air get colder. Bran didn't care. The horse would have to take care of himself. He was drinking, and the comfort of a second-rate horse was not his concern. It was not even a war-horse. He would not have ridden a war-horse to get drunk. The horse never complained—what could he do? It was his fate to be the riding horse of a worn-down Welsh killer with no home or friends.

Ah. Bran tapped the lip of the winecup, smiling grimly to himself. Matty was his friend. He was a Welshman too. Far from his home. But that didn't seem to matter to him, Matty had friends everywhere. Everyone loved him. He could play the harp like Jesus Christ and sing better than any fucking angel. Matty wore the finest clothes, had gold in his purse, and the love of beautiful women.

For a moment Bran hated Matty. He threw back his head and let the wine run down his throat. He himself was just a killer; there wasn't much to love or admire in that. The empty mouth of the cup mocked him. He slammed it into the wall and walked quickly past astonished faces, elbowing past two loiterers at the door, into the cold evening air.

The horse made a noise, greeting him. Bran went into the stable and grabbed up a double handful of grain from the bag inside the door.

The horse slobbered over his hands, feeding greedily, nuzzling Bran's chest for more. He held the horse's head, aware of faint laughter from the inn, a white face watching him from the door. He stroked the horse's soft mane, remembering Sean. The cold air made his eyes fill with tears. He held onto the horse's head, blinking them away, his face tight, like leather.

Fionna watched him from the side door to the kitchen. He looked so lonely standing there with his horse. She seemed to feel his pain and terrible aloneness. Stay away, she told herself. This man is trouble and well you know it. She leaned her cheek against the smooth wood of the doorframe, watching him holding onto the horse's neck in the growing dark.

She sighed. "Ah well," she said to herself, straightening the apron. Stepping carefully through the hardened muck of the yard, she went up to him, stopping a safe distance away; he was such a strange cold man.

He did not see her. Fionna cleared her throat. He turned, eyes widening. She could see that he had been crying.

"Captain . . ." she began. She did not quite know what to say. The black horse moved nervously; one of the hooves scraped against a stone.

The Welshman coughed into his hand. "Mistress MacTieg."

His eyes did not meet hers; he seemed to be staring at her left ear.

"Perhaps you'd like to come into the kitchen," Fionna said. "It's warm there." He smiled and looked into her eyes. "You seem troubled," she said, feeling bolder.

He nodded, pursing his lips. "Trouble is my constant companion."

"I thought that Thirst was your constant companion."

Bran chuckled. "That too. One is always trying to outdo the other."

"Perhaps you and your quarrelsome friends would be more comfortable in the kitchen. We can talk a little."

He pondered that for a moment.

"I don't want to disturb you in your work," he said finally. "I'll just get in your way."

"Not at all," Fionna said, amazed at her boldness. "I'll have that lot swept out in an hour or two. Farmers don't stay late. Sean can take their orders; he's really very handy."

"Yes, yes, he is," Bran replied, slurring a little. "All right, the kitchen it is."

The pain in his head woke him, finally. Bright sunlight stabbed through his clenched eyelids, setting off little paroxysms of agony deep in his brain. The bed he was lying in had a low wooden frame with four stubby posts. He patted the mattress. Down. Like the one he had slept on in Granada, like another he had diced away in Calais. He lifted his head a little from the linen-covered bolster, moaning softly. His head felt enormous. He let it fall gently back into the softness of the bolster.

Whose bed was this? A glance at the half-timbered walls told him that he was not in the castle. He did not remember riding back from the Bird In Hand . . . That was it. He stretched cautiously, the bones of his back creaking and popping. He felt a hundred years old. How long had he slept? The sun streamed through the open shutters at a steep angle. A long time then.

It was sticky hot under the blankets. He kicked them off and swung his legs over the side of the bed. Agony. He cradled his head in his hands, temples throbbing against his fingers like a beating heart. He wished he were dead. He longed for cool, sweet, painless death. Dark. Soft. Without memories.

The heavy leather curtains parted. He looked up. MacTieg's widow carried in a wide bowl of steaming water and set it on the chest at the foot of the bed.

Bran realized that he was naked. The widow did not seem overly concerned, so he decided not to be either.

"Is this your bed?" he asked.

She set a neatly folded washclout and towel by the bowl.

"Yes," she said. Her eyes were merry.

"Jesus." He could not remember.

Bran got up and walked around her to get to the bowl. Dipped his finger tentatively into the water. It was very hot. Bran shook his head. It bothered him that he could not remember. He felt her watching him. Like a wise little bird, watching him. Unafraid.

He was not sure if he liked that. Bran dipped the clout into the steaming water and dabbed at his face gingerly. He felt her eyes steadily upon him.

"Many thanks, Mistress . . . " He was unsure of what to say. He could not remember.

Fionna made a wry half-curtsey and left the room. The curtains moved where she had passed through them. Bran watched the curtains moving for a long time after she left, his jaw hanging open in an idiot's gape. The pain in his head was worse. His ears itched. His face felt greasy and hot. He bent over the bowl and splashed the warm water liberally over his face and chest. That felt good. He straightened up, wiping the water out of his eyes.

His bladder was about to burst. He found the jar under the bed, and bracing it against his thigh, pissed it half full. There was a shiny crust on his prick, the short hairs matted and stiff. So he had fucked MacTieg's widow, but could remember nothing. He slopped some water over his privates, then sat down on the chest with the clean towel knotted in his hands. His head hurt. His mouth tasted like a leper had shit in it. He felt as dried out as an old bone. Sweet Jesus. Bran imagined cool white wine rolling over his tongue.

His clothes lay heaped in one corner, presumably where he had thrown them. He pulled on his trews, fumbling with the laces, thinking of wine cooled in a mountain stream.

Bran wished that his head did not have to hurt so much. When he was young he could outdrink any man he knew and his head would not betray him at all. He thanked God he had not been drinking whiskey. That was worse. A man could die from too much of that. Ah well, he thought. At least he wasn't dead.

"Be sure to scrub those pots out."

"Ach, mither, that's woman's work," Sean said, watching her from the corner of his eye.

She slapped a damp rag at him—he jumped. "It's your work," she said. "Do you think you're going to go riding around like a knight, gambling, and picking fights?"

"Sir Bran said he'd teach me to use a sword, and a knife too. He said—"

"*Sir* Bran is it?" Fionna shrugged her shoulders. "When was he knighted? I didn't hear anything about it."

"You know what I mean . . . he looks like a knight, anyway."

Fionna shook her head, mopping the table top ferociously. It was already clean. "Looking like one doesn't make him one," she said, oddly angry. "Besides, you already know how to use a knife."

"I don't—" Sean protested.

"Yes, you do." she said. "Go slice up those onions like I told you an hour ago. There'll be a lot of men in tonight from Kilconnell."

Sean's eyes shone. "Knights? Will they—"

"Mercenaries," she said flatly. "Scotsmen, like your father."

He squinted up at her, confused. "Like you," he said.

Fionna sighed. "Yes." She did not think of herself as being Scottish any more. That was where much of the problem came from— Men thought of themselves as Normans, or Welsh, Aquitanian, English . . . Scots. But the Irish were still Irish, and the longer anyone stayed here the more Irish they became too. The land marked them. The sooner they accepted that the better. The old Normans like the Burkes and the FitzGeralds were almost Irish; they'd been in Ireland for two hundred years. It took a long time, and the more you fought it the longer it took—still it happened anyway.

She walked over to the next table, feeling tired and heavy, like an old woman. I am not an old woman, she thought. She was tired, and who wouldn't be? She could almost hear the other women saying that the inn was too much for her by herself. Why must there always be a man? She could manage very well alone, with Sean to help.

Fionna smiled, her mood lightening. He really was a great help. But he would be grown in a few years, and where would she be? She could not expect him to spend his youth helping her keep up a miserable little tavern in the middle of nowhere. There would be merchants stopping by on their way to Dublin and Clonmines, perhaps even pilgrims going to Compostela and the Holy Land. And knights. God yes, some of those too. There would be no keeping him. Men were like that; there was no use crying about it . . .

Fionna wiped the tears away with the back of her hand. Sean was gone, good. She could hear him banging things around in the kitchen, pretending to work. She felt silly, crying. The next table top came clean under her vigorous hand. Someone had scratched his initials in it. Men were bound to do that, she supposed. It was the only way some of them had to be remembered. That made her sad. She was far too sad for this early in the day. How would she be remembered? Sean. He would marry and have children, and name one of the girls after her. Fionna. Little Fionna. She remembered her father dandling her on his massive knee. He smelled like horses. She could not remember his face, just the hair, bright and red like her own. Her mother had black hair. Every time she tried to imagine her mother's face she saw her own, with black hair. Fionna had not resembled her mother; it was just a trick of the mind. Her mother had keened for days after her father was killed. He had been killed on a raid into England. Her mother wailed like a banshee, calling his name over and over. Fionna could not remember the name. Her mother had cried until she was hoarse; then she could only make a croaking sound, ugly. Fionna shivered, remembering it.

When MacTieg died she had not cried very much. A little, but mostly for herself. She had been fond of him, but he took a long time dying. He was so shrunken and wasted that he did not look like himself at all, so she hadn't cried very much.

One of the pewter mugs was missing. There had been four on the table, and now only three. It would cost a shilling to replace it. A good day's profit. If this kept up, she would have to chain the mugs to the tables, see if they would like that! She started to swear, and crossed herself. There was no need for that. Enough swearing went on under this roof already. Damn their rough ways! She did not want Sean to be like them. To be like his father. Like the Welshman. Her mouth got dry, remembering how he'd swived her. Drunken, mumbling foreign obscenities—but she'd liked it. MacTieg had been dead such a long time.

It was a sin, but she had liked it. She would not let him do it again, though. She was not a whore. That was the only kind of woman he could understand, she was sure. He must think she was a whore.

Bran dismounted and threw his reins to the straw-haired Irish groom. The groom started to say something cheerful and thought better of it. Bran strode past, headed straight for the tower, cloak flapping behind him.

In the entrance chamber he caught a scull on her way to the kitchen. "Where is Lord Arlen?" he asked grimly, holding on to her arm.

"In . . . in the hall, my lord."

He released her arm and rushed up the winding stone steps, swearing under his breath. The leather curtains were pulled across the main hall entrance, keeping out part of the draft. He breasted through them.

Arlen was sitting at a trestle table in the middle of the hall. There was a flagon out; he had been drinking wine. The crumbled remains of a loaf of bread littered the table. Bran sat down on the bench opposite, collapsing in on himself. He looked at Arlen, waiting for him to speak.

"So you had to kill the horse?" Arlen said finally.

Bran nodded. "Yes, my lord. There was nothing to be done for it, the cannon was cracked in half."

"Sweet Jesus," Arlen frowned. He looked as though he'd swallowed bad wine. "What about Bowman, is he—?"

"Bowyer, sir. He's fine, a little bruised up. Sorry to have lost a horse."

Arlen gave a mirthless laugh. "I'll warrant he is. Well, I don't suppose he's much good to me without a horse. Give him one of the Irish remounts. I don't see why they can't raise tall horses here."

"Possibly to annoy you, my lord."

The corners of Arlen's mouth twitched. "Some of your rare Welsh wit, Captain?"

"Rare indeed, my lord." Bran helped himself to the pitcher of wine on the table. The smell of it was driving him mad. "By your leave, my lord," he said, the cup already half full.

Arlen waved his hand. "Yes, yes. Pour me one. How much do I pay this . . . this Bow—"

Bran handed him the cup of wine. "Bowyer, my lord. Six pence a day, with a quarter of a mark at Christmas, and a new coat in your colours."

"Spare me the details. Six pence a day. Isn't that rather a lot? We're not on campaign, are we?" Arlen hid his face in the winecup. Talking about money embarrassed him.

"Well," Bran said slowly, "in a sense we are. Of course, on a real campaign, there would be ransoms and booty. Not much chance of those out here."

Arlen frowned. "I suppose you're right."

"Thank you, my lord."

"How long has this young ape been with me?"

"Four years, my lord. Since France." Bran rolled some wine back onto his tongue. Last year's Bordeaux, Arlen's been hoarding it. He reached for the flagon and topped off his cup. Arlen appreciated boldness.

Arlen stroked his mustache, weighing the half-empty cup in his hand. "Hmmm. Take it out of his pay. Tuppence a day for six months. That sound all right to you?"

Bran laughed. "He won't like it very much." He refilled Arlen's cup.

"I'm sure he won't. Teach him to ruin good horses. Do you know how it happened?"

Bran sucked his teeth. "They were racing, I think. Nobody would talk about it. The horse's leg probably caught on a wall they were jumping."

Arlen winced, seeing it in his mind. "Was the horse dead when you got there?"

Bran put down his cup. "No. I had to kill it." He remembered their faces watching him, as if they expected him to lay on his hands and heal the horse's shattered leg. Bran stared into the winecup. His distorted image stared back at him, blood red. He had not considered that killing the horse would bother him so much. I'm getting old, he thought.

Arlen leaned forward on his elbows, cup cradled in both hands, watching him. Bran did not like being looked at; it made him nervous. "My lord," he said, staring back at Arlen.

Arlen pushed his cup away. "I'm drinking too much."

Bran chuckled. Was Arlen trying to keep his breath sweet for his bonny bride? "No, my lord. It's good wine."

"Does it remind you of Aquitaine?" Arlen asked.

Bran finished the cup, tilting his head back so that the last drops ran into his mouth. He set down the cup. "Yes, my lord." Arlen was unusually congenial tonight. He must be lonely.

"I think about France a lot," Arlen said.

"My lord?" Bran poured the last of the wine into his own cup. Arlen didn't seem to notice.

"Yes," Arlen said, "those were good times. Good fighting, good comrades . . . "

Good women, Bran thought. Good booty, good ransoms.

" . . . The prince was a great man, you know."

Bran nodded. "Yes." The Prince had been sick a lot the last few years of his life. Bran remembered his face, waxy pale, hollowed out, like a corpse.

Arlen sighed. "Then my brother, God rest him . . . " Arlen crossed himself mechanically. Bran moved to do likewise, but left the gesture half completed when he saw Arlen wasn't looking.

"Left me his Irish lands," Arlen was saying. He shook his head, looking sorrowfully at Bran. "He tried so hard to get a son, you know. His wife was barren, but he wouldn't put her aside for another. He could have bought an annulment. He loved her, I guess. A terrible thing not to have a son to take over your lands."

"Yes," Bran replied. He did not have a son, but then he didn't have much to leave a son, either. Just as well then.

Arlen bent his head forward, conspiratorially. "I hope Alysoun will give me a son, soon," he said, his voice lowered. "She'll make fine boys, don't you think?" Arlen smiled at him.

Bran smiled back, feeling a coldness in his heart. "Yes, my lord. And girls too." He finished the wine, wishing for more.

"Yes, by God." Arlen beamed. "A pretty little girl to dandle on my knee. I'll marry her off to the MacWilliam's youngest boy, Dermott. That would be a fine match." He stood up and called to his page. "More wine for Sir Bran."

Arlen laid his hand on Bran's shoulder. "Well, I'll say good night to you. May as well go up to bed now." He winked at Bran, very pleased with himself. "You should marry," he said, walking away. "Sons, you know."

Alysoun lay deep in the bed, buried in blankets. Her lord and master would be up soon to exercise his marital rights. She had seen it in his face at dinner. She always knew when his lust had overcome his delicate reverence for her. Frowning, she buried her face in the pillow. Perhaps she could plead her flux. Men like Arlen didn't know very much about such things. Last month she had pleaded her flux twice, at the beginning and at the end of the month; that had kept Arlen away from her for eleven days altogether. She giggled against her pillow. He was such a fool. It did not seem fair that she should be married to such a fool. Still, he was well connected, although his friend the Black Prince was dead. A pity, that. To be the wife of a friend of the Prince of Wales and Aquitaine was no light thing. That would go down well with the ladies at the English king's court. If she ever got there. She would have to pick at Arlen until he agreed to take her. Life was so boring here, worse than at home. She reached across the bed, stretching out her fingers for the silver cup of wine her maid had left on the little stand. A drink of wine would help to make Arlen's lovemaking less tedious. The cup off-balanced and tipped over, spilling red wine onto the sheet.

"God's death!" she exclaimed. The sheet was ruined, that stain would never come out. The silver cup rattled on the floor.

The door opened and Arlen came in. He walked over to the side of the bed, surveying the mess. He raised an eyebrow. "What's this, sweeting? You've decided the sheets should be red, instead?"

She hated him for his condescension. "No, my lord," she said pleasantly, "just my clumsiness."

He took hold of her hands, sitting down beside her. "Nonsense," he said. "The cup was too heavy for you. I'll get you a smaller one." Arlen stroked her fingers lightly. His eyes were like a lovesick squire's. He would be forever about it. She decided to help him, to hurry things along.

"Aren't you sleepy, my lord?" she suggested. "Hunting all day . . ."

He relaxed, squeezing her hands firmly. He smiled at her. "Yes, my sweet. I'll join you anon." He stood up and turned his back to her, unbuttoning his tunic. He quickly unlaced his trews and slipped in beside her. She felt him shrug off the trews under the blankets, heard them fall to the floor. Although they'd been married for several months, he still did this, thinking her modest. Leaning on one elbow, he edged in close to her, gently stroking her smooth belly. His hard prick fell against her thigh.

She stiffened, biting her lips, ever the virgin bride. He seemed to expect that. Nuzzling her neck, whispering nonsense, Arlen lowered himself onto her. He was careful with his weight, as if he would crush her. He was so damnably considerate . . . Alysoun felt his prick straining against her. She tightened her muscles, making it difficult for him. He made a tentative thrust. She relaxed a little, admitting the swollen head. He pushed into her steadily, slowly.

"Ahhh. My little coney." He breathed heavily into her ear. "Sweet Madonna . . . sweet lady . . . "

She closed her eyes tightly. Matty's face swam before her. She tried to imagine that the prick moving inside her was his. But Arlen was restraining his passion, for fear of hurting her. It was difficult to pretend that he was Matty, swiving her. Matty would take her with every ounce of his being, filling her completely, stretching her senses to their outer limits. Arlen fucked like an old man. She dared to thrust her hips at him a little, willing him to come. His prick plodded on its steady course, like plowing a furrow. Arlen the ploughman. A giggle welled up in her throat and she fought it down desperately. Tightened around him, milking him. She hoped he would not make her pregnant. There was no fun in being pregnant. Please, Blessed Mary, let it not be. Let it— Arlen groaned and threw his head back; his prick pulsated wildly within her. His weight pressed on her; he gasped faintly, like a fish dying out of water. Alysoun pushed at his shoulders. He grunted apologetically and rolled off her onto his back. He would sleep now. She would not, not for a long while. The wetness spread over her thighs like blood, as if he had dealt her a wound there. She wriggled her buttocks away from the wet spot, and lay on her side, facing away from him. The candle on the stand by the bed had gone out. The dark closed in on her. She sighed, waiting for sleep to take her.

Bran sat hunched over a pot of ale in the Bird In Hand. He had put Arnulf in command, as usual, and ridden out right after supper. The sun was only just going down now. He was in a good mood, he didn't know why.

Fionna was still ignoring him, but she wasn't doing a very good job of it. He caught her looking his way half a dozen times. Bran smiled, felt the tension draining from his face. It was good ale. He felt comfortable, even though men were starting to come into the tavern.

A party of merchants took over a corner of the common room, pushing two of the long trestle tables together. They looked English. All of the men were wearing swords. He could hear their horses stamping and blowing outside by the trough. Four of the younger men look like hired guards. One of them stared across the room at him, lips pursed with insolence. Bran felt a tingle starting in his chest. It felt good. He picked up the mug of ale and touched his lips to the cool pewter, cocking his head back slowly, draining the cup.

"Ahhh." He felt good. Bran snapped his fingers like a Spaniard, signaling Sean from across the room. The insolent young guard turned his head to look at him. Bran stared back, unblinking. He was a boy, really, with tangled yellow hair and windburned cheeks. Under a low flat forehead, the eyes were insolent; insolence fairly poured out of him.

Sean served him, filling the cup expertly to the brim. He always gave Bran full measure. Bran had to remind him to take his money. He smiled at the boy, feeling the tension returning, freezing his face into a mask. The young bravo was still looking at him. Maybe he had seen Bran somewhere before. Maybe Bran had killed his father, or brother, or something. Bran laughed out loud. The ale spilled over onto his trews.

"Look," the young man sneered, pointing at Bran. "He must have a jest. Tell us a jest, stranger." He used the old English word for stranger, which meant Welshman also.

Bran shifted his weight on the stool. So that was it. The old hatred, the feud that never seemed to go out of fashion.

The other men in the party watched them both quietly. Bran wondered if they would help the young man against him.

"Tell us a jest," Yellow Hair repeated. "Tha' can speak, can't tha'?" He was from the border marches. "Can tha', stranger?"

Bran sipped at the ale, forcing himself to relax. Sean watched him wide-eyed, his mouth forming a little O. Fionna stood in the leather curtains, gripping a tray with two filled flagons on it. Bran glanced at her, smiling.

He looked hard at Yellow Hair. "I have no jests to tell you, boy," he said.

A muscle jerked in the young man's face. He stood up. His hair fell into his eyes and he shook it back angrily.

"Welsh pig," he said. He leaned over and spat carefully onto the floor.

Bran stood up suddenly, kicking the stool back out of his way. He drew his sword.

Fionna stepped through the curtains. "Bran . . . no." The tray shook in her hands.

Bran grinned at her. Yellow Hair had drawn his sword and stood waiting. Bran looked up at the rafters and decided that they were too low to use a two-handed grip. It would be safer to make his cuts from side to side, with the quickness and flexibility that a one-handed grip offered.

Bran advanced on him, holding the swordhilt in front of his crotch, point aimed at the boy's throat. The boy charged him, yelling. He swung at Bran's head. Bran sidestepped and ducked out of the blow, slamming the flat of his blade into the marcher lad's back. Some of the men laughed nervously. The young man recovered himself quickly and ran at Bran again, white lips pulled back into a snarling grin. He cut for Bran's legs. Bran caught the blade in his quillons and shoved hard. The boy crashed into a table, but kept his feet. Bran feinted high—and cut low, for the knees. To his surprise the boy blocked him easily and thrust for his chest. Bran ducked out of the thrust, just barely, straining a muscle in his back. That was close, he thought. I should not have played with him. Wary, he circled his young foe, holding his sword low, waiting for the boy to make a mistake.

The boy was not so hotheaded now; he held his sword out, duplicating Bran's guard, keeping the distance between them. He was trying to decide what to do. Bran was content to let him make the first move. The torn muscle in his back throbbed fiercely.

The boy's red face was shiny with sweat. Bran felt sweat running down his own face. The boy's friends were making no move to help him. They stood behind the tables, watching.

The boy grabbed a heavy flagon from the table behind him and threw it. Bran blocked it with his left arm, hissing through his teeth from the pain. He shook his arm. It did not seem to be broken. The boy should have attacked him then, but he had hesitated. The boy's red, sweating, fearful face was offensive to him. Bran wanted to kill him.

He wheeled his sword up from the floor to cut the boy's throat. Somehow, his sword was too slow—the boy's sword smashed into it a foot from the hilt and sent it spinning into the wall.

Bran staggered back, shocked. He had never lost a weapon in a real fight before.

Yellow Hair grinned, moving in for the kill. He waved his sword before him like a cattle goad.

Bran drew his dagger. His hand stung. If he yielded, the boy could not kill him; there were too many witnesses. His reputation would be made—Bran's lost.

Bran grabbed a stool from the floor and charged, yelling obscenities in Welsh. The sword bit heavily into the stool, jarring his wrist. The boy wrenched out the sword and swung again. The stool split; something smashed into Bran's shoulder. Bran reeled, clutching his torn shoulder. Blood spurted through his fingers. He fell down, still gripping the dagger. He lay still, trying to control his breathing, waiting for the boy to get closer.

The boy edged nearer. His companions cheered him, calling for wine, the best in the house. Jamie was a champion swordfighter, he was. Nought could stand against him.

Jamie leaned over for a good look, to see if Bran was really dead. Bran's legs scissored around the young man's ankles, and Jamie came crashing down beside him. Bran rolled him over, and pressed the dagger against his neck.

"Now, boy," he gasped. "I don't jest." He pushed the daggerpoint into Jamie's neck. A fat drop of blood spat out onto the blade.

The boy's eyes rolled. A sheep before the slaughter. "Don't kill me. Please."

Bran nodded, his sweat falling into the boy's face. "All right." He stopped to catch his breath. "I don't want to catch sight of you again. Ever. Do you understand that, English?"

Bran released him and stood up. The pain in his shoulder made him want to scream. He picked up his sword and slammed it back into the scabbard. The young marcher still lay on the floor, afraid to move. Bran gestured with his good arm.

"Out. All of you."

Everyone left the inn, even the two farmers who were not in the merchants' party.

Fionna stood beside him. "You've ruined my business," she said. Her eyes were straining, full of concern. She pressed her hands against his back gently, guiding him to a bench.

"Sit down."

He sat down carefully. His shoulder glittered with bright blood, like a badge. He felt sick. The sweat on his face turned cold. He moaned softly, hoping she wouldn't hear.

"Sean. Get some water and a clean sheet."

Sean was prancing with anxiety. "The hot water, mither?"

"Yes. Quick now, go!"

Fionna put a cup of wine into Bran's hand. His fingers were bloody, smearing the metal. She ripped away the sodden sleeve and threw it on the floor.

"Sweet Mary," she said.

He looked. It was deep, but not as bad as it felt. He could not stand pain as well as he used to. Fionna wiped away the blood; a thin trickle still pulsed down his arm, forming a sizable puddle on the hard-packed floor. He scuffed it with his boot.

"I've had worse," he said.

"I can see," Fionna said. There was an old, deep scar already in his shoulder, below the new wound.

Sean returned with the linen sheet and a bowl of hot water from the kitchen kettle. Fionna began to wash out the cut.

Bran gritted his teeth. "I got that one through armour," he said, remembering.

"Ah," she said, binding his shoulder with strips torn from the sheet. "That must have been a bad one."

Sean watched, holding the big bowl to his chest, awed by the blood and laid-open flesh.

"It was," Bran agreed. The water in the bowl was filmy and pink. He passed out.

Bran woke alone in Fionna's bed. His shoulder ached as if a devil was trying to gnaw its way out from the inside. He buried his face in the bolster and moaned. Bran pressed his right hand lightly over the thick bandage covering the wound.

"Ah, sweet blessed Jesus." His lips were cracked and dry. He needed a drink of something, anything. Water would do.

He was afraid to move. Where was Fionna? She had to be somewhere close by; he judged that it was the middle of the night.

He was so thirsty he could not sleep. There was nothing for it but to get up and look for a drink of water. His left arm was bound against his chest; that was good, any movement in the shoulder would be worse than the furies of Hell. Bran pulled himself up into a sitting position and carefully maneuvered his legs over the side of the bed. He was breathing hard. Sweat poured out of him. He put his feet on the cold floor and dared himself to stand up.

"I can't," he whispered hoarsely. He was too weak. If he stood up he would only fall on his face and rip the wound open, lie bleeding to death on a cold clay floor in the Back of Beyond. Bran wept. He bit his lips, trying not to make any sound.

Fionna was there suddenly, standing in front of him.

"Here."

Bran's blood hammered in his ears. The cool rim of a pewter mug pressed against his lips. He put his hand over hers, tilting the mug up, sucking greedily at the cold water that flooded over his chin.

"God, that's good," he gasped. His chest was wet from the splash.

"Get back into bed," Fionna said. "You'll catch cold."

"I'm burning up."

"Do as I say." She moved his legs up onto the mattress and pulled the blankets over him.

"God's blood," said Bran. A great weariness settled onto him. He started to say something which turned into a moan. Fionna's cool hand stroked his forehead.

"Go to sleep."

His body had gotten very heavy. He felt as if he were falling through the bed, down through the packed clay floor, down, down, into black nothingness. Peace.

The day wore on like most days. Alysoun sat in the window seat in her sewing room, watching her maids piece together a new riding outfit for Arlen. She contented herself with an insipid needlework design she had started over two years ago. "Tristan and Isolde" seemed to stare back, pathetic stick figures, mocking her with their imperfect perfect love. She was sick to death of their coyness. The empty mouth of the winecup seemed to call for more wine. She rose heavily, feeling like an old woman, feeling like she'd been married a thousand years. A thousand years in Arlen's church-blessed bed. She was tired of it all.

The flagon was empty, so she allowed herself the hollow luxury of screaming at her maids.

"You useless base-born sluts! How many times have I told you to keep this filled with wine?"

The oldest of them, gaunt gray-haired Mathilde, rose from her sewing. "My lord said that you were to have no more than a quart a day . . . " She made a little curtsey. "My lady."

Alysoun's rage jerked her from the window seat and set her flying at the older woman. Mathilde raised her arms to protect her face but Alysoun beat them down with her fists and slapped her hard on the mouth.

"Your lord!" Alysoun screamed. "Your lord! I am your mistress, you shriveled sack of shit. Never *lord* me, do you hear?" she shrilled, her voice rising with hysteria. "Do you hear?!!" Her blood was on fire. She knew she could kill at a word.

Mathilde staggered back and sat down heavily on a bench. A thin line of blood ran from her mouth to her chin, moving slowly down the front of her throat. "Yes, my lady," she mumbled thickly, looking away.

"Good. That's good," Alysoun said. The tingling fire in her blood was all gone now. She trembled.

Sensing that her rage was spent, the younger maids gathered round Mathilde like a covey of hens. One of them dabbed at the blood with a strip of white cloth. Alysoun stepped forward without realizing it. Her mouth was dry and her out-sized, incapable tongue stuck to the roof of it. Their eyes avoided her.

"I'm sorry," she said.

Mathilde nodded slightly. Fifteen-year-old Bridget, the bastard of Alysoun's second cousin, Rory MacWilliam, stepped forward and picked up the flagon.

"I'll get you some wine, my lady," Bridget said in a small voice.

"Yes, thank you. Yes." Alysoun went back to her window seat and sat down. Such a stupid, childish thing to do. Arlen was right. She *was* drinking too much wine. Soon she'd be like the Welsh captain, lapping it up like a dog. With little broken strawberry marks on her nose and cheeks, to be covered by white paste. Then Matty would not love her. He would take his harp and his love and go far away. But still, she wanted the wine. Tomorrow she would drink less and be a kind mistress to her maids. Tomorrow.

The cut in his shoulder healed slowly. It has been such a long time since he'd last been wounded—he didn't remember how long it should take to heal. He let Fionna look after him. Arnulf had come from the castle to take him back, but Bran had sent him away. He did not want the men to see him like this, at times so weak he could hardly stand.

The fever hit him on the third day. Fionna bathed his face with cold water, and laid soothing poultices against the wound.

All women had a little of the witch in them. The fever lasted for only two days. He felt weak, but in absurdly high spirits. He liked being looked after, he supposed.

He braced his right hand against the wall and stretched carefully in the bed, his spine crackled pleasantly. His bladder had been painfully full for two or three hours, but he had ignored it as best he could, conserving his strength for the main effort of getting out of bed. Fionna would probably tell him not to, but he was set on the idea. The thought of sitting in the kitchen, sipping ale, while she went about her work appealed to him. The inn was so much warmer than the castle. He decided that his shoulder would be a long time healing. Arnulf could look after the men all right. They would be a little wild when he got back, but he could deal with that.

It had rained all morning, but now he could see a little sunlight through the crack in the shutter, and he longed for some fresh air. A foul smell hung around him. He had gotten out of the habit of bathing, but perhaps it was warranted.

Bran swung his legs over the side of the bed, touching his naked feet to the floor. The packed clay was cool but not cold. Using the bedpost as a brace, he stood up slowly, gasping as the wound stretched a little. His trews were hanging from a peg on the wall. He pulled them on one-handed, and managed to lace them up thoroughly before he remembered he needed to piss. Cursing, he fumbled the laces free. The stream hit the bottom of the pot so hard that it nearly jumped back at him. He sighed like a man entering Paradise. There was nothing quite so good as a well-warranted piss. It seemed to take half an hour for his bladder to empty. He felt a bit lightheaded. He sat on the bed, waiting for the feeling to pass, then got up and emptied the pot out the window.

A while later, Bran walked carefully into the kitchen and sat down on a stool near the bread ovens. Fionna nodded to him. Bran nodded back. She went to a huge, black iron kettle and ladled steaming water into a bowl. Bran watched her warily.

Fionna set down the bowl of water. "So, how do you feel?" She draped a towel around his shoulders.

"Like hell," Bran said. His shoulder ached abysmally. He picked up a corner of the towel. "What's this for?"

"I'm going to shave you," she replied. "You look like an old bear." The razor looked sharp.

Bran laughed, the shoulder made him wince. "I feel like an old bear. A dirty old bear."

"I'll wash you later, after you've eaten." She looked at him slyly through the corner of her eye. Sweet Jesus, he thought. Wounded half to death and she can still put a tingle in your rod.

"Are you really going to shave me?" he asked. The razor looked very sharp indeed.

"Ach," she said. "I've shaved a man plenty of times. I can do it better than you can."

"Probably," he allowed. "I've never shaved a man, myself."

Fionna shook her head. "You're a game one, aren't you? Does it take wounding to bring out your good nature?" She began stropping the razor on a thick strip of leather.

"I suppose it does," Bran replied. "I'll have to arrange it more often."

Fionna applied a hot, soaking cloth to one side of his face. "No, thank you. I couldn't afford it. Hold still." She turned his head to the side and took most of half his beard with one motion. It stung a bit, but there was no blood on the razor. She dabbed the cloth in the hot water and held it to the other side of his face, softening the bristles. Another deft stroke, and she was nearly finished.

"There," she said. "Better than you could do it." She took the towel from his shoulders and shook it out.

"I don't deny it," Bran said, rubbing his jaw. His face felt clean and tight. "I'd've lost half a pint of blood by now. Why don't you open a shop?" He snapped his fingers. "Right here in the inn. You could do a bit of bloodletting on the side. Lance boils—that kind of thing."

Fionna swatted him with the towel. "Enough of that, sirrah. What do you want for your supper?"

Bran patted the bandages on his shoulder. "Ah now, if it wasn't for this, I know what I'd like . . . "

She frowned. "Now don't start getting ideas. Just because I'm helping you—"

"*Mmmm.*" Bran stroked her hip through the dress. "I'd like you to help me."

Fionna twisted out of his reach. "I'm serious. What do you suppose people will say about me?" She put her hands on her hips.

He grinned. "They'll say that Fionna MacTieg has the finest ale for twenty miles around."

Her eyes narrowed. "They will not. But I know what they will say."

He reached out for her. "Fionna . . . "

"What do you want for your supper?" She backed toward the doorway.

Bran sighed. Damned woman. "Oh . . . " he waved his good arm, "anything. Anything handy. Stew, I guess."

"I'll make you a rabbit pie." The leather curtains flapped shut. She was gone.

"Fine," Bran said. His shoulder throbbed wildly. He thought about calling after her for wine, and thought better of it. Damned woman. There was an empty, yawning hole in his gut, but he wasn't at all hungry.

Bran broke open the pie with his spoon, bending close to inhale the fragrant steam escaping. "Mmm. Fabulous. A marvel, truly." He broke up the crust; the gravy streamed out onto the flat manchet bread, trailing vegetables. His belly murmured urgently; he was suddenly quite ravenous. He ladled out some of the bigger pieces of meat to cool on the manchet.

"Careful, it's hot now," Fionna told him.

"Of course it's bloody hot," he swore. Sean giggled, watching bright-eyed from his stool. Bran gave him a wry look, which made him giggle the more. He wasn't a bad lad at all. Didn't look like his father in the least. That made it better for some reason, though Bran didn't know why. He supposed Sean had a right to look like his father.

"Arrwww!" The heaping spoonful of pie he'd just shoved into his mouth was searing like a coal. He danced it around on his tongue, sucking in air to cool it. It would not do to spit it out. Sean struggled with silent laughter, red-faced, swaying on the stool. Fionna looked down at her food, her mouth twitching at the corners.

Bran gulped his winecup dry, swirling the food safely down his throat. "Don't say anything," he said to them both. Sean got up and refilled Bran's cup from the flagon.

"Good lad."

Sean sat down, beaming. Didn't take much to make him happy. Bran swished the wine around in his mouth. Shreds of burned skin hung down from his palate. He tried another bite of pie, blowing on it a long time before he put it into his mouth.

"*Hmm.* This is good."

He drank more wine. This was the life. He liked the copper pots and bunches of herbs hanging from the low beams. The cook-fire threw off a lot of heat. He was sweating, but a lot of that was from the wine. He drank again. The cup was nearly empty. Fionna watched him eat. She seemed to like watching him eat. He'd noticed that before with women. The pie was cooling nicely. He finished the meat and started scraping together the peas and chopped carrots. He broke off a corner of the manchet bread and used it to herd the peas together. Something struck his leg. Sean's dog. The dog thrust his nose toward the food, his tail thumping loudly against the underside of the table. Bran thrust him away with his boot.

"He likes you," Sean said.

Bran snorted. "He likes rabbit pie." He broke off a piece of the manchet, dripping with gravy, and fed it to the dog. "Now go away."

The dog whined, pleading with its eyes.

"Sweet Jesus." Bran fed him another bit of the manchet.

A week after the fight in the Bird In Hand, Bran and Sean went walking together in the woods. Sean showed Bran how he set his snares. Bran listened gravely, pretending to ask questions. He and Rhodri had set snares for rabbits in just the same way. He was pleased that nothing had changed. Watching Sean check the traps and reset the snares was somehow comforting. The link with his childhood in Wales reassured him that he really had been a boy once, although he could not remember what it felt like.

The third trap they checked had a hare caught in it. The hare hung from one of its hind legs, hopping feebly on its forelegs when it saw them. Sean grabbed it by the ears and killed it with his knife.

"He's a big one," Sean said, grinning up at Bran.

"Oh, aye," Bran agreed. The hare twitched at the end of the cord, blood spurting from its neck. Sean loosed the snare and reset it. He tied the hare's hind feet together and slung it over his shoulder. Hanging down, fully stretched, the hare was nearly as long as the boy.

Bran was cold. He was not used to walking so much.

"How many more do you have to check?" he asked the boy. His shoulder ached abysmally. The left arm was numb and useless inside the wide cloth sling.

Understanding flashed into the boy's eyes. "Ach! There aren't any more at all!" he lied. "Are you tired?"

Bran shook his head. "No. Just a little hungry. Aren't you hungry?"

"Sure I am," Sean said, his cheeks flushed with the cold. He held out the dead hare. "I could eat him and twenty more of his friends!"

Bran laughed. "Well, we'd better be getting back then. It'll take your mother a long time to roast that many."

They walked back toward the Bird In Hand, heading for the white curl of smoke from the kitchen fire, hanging over the treetops like a fallen cloud. Bran filled his lungs with the fine cold air, tinged with the fragrant tang of turf smoke. The cold air made his eyes sparkle with tears. He turned his face away from Sean, blinking hard.

Alysoun's breath fogged in front of her as she held the roan mare still in the forest clearing, waiting for Matty to come. It was cold, but not too cold for comfort, with the thick wool cloak wrapped cozily around her like a mother's embrace. She thought of her mother in the north country castle, where the winter wind tooled lines into a woman's face.

"So-o-o . . . " she sighed, making another little cloud in front of her face. She ran her cold fingertip along the edge of her jaw. Growing old with Arlen would not be pleasant. He was so damned healthy that he would probably outlive her and marry again. Another little "coney" to warm his bed and live out her life in contemptible boredom.

The roan lifted her head and grunted. Her ears flicked back

and forth briefly. Then Alysoun heard the other horse too. She held her breath, knowing that it had to be Matty, but fearing anyway. Always afraid.

Matty guided his white horse into the clearing, ducking under a low branch. He lifted his head and smiled at her.

"Good morrow, my lady. My dearest lady."

Alysoun's chest felt tight. "Good morrow, my lord," she replied huskily.

He brought his horse next to hers and held out his hand. She brought one of her hands out of the warmth of the cloak and placed it in his wide palm. The roan mare shifted uneasily.

"Shhh, there," Matty said in Irish. He stroked the mare's mane with his free hand.

Alysoun let go of his fingers and cupped his face in her hands. Matty leaned over and kissed her hard, his tongue thrusting between her lips. The warm honey flow started between her legs.

"Ah, sweet . . . sweet," she breathed.

Matty let her go, rode closer to the woods and dismounted. "Come down," he said.

Alysoun swung down from the roan mare and ran toward him, cloak billowing behind her. He caught her up and crushed her against his hard chest. Their mouths joined fiercely. Matty pushed against her, forcing her backwards right up to the tree line.

She pulled her lips away from him, gasping for air. "I can scarcely breathe . . . "

"What need of breath?" Matty purred, his voice thick with lust.

Rough tree bark scraped her back through the cloak. Matty fumbled with the heavy winter dress. She felt his hardness against her belly.

"Yes-s-s . . . sweet Jesus." Alysoun reached down and hauled the front of her dress up to her waist, holding it bunched below her breasts with one hand while the other guided Matty's thrusting cock. He speared her easily, moving her thighs wider apart with his tightly gripping hands, lifting her higher onto the tree's trunk.

Drunk with passion, Alysoun started to bite his neck, but thought better of it. The marks. There should be no marks.

Afterward, riding back to the castle alone, she thought of her sin as Matty's seed trickled and cooled along her legs. *I am a wicked woman,* she told herself. *A faithless wife.* There was a stir of anxiety at the thought. She pretended that she did not care. The marriage had been forced upon her. She could not be blamed for loving Matty Groves. Not when everyone loved him.

But Arlen would not love him, if he found them out. That was certain. There would be no love in him for either of them.

She considered escape. Just running away. But Matty would never allow that. He did not want his reputation ruined over her. Stealing a lord's wife from under his own roof. That would not go well with Matty's patrons, lords themselves. There would be no welcome for them in courts or castle halls, no gold rings and silver cups and clinking purses . . . just the cold comfort of a bug-ridden straw tick in a tavern loft, while Matty played below for yokels and greasy-faced kitchen boys. Well, that would never do. For either of them. They were used to finer things.

Alysoun sighed, looking up at the tower showing through the winter-dead trees. White turf smoke from the village blew across her path, making everything ghostly. She was hungry. Wondered what it would be like to starve with Matty under an open sky. A few cold raindrops spattered her cheeks. She pulled the hood of her cloak closer, shivering. There would be no escape. None.

Hidden in the trees and scrub bushes, Conor waited, listening to the hoofbeats getting louder and nearer. He was cold but not too cold. The day was fair enough really, except that he was hungry. But the hunger was such a part of him now that he barely minded it. Or so he told himself.

Conor stepped out of the trees into the road in front of the approaching horseman. He held his hand away from the long dagger in his belt.

"So. We meet again," said Matty Groves, patting the neck of his suddenly nervous horse.

Conor nodded. "Right enough, harper. You look well." As well you might, he told himself. With your fine feasts and wine and warm bed to sleep in.

"You don't," Matty told him.

Conor forced a hearty laugh. "Right there too. My life is much harder than yours, I fear."

Matty grinned wryly. "By your own choice, Conor-In-Iron."

"Oh, I like that," said Conor. "I don't hear that name very much these days."

"Again, by your own choice," the harper said daringly.

Conor let the barb roll off him and nodded sharply at the harper. "You might be very wise. But very foolish too, I think. Anyway, I'm glad to see that you're well."

"And I'm glad to see that my well-being is of such concern to you," said Matty. "Otherwise I might be dead."

"Right again," said Conor.

The harper shifted in his saddle and looked around him. The horse snorted uneasily.

"I'm alone," Conor said, sensing his thought. The bulging wineskin hanging from Matty's saddlebow attracted his attention. "Would you have a drop on you?"

"I do," Matty agreed. He freed the slipknot and tossed the heavy skin across to Conor.

Conor drew the stopper eagerly and threw his head back, letting a stream of wine into his throat.

"Ah! Jesus, that's good. You have the best of everything, don't you, harper?"

Matty grimaced. "Come on, Conor. Don't try to make me feel sorry for you. No one forced you into this life."

Conor wiped his mouth on the back of his hand. Suddenly he did not feel so playful. It was as well that he owed this man his life. "Ha!" he said finally, scornfully. "You're forgetting a lot, Welshman. I *have* been forced into this life, as well you know."

Matty shook his head, "I don't agree. You're playing at being a hero. Some kind of Roland."

"Who?" Conor's ears pricked up, alert for insults.

"One of Charlemagne's knights. Never mind."

"The only knights I know are Norman," Conor said. "Don't compare me with them. You'll strain our friendship."

Matty smiled, chuckling to himself. "Is that what it is? By God's beard, I have some strange friends."

Conor handed up the wineskin. "Thanks for the drink."

Matty offered it back. "Why not take it?"

It was tempting. He wanted to drink it all, he had been so long without wine. Or decent food. Or a woman . . .

"No," Conor said firmly. "Thanks. Now I'll give you a piece of advice."

"What's that?" Matty asked suspiciously, narrowing his eyes.

"It's well known that you love Alysoun Burke." Conor watched Matty's face for a reaction. None came.

"This is your advice?" the harper said drolly.

"It is not," Conor said. He was beginning to feel a little angry. "My advice is to forget her. Nothing good will come of it."

"So you say."

Conor drew a deep breath and let it out slowly. The wine had made him hungrier than he was, if that was possible.

"Look," he told the harper. "Arlen will know, he *must* know. Why he hasn't killed you, I can't guess. I would."

"You'd kill me?" Matty asked, interested.

"Of course I would." Conor scratched his head and looked sideways at him. "You'd be better off going. You know that, don't you?"

Matty nodded. "Are you sure you won't take the wine?" He gathered up his reins.

Saliva spurted inside Conor's mouth. "Thanks. Thanks, I will not. Watch your back, Matty Groves."

The harper smiled and nudged his spurs into the horse's flanks. "And watch your back, Conor-In-Iron. Good luck to you."

Conor watched him ride off down the road, until he disappeared behind a stand of trees at the bend. A heavy feeling weighed on him, so strong he could almost touch it. He half expected to hear a banshee wailing. But it was midday, and banshees only wailed at night. Still, it was a cold, grave-clay kind of feeling. Not for himself, but for the harper Matty Groves. Such a proud, foolish man. Good at giving advice, but not at taking it. He sighed heavily and started back into the woods. He hoped that Padraig had caught a rabbit in one of his traps. Regretted not taking the Welshman's wine when it was offered.

In the middle of the second week Arnulf came into the tavern with three of the men, including Mark Bowyer. Bran was seated at his usual place by the central hearth, watching the cottars drink up their seed money. A few of the Kilconnell men sat in the farthest corner, grumbling over their ale. They stopped talking altogether when Arnulf and his men made their appearance.

"Well met," said Bran, nodding at Arnulf.

Arnulf pulled up a stool and sat down. The other men stood behind him looking awkward. Bowyer made a face at the Kilconnelll men, rolling his eyes like an idiot.

"I'm thirsty," Arnulf said.

Bran pushed the flagon across to him. "Drink." He stood up halfway and caught Sean's eye. "Cups!" he shouted.

Sean immediately brought four cups and set them on the small table. He filled each cup, sharing the wine out evenly until the flagon was empty, then darted back to the kitchen for another. Arnulf drank off half his cup, looking at Bran over the rim with worried eyes. He set the cup down carefully and belched.

"All right," Bran asked. "What is it?"

Arnulf cleared his throat. "You've got to come back to the castle, Captain."

Bran frowned. "I like it here. What's the matter, Arnulf?"

Arnulf leaned forward. "It's your friend, Matty Groves," he whispered conspiratorially.

"What about him?" Bran picked up his cup and studied the dimpled imperfections in the metal. So they knew.

Arnulf shifted uncomfortably on the stool. "I— We think that he and Lady Alysoun . . . well . . . we think they are—"

Mark Bowyer broke in. "We think he's swiving her, and he's going to get himself killed if he doesn't watch out."

"Arlen doesn't know?" Bran asked, relieved.

"No," Arnulf said. "I don't think so. If he does, he's hiding it well."

"Arlen isn't that devious," Bran said.

"No, he's not," Bowyer agreed.

Bran narrowed his eyes. "Shut up."

Bowyer looked away, his face flushing with anger.

"Don't let this bother you," Bran said, patting his wounded

shoulder. "If you've got anything to say, say it now. I'm still more than a match for you, puppy, with one arm or two. It makes no difference."

"Come on, Captain," Arnulf said. He looked over his shoulder at the men. "Go and find a place to sit down."

When they were alone, Arnulf said, "You're too hard on him."

"Phaugh!" Bran sneered. "You talk like an old woman!"

Arnulf's face tightened. He stared down at the cup in front of him.

"I'm sorry," Bran said. "I'm in a hell of a bad mood."

"I know," Arnulf said. "It's all right. Are you coming back?"

"Yes, damn it. I'll come back."

Sean returned with the fresh flagon of wine.

Bran blew through his mustache. "Saddle my horse," he told the boy. "I'm leaving."

Sean's face fell. He set the flagon down on the table.

"Does mither know?"

"No," Bran said. "I've just decided. Fill up our cups and take this around to my men over there. Then get my gear together and saddle the horse, all right?"

Sean nodded glumly. "All right. I'll go and tell mither."

"You do that."

After Sean left, Arnulf said, "That's a good lad. MacTieg's boy, isn't he?"

"Aye," Bran said, rolling the wine around in his cup. "He's MacTieg's boy." He gripped the cup tighter to stop his hand from shaking.

Arnulf yawned. "The mother's handsome enough. Small wonder that you want to stay."

Bran looked hard at him. "Enough of that."

"All right, Captain," Arnulf said, hiding his grin in the winecup.

"I mean it," Bran said.

"All right, Captain. All right."

Bran sat on the bed in his cramped chamber, staring into the blank wall. It was not good to be home. A red glow from the dying sun found its way through the narrow slit in the wall. He would have to light a candle soon, or go down to the hall. He didn't feel like doing either.

"Ah well," he said to himself. He wiggled his toes inside the left boot, squinting to see the new patch Fionna had sewn on. No more leaky boot. That was something anyway.

He heard someone walking along the corridor, soft leather scuffing on the stones. Bran looked up, expecting Arnulf.

"Hallo," said Matty, stepping inside. "You look well enough."

"Liar," Bran said. "Is that a bottle of wine?"

"It's dark in here," Matty said, pulling out the stopper. "Do you have any cups?"

"No, I don't think so. I don't know."

Matty took a slug straight from the bottle. "Ahh. The good stuff. Here, you look a bit sad."

Bran took the bottle and drank. The wine bit his tongue. He drank again. The second swallow was better. His stomach rumbled, demanding food.

Matty took the bottle out of his hand. "So-o-o," Matty drew out, holding the bottle against his chest. "I didn't think you were coming back."

"Hunh! I didn't think I was either. Duty called . . . "

Matty sat down on the bed next to Bran.

"You came back to spy on me," Matty said, not unkindly. He passed the bottle to Bran.

"You need . . . watching," Bran said. You need a boot in the arse, he thought.

Matty laughed. "Everything's all right."

Bran looked at him. "Is it? The whole castle knows."

"No." Matty shook his head. "I'm sure of it. No one knows but you."

Bran set the bottle down on the floor.

"Everyone knows. You can't keep a secret in a castle very long. Everyone knows who's fucking who and how often. You should know that."

"I don't believe it," Matty said. Bran could tell from his voice that he did.

They passed the bottle back and forth. The red glow in the arrow slit had disappeared. It was completely dark. Bran felt as though they were sitting in a tomb. Two amiable corpses sharing a bottle of wine.

"Do you think Arlen knows?" Matty asked. "He must. Someone would have told him."

"No," said Bran. He felt as if a weight were dragging on his heart. "Sad Hugh is the only one who might and he's too much of a gentleman. None of the servants would dare. He wouldn't believe them anyway."

"What about your men?"

"No. They won't say anything." Bran tilted the bottle up and drained off the last of the wine. The dregs gritted in his teeth like fine sand.

"Why not?" Matty challenged. "Arlen pays them, doesn't he? They might feel obligated to tell him."

"Arlen pays them, but they're my men," Bran said.

"What an admirable arrangement," Matty said. "For you."

"You should be glad of it," Bran retorted, getting angry. "By all rights you should be dead by now."

"Then I thank you," Matty said. "And your men, for their loyalty."

Bran could feel him smiling in the dark.

"It won't work, Matty," he said.

"Ah, but it will. It has and it will."

Bran blew air through his mustache. "He'll find out. He's

got to, eventually. He's not stupid."

"Then I'll ride like hell. He won't dare follow me into Thomond. Everyone knows that the Earl is my friend."

Bran snorted. "I take it that he has an ugly wife."

"Clever Sir Gallowglass. You should have been a philosopher. Soldiering's not really your trade at all. Bashing a man's brains out with a mace lacks a certain, ah, wit . . . Don't you think?"

"Oh, aye," Bran smiled. "I've wasted my life all right. I should have learned to play the harp."

"I'm glad you did not," Matty said. "You'd give the rest of us a bad name."

"When did you ever have a good one?" Bran asked. "I never heard of it."

"You're just envious." Matty picked up the bottle. "You've drunk all the wine."

"Forget the wine," Bran said. He was tired of playing. "You've got to leave. Arlen won't stay blind forever. He'll kill you, Matty."

"He doesn't seem like that kind of man."

"Phaugh! Like what kind of man? Any man would kill you for tupping his ewe. Especially Arlen. He loves her, you know."

"I know."

"In another week it will be Candlemas. Leave after the feast. Say that you're restless. That you want to go down to Thomond early. Arlen will let you go."

"I can't," Matty said. "Besides, he'd be suspicious."

"No more suspicious than he's going to be."

"I'll be more careful, Bran."

"Sweet Jesus, Matty! Just go. Go while you're still in one piece."

"You're just trying to scare me. It won't work. Arlen's expecting me to stay until April and that's what I'll do. Are you going to tell him?"

Bran felt like striking him. "Get out of here, little Matty

Groves. Get out of here before I break your foolish head."

Matty laughed. "All right. I'm hungry. Let's go down and see what's left in the kitchen." He stood up and held out his hand.

"It's your head," Bran said. He grabbed Matty's hand and pulled himself up.

"That's right," Matty said, relieved. "It's my head and I take full responsibility for it."

"Don't come crying to me when he's killed you."

"I won't, I promise."

They both laughed at that.

The Fourth Month

Ballinasloe
February 1382

Arlen was still asleep beside her, snoring softly. His heavy arm lay across her chest, as it did nearly every night. She hated the feel of it on her. Sometimes she would wriggle out from under it, or gently push it away. At other times—like now—she left it alone, afraid he would wake. Then he would want to talk, or worse.

The curtains had not been pulled together all the way the night before. Sunlight edged through, cutting across her body like a dusty pane of thin, yellow glass. The winter was almost over. Matty would soon be gone, and she would be utterly alone.

Alysoun's chest heaved sharply at the thought. Arlen mumbled something under his breath and shifted a little. She was afraid he might wake. She did not want to lie there with him, but the idea of getting up did not appeal either. Another long day to while away. She knew that there were many things she should be attending to—many tasks to supervise   many decisions to be made, for herself and others. She was the mistress of this household, responsible for a hundred and one duties and details. If the beer was brewed sour, it was her fault. If a scullery maid was seeded by one of the stable boys, the blame would ultimately fall on Lady Alysoun. If scissors needed mending, or the cook's son had a stye in his eye, then the mistress would see to it. It was something she had been bred to, been prepared for, since she was small. And if it had not been for Matty Groves, she would have been content enough to do it.

137

It was easier to blame Matty, whom she loved, than to blame herself. He was older, more experienced. He should not have taken her, and having taken her, stayed to bring shame and misery and discontent. He had no *right* . . .

Alysoun squeezed her eyes shut on the smarting tears, gulping back a sob. DearsweetMarymotherofGod . . . she had sunk so low as to blame *him* for the mess she'd made of it. Who was it that begged him not to go, that twisted Arlen into asking him to spend the winter? Who was it that held onto him like a drowning woman, or a frightened child afraid of the dark? Who was really to blame?

Alysoun was shaking with the strain of trying not to wake Arlen. There would be plenty of time later to blame herself and cry into her pillow. Arlen always wanted to know why she was crying, and she nearly always lied to him. He had been very considerate for a long time, but less and less in the last month or so. Sometimes she frightened herself by pretending that he knew. She would see it in his eyes—he *knew*. But nothing he said or did betrayed this. He was polite and generous to Matty, and treated her well, although not as warmly as before. And then she would decide that he could not really know, probably didn't even suspect. How could he? They were as careful as they could be. Only the Welsh captain knew. And probably her maids, damn them. And their lovers, and the other servants . . . everyone had to know.

Arlen was awake, looking at her.

"Good morrow, my lord," she said sweetly.

He rubbed his eyes—for form's sake, she thought. Perhaps he had not been asleep after all.

"Good morrow, my lady."

She reached for something to say. "The sun is very bright today, husband. Will you ride?"

Arlen shook his head slightly. "No. It's too late to hunt. What will you do?"

"Oh, there are always many things for me to do, my lord." At the moment, she couldn't think of *which one,* and hoped he wouldn't ask.

Arlen rolled her nipple between his finger and thumb. As his reverence for her diminished, he had become freer, more familiar. Alysoun felt nothing.

"We lack fresh meat," she said, daring greatly. "It's a fine day to be out hunting."

He frowned. "I don't want to hunt. You never hunt with me. Didn't those half-breed cousins of yours show you how? I hear there's good sport up there."

"You're talking about my family," she said coldly. "My cousins could teach you a thing or two about hunting, sir. Aye, and good manners too."

Arlen took his hand from her breast. His face seemed to collapse; he looked very old. She thought that he might cry. Alysoun had never seen him cry before. If he did, she could not bear it.

"I love you, Alys," he said in a little voice. "Can't you love me . . . just a little?"

A sick feeling spread in her belly. She pitied him, just for a moment. Then— "I do my duty, sir. As you do."

Arlen chewed his lower lip, watery eyes unfocused, staring beyond her. "Can there be nothing else," he asked her, "only duty? I need you, my lady."

This was getting dangerous. She knew she had to give him something, a show of affection. Alsyoun felt she was gaining lost ground. She shifted closer to him and laid her cheek against his shoulder.

"Forgive me," she said. "I was angry with you. What you said about my family—"

"I know, I'm sorry." Arlen put his arm around her. "It was wrong of me to say it."

The tears came quite easily to her. She felt very relieved.

He was comforting her. She wanted to laugh, but it was so sad, so sad. He deserved more than this. She did not love him, could not love him, but he deserved more than this.

Arlen petted her like a child. "Sweet Alys. Sweet, sweet Alys."

Matty had one of Arlen's sparrow hawks on his wrist and invited Bran to join him. Bran didn't much care for hawking, but he went for the company. It was good to get outside again after the snow and freezing rain. Good to speak his own language again too, although his tongue was rusty and fumbling unless properly oiled with wine. When he was drunk he spoke well enough.

"What a fine day," Matty said, smoothing the hawk's feathers as he rode.

"It'll do," Bran said.

"I suppose you think it's too cold," Matty said, baiting him.

Bran watched him preen the young hawk. "I suppose I do. It was cold in Spain too, sometimes. The wind blows the cold down off the mountains. Snow up there all year round."

Matty broke a short silence. "They say that this is the worst winter anyone can remember."

"It's the worst I can remember," Bran returned. He felt very old having said it. Besides, it was a lie. He had seen worse winters in Wales when he was a boy. Much worse. At least here you wouldn't get trapped in the mountains for months on end. But he didn't seem to mind the cold as much when he was young.

"You need a woman," Matty said. The hawk stirred on his wrist, jingling the tiny silver bells fastened to its spurs.

Bran looked at him. "Do you have any to spare, harper?"

"None," Matty told him. "Do you need me to find women for you?"

"Fuck yourself," Bran said genially. "I've brought some wine. Do you want any?" He slipped the knot of the wineskin and held it out. The hawk shivered, blind inside its leather hood.

Matty soothed her with his voice. "There, there, sweet. My little beauty."

Bran shrugged and pulled the stopper. The rich blood-red wine flooded his mouth. He felt better for it. "Jesus, that's good," he said, still swallowing. "Arlen's private stock."

"I'm sure he won't mind," Matty said, smiling.

Bran laughed. "Ah, no. How could he?"

They laughed together. The hawk was quiet now, waiting for Matty to loose the hood and let it fly. Bran could never understand why they came back after being cast. Sometimes they didn't.

"I don't see anything," Bran said, scanning the sky for prey. The watery sun made everything unreal. He wondered if this was how the sky would look after he was dead.

"There," Matty said quickly. "There—look!"

A kingfisher flew lazily above a small pond, with a little fish flapping in its pointed beak.

Matty unlaced the leather hood. The hawk blinked slowly, looking very wise and very cruel. Matty lifted his hand and the hawk flew up from his glove. They watched it climb high above the kingfisher.

"She's going a long way up," Bran said. His stomach tightened with anticipation. He did not like hawking, but he was fascinated with the kill. There was something very clean, almost pure about it.

Matty curved his hands around his eyes to focus on the hawk, already a barely perceptible speck in the cloudless sky. The kingfisher was heading away from the pond, going home.

"There," Matty said excitedly. "She's diving now, look at her!"

Bran had lost sight of her, but now he could see the hawk

diving, becoming larger, dropping toward the kingfisher like a flight arrow. "She'll miss," he said. "She started too far up."

Matty shook his head. "She won't miss. Not that one."

The kingfisher darted sideways suddenly, sensing the hawk above it. The hawk moved her wings slightly, changing the angle of her descent. The kingfisher turned and dove for the trees. Bran's heart beat wildly, painfully. The hawk struck the kingfisher in the back, exploding feathers. The little fish dropped out of the kingfisher's beak and fell into the trees.

"Good girl," Matty murmured under his breath. "Good girl."

"That was well done," Bran agreed. He felt his hands tremble.

Matty swung the lure above his head and the hawk returned to his wrist. He fastened the hood over her head. "We'll ride over and see the kingfisher," he said, "I'll let her have a few bits. Not too much if we want to cast her again."

"It's up to you," Bran said, unstopping the wineskin. "That was a good kill. She won't top that today."

"Maybe. Maybe not," said Matty, grinning fondly at the hawk. "God, I wish she were mine."

Bran stood on the ramparts of the tower, looking beyond the little village into the dark trees. The sun was almost down. A long line of red showed above the treetops, bleeding into the bottom edge of the deep blue sky. White turf smoke drifted up from the village like fog.

Smelling the turf smoke made him hungry. It was a pleasant kind of hunger, not like starving in the saddle on a forced march with the enemy closing in behind you. He knew he would go down to the kitchen in a few minutes and get some cold beef and mustard and a hunk of bread. He rested his palms against the cold stones, wishing that he had ridden out to the tavern for a hot meal and a flagon of Fionna's excellent ale—but he couldn't be doing that every day, like some love-struck squire. The men were already laughing, he was sure. His hands were numb from the stones, so he blew hot breath on them and clamped them in his armpits. Some of the stars were out already he noticed, the big one that never moved and the Warrior's Belt.

He started thinking about a battle he had been in a long time ago. In France, but he couldn't remember exactly where. He couldn't even remember how old he had been, but he had the big Angevin war-horse, so he must have been twenty at least. As usual, he couldn't recall the horse's name. Bran couldn't remember calling the horse anything. He leaned forward on his elbows, shutting his eyes, drifting back . . .

Dodging a thrown axe, Bran rammed the huge Angevin war-horse broadside into a mounted man-at-arms; the soldier and his mount rolled over twice in an untidy tangle of broken legs and flapping armour.

A crossbow bolt smashed through his shield, numbing his arm to the elbow. The thick, pointed head grated in one of the joints of his arm harness. He did not think it had penetrated. Another bolt skipped off the front of the saddle.

Bran whirled the horse about, charging the two reloading crossbowmen, Italian mercenaries by the look of them. They dropped their bows just before he hit them. One managed to draw a sword before Bran rode him down. The other man tried to run and died, staggering blindly, with the brains and lungs hacked out of him from behind.

Bran reined the horse in and looked around at the carnage, bracing the bloody sword against his hip. Thick Italian blood ran down the length of the blade, dripping onto his gauntlet. The war-horse's flanks were spotted with gore. Bran looked around quickly. The nearest fighting was at least two bowshots away. He dismounted and bent over the first man he'd killed, slashing open the front of the doublet with his dagger. He found the little purse where he expected it to be, filled with newly minted gold ducats. Paid in advance, he thought. He stuffed it behind his swordbelt and leapt back into the saddle; the war-horse reared, kicking out, maddened by the smell of blood.

As Bran fought to control the horse, a knight detached himself from the melee and charged toward him, whirling a flail above his head. Bran spurred his war-horse into a countercharge, raking the underside of the horse's barrel with the sharp rowels; he would not let the knight catch him flat-footed. As the Frenchman bounced along in his saddle toward him, Bran calculated the value of his finely made German armour. He would try for a head kill if he could, he decided, pulling the axe from its ring in the saddle. The Frenchman was almost upon him, red and white plumes bobbing above his closed bascinet. Bran's visor was up but it was too late to do anything about it. He swung his shield to cover his back as the horses half collided, but the spiked ball caught him anyway, crunching in his thin iron backplate, blasting the air from his lungs. He reeled in the saddle, black spots dancing before his eyes. For a moment he browned out completely, and spurred the horse forward blindly, hoping that he wasn't riding into the knight's second charge.

His vision cleared. The knight was on him again, swinging his deadly flail. The chain caught on the edge of Bran's shield— the steel ball glanced off his shoulder cop with a clang, drawing sparks. Bran swung wildly; his axe bit into the Frenchman's shield. He wrenched it free, ducking as the spiked ball blurred past his head. Bran chopped at it instinctively. The chain wrapped around the haft of his axe. He pulled hard and sent both weapons spinning away. They drew their swords at the same time, pulling the horses away from each other. Now that swords were being employed, it was more dangerous for the horses. They circled each other warily, controlling the horses with their knees, watching for an opening.

Bran slammed his visor shut and attacked the knight without thinking. He was unaware of the blows splintering his shield. He only wanted to kill the man and then ride out of the battle and find a place to lie down. His back hurt where the spiked ball had forced the thin iron into his flesh. Cracked ribs again, he was getting tired of that. His sword sheared away part of the knight's shield. Bran smashed at the smooth, featureless visor, hating the man behind it for cracking his ribs. A month of misery to look forward to, lying on the cold hard ground at night with two or three cracked ribs.

He parried the next blow on his blade and thrust down quickly into the neck of his opponent's horse. Bloody froth exploded from the horse's nostrils; its forelegs buckled and it fell onto its knees. Bran reined his war-horse back onto its powerful rear legs and let him drop. The great steel-shod hooves crashed down on horse and knight like hammers. The knight's horse screamed, a terrible sound. The knight dropped his sword, clutching the front of his saddle with both hands. The dying horse struggled to rise. Bran could see the man's eyes behind the visor, frightened, pleading. He cocked his sword back and hit him as hard as he could in the gap between helm and breastplate. The fine chain mail kept the blade from penetrating, but the force of the blow broke the knight's neck. The knight jerked and fell out of the saddle.

Bran hurt too much to bother with the dead man's armour. The main battle had moved farther away. The only banners that he could see were English. There was a windmill turning slowly on the hill above him. He remembered seeing a farmhouse in the hollow behind it. Bran turned the war-horse toward the mill, urging him up the steep slope, swearing mechanically as the buckled iron ground into his ribs . . .

"Sean! Seaneen! Come in now and take your bath!"

Sean crouched in the loft above the stables, determined not to come out until he was good and ready. His heart beat wildly in his chest like a little drum. Defying his mother like this made him feel more grown up, more independent.

"Sean! I mean it! I know you're around here somewhere, I can smell you! Come on now!"

He wished that Sir Bran had not gone away. It was good to have another man around to talk to. Not that there weren't men around nearly every night, swilling his mother's good ale, but they treated him like a nithing little boy, when they noticed him at all. Sir Bran made him feel important, and listened to the things that he had to say. Even his mother didn't do that any more, not really. She treated him like a child, as if he were still her "wee bitsy bairn." He supposed all mothers did that, but he didn't like it.

"Sean!" Her voice had changed, much lower now. "I'm getting angry!"

Sir Bran had not visited the tavern for three weeks at least. Sean was getting worried about him. He supposed that Sir Bran had gotten into another fight and was lying wounded somewhere, waiting for Sean to come by and find him, and care for him like his mother had. When he was better he would ask Sean to ride away to the wars with him and be his squire. Sir Bran was always talking about wars that he had fought in, and Sean couldn't imagine that he would stay around too much longer before going in search of another one.

His mother had stopped shouting. This scared him a little, more than the shouting had. It was fun to hear her calling for him and not to answer back, wicked almost. The priest said to always "honour and obey thy parents," but he was tired of being a good boy all the time. He did not think that Sir Bran had been a good boy all the time.

The silence frightened him. It was delicious in a way, but

he was starting to wish he had not waited so long. The fat pony shuffled and snorted in the stall below. His pony. His father had bought it for him last year. Sean hugged his knees, remembering MacTieg's broad red face, and how his wide shouting mouth would seem to split it apart. When Sean was bad, MacTieg would swear at him and blacken his bottom with a stick or his thick leather belt, doubled over in his fist like a weapon. He had been afraid of his father, but he missed him anyway. Not so much now that Sir Bran was around, of course. Sometimes Sean had to remind himself that MacTieg ever really existed; it seemed almost that he had imagined him, there was so little trace of him left. MacTieg had been dead such a long time, almost a year. He thought it strange that a bellowing bull of a man like his father should shrivel up and die so quickly. It didn't make any sense. Sir Bran was not as big as his father, but big enough, and he didn't shout so much. Sean hoped that Sir Bran would not die too soon.

He hung from the edge of the loft and dropped noiselessly into the hay. Well, he'd been hiding long enough. His mother had been heating water for hours to make a good hot bath for him. It felt good to take a bath every now and then. Sir Bran said that he took baths all the time in Granada. Sean thought that Granada was in France somewhere, except that Moors lived there instead of Frenchmen.

Sean crept around the corner and went through the kitchen door. Fionna stood with her hands on her hips, glaring at him. "Where have you been? I've been calling you for half an hour."

Sean swallowed the lump in his throat. "I was down by the river looking at the swan."

Fionna's eyebrows rose. "I thought you said the swan was dead."

"This was another swan," he said hastily. "A black one."

"I see. A black swan. We'll get people coming in from miles around to see it. I'd like to see it myself."

She took off her apron and started toward the door.

"Ach, no," Sean cried. "It swam off down the river. I think it's going back to the sea."

"Oh?" Fionna said, a smile tugging at the corners of her mouth. "Back to the sea, is it? Did it tell you this?"

"Ach, no, mither," Sean protested, red-faced. "Swans can't talk."

"Enough of your lies," Fionna said, swatting him with the towel. "Get those clothes off and into the tub with you."

Sean undressed quickly and sat down in the low wooden tub. The water was very hot. "Owww," he cried. "Pour some cold water in!"

Fionna shook her head. "I'll pour the lot outside, and you with it. Close your eyes." She poured cold water from the bucket over Sean's bent head. His long hair streamed down into his face, like that of a drowned man. The thought put a sudden chill in her heart.

"Did you really see a swan?" she asked gently, the warmth coming back into her voice.

Sean looked up at her, sputtering from the cold water. "Oh! I'm certain I did. At least I think it was a swan."

Fionna laughed, emptying the rest of the bucket over his head.

Lord Arlen stood on the battlements of his tower and surveyed his domain, what he could see of it. It had rained earlier in the day, leaving a freshness in the air that he enjoyed very much.

It was a sad thing, inheriting these lands as he had. He had liked his brother, although he had not seen him for many years. Perhaps that was why he liked him.

Like most young knights, Arlen had hoped to win lands for

himself in the King's service. But land was land, he could not complain. He was a little too old now to be dodging arrows and eating bad food on the march, relying on the King's paymaster for his few comforts. He was his own paymaster now, and he liked that very much indeed. He could not complain.

Too bad that the colony was not holding up better. The old Normans had only half conquered it to begin with, and now the ones that came after were paying for that mistake. The Gaelic chieftains were regaining their influence and a lot of their territory. He and three other lords and their vassals formed a little island in the midst of O'Dowds and O'Kellys, separated from the borders of the true Pale by sixty miles. At least the trading routes were still open, joining the English towns and fortified enclaves together after a fashion. That was mostly due to the "black rents" that almost everyone paid to the chieftains. Even Arlen paid. The O'Kelly was not such a bad fellow, and the "rent" that Arlen paid him, in money and cattle, was not unreasonable. Still he did not like paying it.

It was a fine day. He decided to let nothing bother him. Some of his men were on horseback in the village common. He squinted his eyes and made out the figure of the Welsh captain, wrapped in his black cloak, watching them from the side of the meadow. Arlen was glad to have such a capable man in these uncertain times. True, it was quiet now, but war could break out at any time, and it was comforting to have seasoned soldiers to defend his lands and drive back the enemy if need be.

He caught himself worrying again. It was not good to worry so much. He did not remember worrying at all when he was just a landless knight in the Prince's retinue. Life had been simpler then.

He had a lot to be thankful for. He paced along the narrow walkway between the peaked roof and the battlements. A lot to be thankful for. He had his lovely lady, who was surely too fine for him. Arlen worried about that too. She was almost too beautiful, but wasn't that why he had married her? Surely she had expected a lot more, though. Arlen sometimes had the feeling that she was bored by him. It was a lucky thing that he had been able to bring the harper along for the winter, to amuse her.

Arlen took off his glove and touched his fingers to the cold stone. Mine. All of this.

His fear that he bored her came back into his head. Soon the harper would leave. It was unlikely that he could persuade a man like that to stay longer, when richer, more important men were waiting to welcome him. Still, he would try, for Alysoun's sake.

Two of the horsemen had reined their horses close together, turning in slow circles. He saw that each was trying to pull the other off his horse. He could not make out who the men were, but he could see from the way that they moved that they were young. Arlen smiled. He decided to go inside for a drink of wine.

When he came into the hall, Sad Hugh was there at one of the tables, straining over his ledgers. Like a clerk, Arlen thought. He is a belted knight, and yet I doubt he's ever been in a battle, or felt his teeth rattle under a blow. That was unfair, he probably had. Still, knighthood was not what it once was. The world was changing. Arlen did not think that he liked the changes.

"How does it, Hugh?" Arlen asked. He sat down on the bench opposite.

Hugh looked up, blinking. "Well enough, my lord." He looked down at the ledgers, frowning. "Well, not actually. It's been a bad year."

"I know," Arlen said. "Next year will be better."

Hugh said nothing. He bent his head over his ledgers self-consciously, rolling one of the freshly cut quills between his fingers. Arlen saw that he had spots of ink on his hands. A clerk, no better than the young priest he had hired away from the Law Courts in Dublin. The priest was Hugh's chief assistant, preferring rent-rolls and cattle tallies to the proper work of the Church. Strange, strange world, Arlen thought.

He caught sight of a lurking pot-boy out of the corner of his eye and called him over.

"Bring a flagon of wine for Sir Hugh and myself. Quickly!" The pot-boy ran off to fetch the wine.

Hugh looked up from his ledger. Arlen thought that he looked like an old hound— You are well named, Sad Hugh. He knew that his steward did not want his company just now, but he would have it anyway. A little wine would do them both good, help drive away the bad humours.

"You should get out more, Hugh, now that the weather has cleared. You look as white as a corpse."

"I've been out nearly every day this week, my lord, attending to your business."

Bloody man. "Well, I suppose you have. Still, you look pale, you should take better care of yourself. Why don't you go hunting with me? Let your clerk do the dirty work for a while."

"My lord is very kind."

He did not like the way that Hugh avoided his eyes. Arlen did not trust men that would not look him in the eye, but he knew that he could trust Hugh, so something must be wrong. Maybe things were worse than the steward would admit. Arlen knew that there was a lot of money going out and very little coming in. That could be it, he supposed.

"What's the matter, Hugh?"

"My lord?" Hugh looked startled.

"Ah, the wine," Arlen said. The pot-boy set one of the silver flagons on the table between them. The steward moved his precious ledgers to one side, where they would be safer.

The boy poured wine into Arlen's cup. Arlen picked it up and drank. "Ahhh. Nothing like good wine to wash away the cares of the world."

"Just a little," Hugh said as the boy poured wine into his cup. "Half. That's enough."

"Fill up his cup," Arlen ordered.

Hugh nodded. "My lord."

"You may go," Arlen said. The pot-boy scurried out of sight.

Hugh raised his cup. "Your health, my good lord."

"And yours." Arlen drank deeply. Wine is good for the soul, he thought.

Hugh played with the rim of his cup. He looked troubled. "My lord—" he began.

"Yes, Sir Hugh, what is it?"

Hugh clenched his fingers around the base of the cup. He sighed. He pushed the cup away and folded his hands in front of him. "Nothing, my lord. Nothing."

A warm haze expanded inside Arlen's head. He was wrong to worry so much over trifles. Alysoun was his wife, he loved her, he treated her well, there was nothing more that he could do. He leaned forward on his elbows and smiled at Hugh. All in all, he was a very lucky man.

The weeks passed very slowly for Bran. Everything was the same, day after day. It was not so cold any more. Arnulf had the men practicing with their weapons in the bawn, or working with the horses in the flat common in front of the village. Bran stood on the edge of the field and watched. He did not want the wound to break open. It had taken almost three weeks to close. Every couple of days he would change the dressing and look at the wound, willing it to close. The edges seemed to be joined solid now, but he knew that it could still break open if he did something stupid.

The first time he had been wounded in the shoulder he thought he would lose the arm. That wound was much more serious. An axe had shattered the thin iron shoulder cop and broken through the mail links underneath. Griffith had picked out the broken links with the point of his dagger. They made Bran drunk first. Then Griffith put the dagger blade into the fire until it was white hot and cauterized the wound. Bran could not remember how long it had taken to heal, but it had pulled open several times because he had to ride all the time. He did not use a shield for nearly a year after that; he always rode in the third rank of the cavalry, with the light-armed hobilars and the javelin men. Eventually he found a lighter shield that he could use, but the shoulder had still given him trouble, especially in damp weather.

Bran pressed his right hand over the padded bandage. Bad luck getting hit there again. The sling made him self-conscious, so this morning he had decided not to wear it any more. He kept his left hand tucked into his swordbelt, but the shoulder ached anyway. As long as he didn't do anything stupid, it would be all right.

Mark Bowyer and one of the young Gascon men-at-arms were trying to knock each other off their horses. Bran watched, urging the Gascon on with his eyes.

"Come on, you frog-eating bastard . . . " he muttered.

Bowyer grabbed the Gascon by the front of his breastplate and pulled him out of the saddle.

"God's death!" Bran snorted. Gascons weren't worth a damn.

Arnulf came riding up. His face was flushed, he was not used to the exercise.

"Did you see that?" he shouted at Bran, laughing.

"Oh, aye," Bran said. "Very impressive." Boys playing at men. "Let's see some blood, Arnulf. They've had it too easy."

Arnulf shook his head, smiling. "You're in a sour mood, Captain."

Bran scowled at him. "Who would not be, watching these . . . knaves playing at being soldiers? Who would not?"

"I know the remedy for your malady," said Arnulf, nodding sagely.

"For God's sake . . . "

"Go and see her, Captain. It's only pride that's stopping you. She'll be glad to see you."

"When I want your advice, I'll ask for it," Bran said. He decided that he would go and see Fionna. She had to be missing him by now.

"Well," she said, as he came through the main door, "it's been a while. I thought you were dead."

"Something very like," Bran said. He threw his cloak back over his shoulders and walked to the hearth. "Ahhh, that's good," he said, cupping his palms over the heat. "I forgot my gloves."

"You've forgotten a lot of things," she said.

He looked at her. She frowned and turned back toward the kitchen.

"What do you want to drink?" she asked.

"I didn't know if you'd want to see me," Bran said.

Her head snapped around, eyes blazing. "And why didn't you ask? I'd've told you if I wanted to see you or not!"

"I . . . just don't understand," Bran said weakly, hating himself for it. Why did the woman have to be so damned mysterious about it? He held out his hand. "I'm sorry."

"Ach, never mind," she said, grinning suddenly. "I'm glad to see you anyway. Sean will be glad to see you."

"Where is he?"

She went back toward the kitchen. "Oh, he's around. When he sees your horse he'll be in—" she snapped her fingers, "like that."

"I'll have whatever you've got handy," Bran called after her, "as long as it's wet!"

Fionna disappeared into the kitchen. Bran sat down in his usual place, tilting the stool until his back rested against the warm wall of the hearth. He was glad that he had come. She had missed him after all. He found it hard to believe that she really cared for him, but it was obvious. He did not know why anyone should care for him any more. Still, he was glad that she did.

Sean came in later, after they had drunk most of the second flagon together. Fionna was very merry. Bran felt like kissing her, but then Sean had come in.

"My lord," Sean said formally, "I'm glad that you are well."

Bran laughed. "God, what manners this boy has."

"He wants to be a knight," Fionna said. She winked. "Like you."

"Oh," Bran said, pleased. "Then we'd better start his training."

"Do you mean it?" Sean shouted.

Fionna looked at Bran suspiciously. "Yes, what do you mean?"

Bran stroked her hand. "Let me take him over to the castle and show him around. You'd like that, wouldn't you, Sean?"

"Ple-e-ease, mither!"

Fionna sighed. "You devil," she said, looking at Bran. "All right. Tomorrow. You can come for him tomorrow."

"I don't have to come for him tomorrow," Bran said suggestively, squeezing her hand, "if you follow my meaning."

She slipped her hand away delicately. "Come for him tomorrow, Sir Bran, if you will."

"There. Left a bit. Hold steady. Hold steady. Now!"

They fired the crossbow together, Bran's fingers guiding

Sean's. The heavy bolt clanged through the front of a rusty breastplate set up on a post thirty paces away.

"Good," said Bran, taking the crossbow. He put his boot through the iron stirrup on the end and bent down low to slip the goat's foot hook under the cord. The hook was attached to a stout strap that hung from the center ring of his crossbowman's belt. He braced the stock against his knee and straightened up; the hook drew the cord back along the stock until it locked behind the nut. Bran slipped the hook off and stood up all the way. His shoulder hurt.

Sean reached for the weapon, eyes wild with excitement. "Let me do it this time." The soldiers standing around them laughed.

"That's a likely lad," said Arnulf, chuckling. "Are you going to sign him on?"

Bran shook his head, handing the crossbow to Sean. "His mother would kill me." He took a bolt from the short, box-like quiver on his belt and set it in the groove.

Mark Bowyer nudged the old Gascon standing beside him. "Two to one he doesn't make it, Armand." He held out four silver pennies.

Armand shrugged, pulling on his grizzled white beard. "No. That's a fool's wager."

"Go on," urged Mark, "Tuppence." The Gascon shook his head.

Sean sighted along the crossbow; his left arm shook a little from the strain of holding it steady. Bran was afraid he would miss.

The boy twitched the long iron trigger with the first two fingers of his right hand. The bow snapped out nearly straight— Clang! The breastplate swayed on the post. The wooden fletches from the two bolts were a hand-span apart.

"Good lad!" shouted Arnulf. The other men nodded and grinned, even Bowyer.

Bran laid his hand on Sean's shoulder. "Very good. You want to quit while you're ahead?"

"Ach, no! Do you?" Sean looked up anxiously, fearing he would.

Bran laughed. "No. No. Here, I'll span the bow for you." He took hold of the stock. Sean tugged it back.

"No. I'll do it," he said.

Arnulf laughed, the other men laughed with him. "He's his own man, Captain, let him be!"

Bran nodded. His face felt hot; he was strangely ill at ease. "Pull up hard," he told Sean. "Hard as you can."

Sean strained at the cord. The other men bent forward, urging him on with their eyes. Bran hooked his thumbs in his belt, trying not to look at Sean. He concentrated on the battered breastplate, punched full of little square holes. He heard the cord click into place. Sean raised the crossbow, already sighting on the target.

"Here," Bran said, fitting a bolt onto the stock. "You may need this." Arnulf laughed good-naturedly, winking at Bran.

Sean flushed, the crossbow wobbled dangerously.

"Relax," said Bran. "Steady. That's right. Easy, easy—"

The bolt spanged off the curved side of the breastplate.

Arnulf blew out a gust of air. "Well," he said, "You scared the shit out of him, anyway!" Everyone laughed. Bran ruffled the boy's hair.

"That's all right," he said. "You've got to hit plate armour straight on, not the easiest thing to do—"

"Thank God!" Arnulf interjected. "Otherwise half of us would be dead right now!" He laughed. "God! I've got a thirst that would kill a lesser man! Let's ride out to the Bird In Hand—" He winked at Bran. "I hear the landlady there is pretty enough to make you weep!" Arnulf slapped Bran on the back. "Any truth to that, Sir Bran?"

Bran cleared his throat. "Well . . . that's what I'm told, yes."

"That's what I'm told," Arnulf mimicked. "Sometimes I think

you've got sea-water in your veins instead of blood—with all respect!"

Bran gave him a hard look. "Of course."

"Mither will be glad to see you," Sean said innocently.

"I'm sure she will," said Arnulf gaily, "I'm sure she will—"

"Arnulf!" Bran barked sharply. He did not care to be trifled with in front of his men.

Arnulf mumbled something that sounded vaguely apologetic. The men were quiet, all the jollity gone from them. Bran was almost sorry he's said anything. Never let them like you over much, he thought. They'll sneer at you behind your back.

"Let's pick up the bolts," he said to Sean.

"We'll get the horses," Arnulf said.

"Fine," said Bran. His shoulder ached miserably.

Sean ran into the wide field beyond the post, searching for the lost bolt. Bran faced the rusty breastplate with the two bolts sticking out of it, remembering the men he'd seen killed that way.

Sean let out a whoop. He held up the bolt. Bran waved at him, forcing a smile.

The bolts were wedged tightly in the rusted steel. He worked the first one loose carefully, trying not to damage it any further. He gripped it ahead of the wooden vanes and tugged gently—it slid free. The chunky pyramid-shaped head was flattened at the point. Bran swore under his breath and dropped it into the quiver.

Bran reined back the black horse so that Sean's fat, ambling pony could keep up. Arnulf and the three soldiers with him had gone on ahead to the inn, impatient with thirst. Bran was still annoyed with Arnulf's familiarity. He felt his authority slipping, and thinking about that kept him awake at night.

For twenty years he'd had the professional soldier's knack of falling asleep immediately, under any circumstances, and now that too had left him.

The boy bounced along on the oversized saddle, scanning the trees on the side of the road, birds flying overhead, a ploughman and his beast—everything with equal interest.

Bran tried to remember if he had felt that way once about the mundane trifles of life. All boys did, he supposed. Something of that feeling had returned when he lived in Granada, with its exotic smells and tastes and sounds. Everything was so different that he was forced to experience it. But that dream had suddenly shattered, and he had found himself back in war-ripped France, scarred and half starved, the colour and excitement already fading from his mind like an old, old memory. He'd taken so much for granted. All gone.

Cool air brushed against his cheek, making him shiver. A fur-lined hood for his cloak would be a good investment. He'd suffered through the winter without one, but the thought of doing so again next winter depressed him. He would shoot a string of coneys and give them to Arnulf's wife to line the hood. No. Arnulf's wife was dead.

"Look!" said Sean, pointing skyward.

A wild hawk dropped out of the sky onto a low-flying heron. The heron died with a brief shudder and fell into a field next to the river. The hawk followed it down, hidden by the tall rushes.

"I'd like to have a hawk," Sean said admiringly.

Bran squinted at where the hawk was hidden with its prey. He imagined it ripping the heron's throat, pecking out its eyes. "Only noblemen keep hawks," he said.

Sean looked at him. "Are you a nobleman?"

Bran laughed, startled. His heart felt like lead. "Sort of," he replied. "In my own country I'd be, for what it's worth, which isn't much."

"Why?"

Boys asked too many questions. "It's like Ireland; everyone is a king, or the son of a king, or descended from kings. It's not such a great thing to be noble there."

Sean frowned. "Oh."

"Is that so important?" Bran asked gently.

"No," Sean lied, "I was just thinking—you have to be noble to be a knight, don't you?"

Bran nodded, pursing his lips. "Usually, yes. But commoners get knighted all the time. Well, sometimes. Is that what you want to be—a knight?" The lad had spirit all right.

"Yes!" Sean's eyes shone. "Do you think I can?"

Bran remembered the fantasy with Arlen and the fief. A brass slab with his name on it. "Maybe," he said, half believing it. "It's not easy though. Your mother won't like it."

Sean grinned. "Ach, let me worry about that!"

Bran laughed. "God's blood, boy! And I thought you were . . . never mind." He reached over and punched Sean's shoulder.

"You thought I was what?" Sean asked, frowning.

Bran shook his head. "Nothing. Nothing. I thought you were such a good boy, that's all."

"I am," said Sean. "I just want to be a knight."

"Well, where have you been?" Fionna swatted Sean playfully with a dishclout. Sean ducked away, running into Bran.

"Whoa, now," said Bran, pushing him away. "You're the one who can handle her, remember?"

"What does that mean?" Fionna asked, hands on hips.

Arnulf pounded his mug on the table top. "More ale, landlady!" He winked at Bran.

Fionna took a flagon and went over to fill his mug. Bran hooked a stool with his foot and dragged it to an empty table. Sean had disappeared. He tilted the stool, resting his back against the edge of the table. The room was warm with sweating, drinking men and the banked turf fire. He closed his eyes, letting the day drain out of him.

"What will you have?" Fionna asked, suddenly beside him.

Bran looked up into her freckled face. He wanted to hold her. "Mead. If you've got it. I haven't drunk any in six months."

"You won't drink any tonight, either. I sold the last drop on Martinmas. I'll have some ready in a month or so."

He put his hands behind his head, stretching. "I'll be awfully thirsty by then. Bring me some ale."

Fionna raised her eyebrows. "At once, good sir. I only hope you're still alive when I bring it to you. A terrible thirst you must have."

Bran patted her hip, feeling awkward. "Oh, it is. I'm perishing with thirst."

She smiled and went away to fetch the ale. He felt good. He wished that all the men there would suddenly find something better to do, but he knew they wouldn't. Smoke from the turf fire made the air thick, tickling his throat. He imagined the cool ale rolling down his throat.

Sean staggered toward him, bearing a huge leather jack of ale. Bran laughed. "Your mother has a fine wit."

"She said you were thirsty." Sean thumped the jack onto the table.

"So I am." Bran grabbed hold of the jack. It was heavy. He tried to pour some ale into the mug Sean had set on the table top.

"Oh, watch out!" said Sean. The ale foamed alarmingly over the sides of the mug, spilling across the table.

"What a waste!" Bran exclaimed. He quickly sprang to his feet and drank from the jack. Arnulf and the others cheered. Bran set the jack down and wiped his mouth extravagantly on his sleeve. "Ahhh. I feel like a new man."

Sean grinned. "You don't look any different."

"Such insolence. Go get me something to eat." Bran waved him away. He sat back down on the stool, feeling pleased with himself.

The sun glowed red through the oiled cloth windows. Another day down. Would Fionna let him stay the night? He doubted that she would. Her cursed reputation. The thought of going back to his cramped, cold closet in the castle depressed him. There was nothing to do but look at the wall and wish he'd done things differently. Maybe she would let him stay.

Sean brought him a spit-roasted chicken and a round loaf of bread. Bran ripped off one of the legs, chewing ferociously, concentrating only on eating and drinking. He gulped down a throatful of ale, nearly choking. Eating and drinking and shitting and pissing. Life was pretty simple after all. Why did he let things bother him now, when it was too late? His lips twisted in a wry grin, dripping with grease. He picked up the jack and let another flood of ale down his throat . . .

Bran stirred. Someone was trying to make him stand up. He felt somebody's arm hooked under his armpits, struggling against his weight. "Hunh?" His arms thrashed wildly, independent of the rest of his body. Opening his eyes, he saw only bleary double images, a confusing hodgepodge of light and shadow.

"Help me with him!" He heard Fionna's voice, strained, angry.

Bran tried to put his arms around her; they didn't work properly. His head spun sickeningly. "Garrrgh . . . Jesus . . . Arrw—" He vomited down the front of his tunic. The soldiers were laughing. Everyone was laughing at him. He didn't care, he just wanted to die. He retched again. Fionna pushed his head down between his knees. He fell off the stool, slowly, slowly; it seemed to take a long time before his head thumped on the packed dirt floor. "Sweet fucking Jesus . . . "

The raw stench of beer-sodden vomit clawed at his nostrils. He retched weakly, trying to curl himself into a ball—if only the room would stop moving. If everyone would sit down and stay very, very still, he was sure the room would stop moving.

He felt strong arms lifting him. "Haw!" Arnulf shouted in his ear, "I haven't seen you drink like that in years! You lost me sixpence— Bowyer bet that you'd puke your guts out, but oh, I said, never! That man's been drinking since you were sucking at your mother's teat, I said! Not him—"

Leaning hard on Arnulf's shoulder, Bran struggled to arrange his feet in a logical manner. "Sh-shut up," he murmured, "I'll k-kill you if you say another word."

He felt Arnulf stiffen. "Of course, Captain. Now, we'll just get you to your horse. Sean's got it all saddled up for you."

Bran pushed Arnulf away, swaying against the edge of a table. "No. Stay here." He set his legs farther apart and tried to focus his eyes. Fionna appeared in front of him, like an avenging ghost.

"You're not staying here," she said firmly. Her green eyes blazed furiously.

Bran staggered toward her, arms outstretched. "Stay here," he repeated. He wanted to be held by her, soothed, like a child.

Fionna turned on Arnulf. "He's not staying here. Please take him."

Bran shut his eyes. When he opened them, she was gone. He felt Arnulf's heavy hand on his shoulder.

"Come on, Captain," Arnulf said softly," Let's go home."

Bran dug his chin into his chest and wept. Home. He felt that he might weep for a hundred years.

"Come on, Captain," Arnulf said.

Bran let them lead him outside and put him on his horse. His eyes were matted shut with tears; he was like a blind man. He heard the jingle of harness as the other horses gathered around.

He started to fall off the horse. Arnulf's hand shot out and pushed him gently back into place. He heard the men's low voices, whispering, uncertain. Someone took his reins; the black horse stretched his neck forward and began to walk. The other horses fell in behind, their hooves pinging on the little stones in the road. He sighed, and it came out like a moan. Hunched over the saddle pommel, chin resting on his chest, Bran let himself drift away.

Bran rose reluctantly. It felt late. He pulled on his leather riding breeks and went to the slit window. The cold stones of the floor numbed his feet. The sun was high, what he could see of it; it was nearly noon. He sat on his bed, holding his head in his hands. The simple effort of going to the window had drained him. Cold sweat stood out on his forehead. His stomach rumbled warningly. He felt like throwing up. Wiping the sweat from his face with his balled up tunic, he lay back down on the bed. He would have to move sometime. The thought of moving about the castle, facing them, made him ill. Never again, he swore. Not another drop.

After an hour or so he got up and pissed into the clay pot under his bed. He shivered as the bright yellow stream ran out of him, nearly filling the little pot. Feeling better, he decided to dress and go in search of water. Two or three quarts should quench his thirst. He buckled on his swordbelt. Jesus, he thought, as the sword banged against his calf, it's like a bloody tail. He had worn a sword since he was fifteen. There was a patch of callus over his left hip where he felt nothing, not even a needle driven into the skin.

There was no one in the stairwell when he went down, thank God. He could not bear to look at anyone at such close quarters.

They were roasting something on the hearth in the great

hall. The smell made him gag. He held onto the curving stone wall. Sweet blessed Jesus, he swore, never again.

There were only a few knaves in the storeroom at ground level, dicing between the stacked casks and weapons racks. They did not notice him. He moved past them toward the door.

Outside, the fresh rain-scented air struck him like a blow from God. He filled his lungs with it, rejoicing. Some of the pain in his head blew away. Water. His mouth felt like a dried-up leather purse, and tasted worse. He squelched across the muddy courtyard toward the water trough. He went down on his knees in the clammy mud and plunged his head into the trough. The icy water exploded the haze in his suffering brain. Here I plight my trough, he thought, chuckling. It hurt to laugh, which made him laugh all the more. Stop, stop, I'll die here. He could think quite clearly now, which was a pity. Once again he plunged his head under the water. Without thinking, he opened his mouth to drink, and jerked back out, spluttering and choking. He shook his head like a dog, glistening droplets spinning from his hair in every direction. He sat back on his heels in the mud, laughing.

When he had drunk his fill, half the trough it seemed, Bran walked briskly to the stables and ordered the boy to saddle his horse. That accomplished, he set out on the road to Fionna's tavern.

Along the way he met a dove-catcher, with four or five of the birds thrashing inside his bag. Bran bought a brace from him, tied them together by the legs, and hung them from his saddlebow. It was Providence meeting the dove-catcher; it would not be well to show up empty-handed. He smiled at his good fortune, humming a tune he had learned as a child in Wales. He had not thought of it for years.

The black horse fretted at the bit, angry with him. No one had rubbed him down after last night's ride. Bran decided that the horse must have been fed, or he would have been thrown by now.

He patted the horse's neck. "Good boy." The black horse grunted.

The doves fluttered weakly under the battered saddlebow, scarred by sword tips and constant use. He'd had the saddle since he came back from Spain. Most of the studs were missing. It was time for a new one; the leather seat was worn through to the tree, rippling with little cracks where it had dried out without being oiled.

The doves had nearly had it too. He supposed the blood had gone to their heads, like Saint Peter on the cross. Fionna could make them up into a little pie, or spit-roast them, stuffed with mashed bread crumbs and spices. He felt a spurt of saliva in the dried cavern of his mouth, and knew that he would live. He remembered a stream-cooled Rhenish he'd drunk many years before. Maybe Fionna would have a passable white wine hidden away somewhere.

There was a donkey tied up outside the door of the Bird In Hand, a fat bundle hanging from either side of the well-padded saddle.

Bran put the black horse in the stable next to Sean's pony. The black horse was in a bad mood and was likely to cause trouble. It liked the pony though. There was no sign of Sean; Bran supposed he was somewhere inside the tavern.

He didn't think Sean would stay more than a few years longer with his mother, as things were. Well, maybe he would, but he'd resent it. Sometimes Bran felt like telling him: Look at me, I've seen the world, and I've done all the things you'd like to do, and where has it got me?

If someone had told him that when he was Sean's age, he would not have listened. It was natural for a man to want to go out and make a way for himself. Everything seems easier when you're young. If only he could have bottled the confidence and energy he'd had when he was young. The *knowing* you could be what you wanted to be, do everything you wanted to do.

Bran shut the stable door carefully behind him and walked past the donkey into the tavern. The common room was dark as usual, although there was a small fire going in the hearth. He made out the dim figure of a man, sitting by himself in the corner nearest the fire.

"Good morrow," Bran said in French.

"God be with you," the man replied, with a heavy Flemish accent. One of the townsmen from Galway, Bran thought. The little burgher had a solid looking round belly that hid his belt buckle, and two chins.

Bran decided to be friendly. "Where is the lady of the house?" he asked, leaning against the stone wall of the hearth.

"She is cooking for me . . . she is cooking me a supper." The little Fleming beamed with anticipation.

"Ah," said Bran, resting his hands on the warm stones. The little fire hissed; the glowing, crumbling sods of turf looked like a castle on fire. "Well, I hope she comes out soon; I've got a thirst that would kill an ordinary man."

"*Ja, ja,*" said the Fleming, nodding stupidly, "thirsty man."

Bran laughed. "Much thirsty man. What's that you're drinking?" He reached for the Fleming's pewter cup.

The little man looked doubtfully at him, then the cup, but brightened suddenly and handed it over, smiling. Bran took it, making a little bow. The Fleming bowed back. Silly bastard, Bran thought, what if I don't give it back to you?

He sniffed at the contents. Beer. That figures. He drank deeply and handed the cup back nearly empty. "I guess we're both hoping she'll get back out here soon, aren't we?"

The Fleming smiled, nodding rapidly. "*Ja, ja,* very thirsty!"

"What are you doing here?" said Fionna's voice, suddenly coming from the direction of the kitchen entrance.

Bran pushed himself away from the hearth and turned to

167

face her. He couldn't see her face in the shadow. "Where's Sean?" he asked impulsively.

"Out. Checking his snares. What does it matter to you?"

He stepped toward her. "Fionna . . . " His heart collapsed in on itself. Fionna shook her head and stepped back from him.

"No. Just stay there," she said.

The fat little Fleming watched them delightedly, as if they were actors in a morality play. He smiled at them both, nodding happily.

Bran sighed. "Look—" he said, remembering the doves. "I brought something for you." He rushed past her, out the door and into the stable. The birds were still alive, just barely. Bran patted the black horse for luck. The black horse twisted his head back, trying to bite him.

"Here . . . " he said breathlessly, bursting into the common room. Fionna was gone.

"Where is she?" Bran yelled at the Fleming.

The little man flattened himself against the wall, jowls quivering. "There . . . back there," he stammered, unconsciously grasping his dagger hilt.

Bran thrust through the leather curtains into the kitchen. Fionna stood in front of the baking ovens, arms crossed tightly over her breasts.

"Get out," she said, almost whispering.

Bran's eyes filled suddenly with tears. "God's love . . . " he croaked.

Fionna bit her lips and looked away. "Just go. Please."

Bran saw that she was crying. He held out the dying birds. After what seemed like an hour, Fionna stepped forward and took them.

Bran's outstretched arm was shaking. He hooked his thumbs into his belt, trying to summon up his dignity. It didn't work; dignity seemed out of place here. Fionna untied the doves and laid them gently on the floor. They fluttered helplessly, unable to move.

Fionna shook her head slowly. "Why . . . why?" Impulsively, Bran reached out and held her, crushing her against him. She wrapped her arms around him, sobbing quietly. His mind was blank, completely. He just held her. After a long time Fionna said, "I can't . . . I just can't."

He stroked her hair. "Shush. Shush now. It's all right."

"I can't," she sobbed, holding him tighter.

"Fionna," he whispered, "my sweet lady." He felt as if the world were spinning around him. He wanted to die, just holding her like this. Die and forget everything. Oh Jesus. Sweet, blessed Jesus.

All the way back to the castle, Bran looked up at the early stars, straining his neck, singing an old marching song.

"Oh, she took me by the lily white hand and led me to the table . . . She took me by the lily white hand and led me to the table . . . There's plenty of wine for a soldier boy, to drink it if he's able . . . With a tur-ril-lie . . . "

He patted the black horse, letting the reins slip through his fingers. The black horse would get him home all right. He stared into the glowing face of the moon. Well, he would marry her and that was that. Arlen had said that he should be married—well, he'd be married then! It was time, anyway.

Arlen would give him that fief and knight him, and all would be well. It wasn't so bad really, not what he'd expected at the beginning—but who got that? It would be all right. He felt good just thinking about it, better than he had felt in years. They would keep the inn for a while, then sell it and buy more land. Ireland was full of land. Arlen needed strong vassals—he'd knight him in a minute, as a wedding gift.

Bran laughed out loud, startling the horse. Yes, by God! he thought. *Sir* Bran ap Howell, Knight. He'd build a castle, a little one at first, just to establish his hold on the land. Sean could build a better one.

But what if he and Fionna should have a child? A son? Wouldn't he be the rightful heir? Bran frowned. He'd never considered that before. It was a problem. By Norman law it was a problem. He sucked the cold air into his lungs, clearing his head. Problems, problems. Get the fief first and worry about the problems.

He uncorked the leather bottle of wine Fionna had given him.

An owl hooted disconcertingly. He looked up. The sky was patterned with hundreds of silver clouds. He tilted his head back, sucking greedily on the smooth leather lip of the bottle. The rich, full-bodied wine flooded his mouth.

One of the little silver clouds covered the moon for an instant. He thumbed the stopper back into the bottle. Well, he would marry her, and that was that.

Arlen was frightened. He knew he shouldn't be. But the killing of the Flemish tailor on *his* land was an affront to his authority that he could not ignore. He felt that if Conor and his followers were marauding in force then he could somehow deal with them more effectively. But a handful of dispirited men attacking travellers at whim, and then disappearing back into the silent woods . . . well, that worried him. He knew from experience what men like that could do. Just a handful—and the whole countryside was in jeopardy. And everyone, from his vassals and tenants down to the lowest bog-kerne would feel that Lord Arlen was not in complete control of his lands.

The killing had taken place far enough away from his

immediate demesne for Arlen to pretend that it was not his direct responsibility, but he knew that he couldn't do that. It was really the O'Kelly's problem—and it angered him anew that the O'Kelly had not dealt with it before now.

Sad Hugh came in with some tally sheets for Arlen to look at.

"Not now!" Arlen snapped. "I have real problems to deal with, not these . . . these scratchings on parchment that mean so much to you."

Sad Hugh's face tightened. "These scratchings, my lord, are important, I assure you."

"Yes, yes," Arlen exclaimed, bobbing his head up and down, "I'm sure they are. Find Sir Bran for me, will you?"

"My lord." Sad Hugh gathered his tally sheets and withdrew through the leather curtains.

Arlen reached for his winecup, thought better of it and pushed it away. That was no answer. It was no good getting drunk this early in the day. The problem of Conor had to be faced and dealt with. Conor could not be drunk away like the ache of an old wound or uncollected rents. The Welsh captain would know what to do—or at least he'd better, that was what he was paid for.

Arlen felt a cold draft as the curtains opened. Bran walked into the room and sat down at the table next to him. The Welshman's familiarity irritated him, but Arlen decided that this was not the time to mention it.

"You sent for me, my lord?" The mercenary shook out one of the goblets and filled it from the flagon.

"I can't have this young lout killing travellers on my highway. What are you going to do about it?"

The Welshman smiled. "I've been thinking about that. He's robbed four or five others before this—"

"I didn't know that," Arlen said, annoyed. "Why wasn't I told?"

The Welshman's hard eyes held him fast. "Because it wasn't important . . . my lord."

Arlen felt a hot blush rising in his forehead. "But now it is. You think that killing a man on my land is important? I'm relieved to hear it."

Bran nodded, accepting Arlen's sarcasm without comment. He drank the wine in his cup and poured more from the flagon. Arlen had a sudden urge to strike him.

"Well?" Arlen demanded.

Bran held the winecup in both hands, regarding it with bemused indifference. His eyes were like stones, Arlen thought. At times the Welshman made him uneasy. This was one of those times. Arlen did not love him for it.

"I have a plan in mind," Bran said finally. "Not a good plan, but it might work. Would you rather have Conor alive or dead?"

"Whichever," Arlen said. Bran shot him a skeptical look. "All right," Arlen conceded, "alive if possible. The O'Kelly will appreciate it."

Bran chuckled. "Perhaps. I'll see what I can do."

"I'm tired of the rain and cold," Alysoun said. "I'm bored too."

Matty grinned at her. "Poor little dove," he crooned, "poor sweet Alys."

"Do you mock me, sirrah?" she asked, her voice rising.

But Matty always knew when to be tender with her, when to play. "How could I do that?" he countered softly, brushing her cheek with his hand. "You're my sweet flower," he said in Italian.

She wanted him to hold her, but Bridget and two others were in the room, sewing. Alysoun sighed. "I wish it was spring."

"Do you now?" Matty asked slyly.

She realized what she'd said. "No, no. I don't. I hope spring never comes." Her heart beat painfully. She felt herself losing control.

"It will, you know," Matty told her.

"No," she said. "It can't. I couldn't bear it."

"Steady now," Matty said, looking over at the maids.

Alysoun reached for her goblet of wine. Her hand was shaking as she picked it up. She gripped it tightly in both hands and drank. Matty was looking at her, full of concern. "I'm sorry," she said, setting the goblet down carefully.

"Don't be," he told her. "It can't be helped. Do you want me to play for you?" He started to pick the harp up from the floor.

"No. No. I just want to look at you," she cooed in the lover's Italian he'd taught her. Alysoun brushed the first tear away. He was so beautiful. The pain of it pushed into her stomach like a dull blade.

"And I just want to look at you," Matty said softly.

The wetness started between her legs. She dipped her eyes at him, nostrils flaring. "Is that all, my lord?"

"Don't," he begged her. "Please."

"*Yes,*" she mouthed at him. "*I want you.*"

"No," he whispered. "Tomorrow, perhaps. You risk too much."

"Are you afraid?" she asked him in Italian.

"Yes," he told her. "Always."

She nodded. "Tomorrow, then."

Alysoun picked up the goblet. Her hand was steadier. Hearing him admit his fear made her less afraid. It was strange. She hoped that Arlen would hunt tomorrow, or go out looking for the Irish rebels. Then they would have a good chance. Even the Welsh captain did not worry her any more. He was Matty's friend, and would not betray them.

"Play for me," she commanded.

Conor lay crouched under a flat stone jutting from the hillside. Raindrops splashed into his face, making him blink. Somewhere below he could hear them chasing Declan. The others were all away safely, he hoped. The hollow under the stone was beginning to fill with water. Conor pulled himself into a tighter ball, moving his ragged boots away from the worst of the mud. He hoped they would not climb the hill looking for him. He would stay put for a couple of hours in case they were watching.

Declan screamed farther down the little valley. The shangoll were killing him. Conor gripped the hilt of his broken sword. His hand was still numbed from blocking the axe stroke that had shattered the too-thin blade. He peered at the marks punched into the forte near the gilded crosspiece. *Italian.* The Italians usually made better swords. He had taken the sword from a Flemish tailor on the road to Galway. The tailor would not miss it in any case, being dead. He had tried to bribe his way out of his trouble while the pretty sword stayed safely in its scabbard. A mistake. They had taken his money anyway, so he may as well have fought.

Today was not so lucky. Conor had taken everyone but Padraig to the Athlone Road in the hope of robbing two English merchants who had passed the night in the Bird In Hand. Instead they'd been counter-ambushed by half a dozen horsemen in Arlen's livery. But the hillsides were steep, and everyone had gotten away except Declan. The wind was driving the rain harder now, but Conor could still hear the man's screams, just barely. He stuck the broken blade into the clay beside him and pressed his hands tightly over his ears, trying not to think. Rage welled up inside him and he welcomed it, shaping and polishing it to fit the few unfilled gaps in his hatred for the shangoll.

Bran rode into Fellbrigg's palisaded bawn with four men, young Bowyer among them. Arnulf's man had reached them an hour before to tell them that one of the reivers had been taken. Bran hoped it was the great Conor-In-Iron himself, but that would have been too much luck in one day. He had won nearly two shillings from Bowyer just after breakfast, using Bowyer's dice. That was enough good fortune to satisfy him until supper at least.

A boy ran forward to hold his horse. Bran dismounted and dropped the reins over the boy's shoulder. "He bites," he told the boy in Irish.

Fellbrigg came out of the tower and met him in the middle of the bawn. He had put his armour on for the occasion, although Bran doubted that he had been out riding after the reivers.

"Captain, I'm very glad you've come," Fellbrigg said, looking worried.

Bran nodded. "Sir Robert. Where do they have him?"

"In the storeroom. Your man has been questioning him but he won't talk." Fellbrigg's eyes were twitchy. Bran doubted that he approved of Arnulf's methods of questioning.

"God's teeth," Bran said, chuckling. "He'll talk all right. He'll betray his dear mother when Arnulf's done with him."

Fellbrigg's jaw tightened. "I don't like this, Captain."

Bran looked at him sideways. "No. I'm sure you don't, Sir Robert. But we must do all in our power to rid this land of murdering kernes, mustn't we? Conor's getting too bold."

"Yes," Fellbrigg agreed. "You're right, of course. I wish that his father would do something."

Bran laughed gruffly. "Well, blood is blood. The old man was quite a reiver himself in his day, only he wasn't quite so particular. Robbing his fellow Irish didn't bother him at all. Conor's different though, they say." Bran laughed again. "He doesn't like strangers."

"He's got to be dealt with," Fellbrigg murmured. Bran noticed that he was chewing one end of his long mustache.

"Conor will be dealt with, never fear," Bran told him. "But the old man won't be much help. They say he doesn't give him weapons or food, but that could be a lie."

"I don't know," Fellbrigg said doubtfully. "This one hasn't eaten in a while, by the look of him. He had a dirk and cudgel when your men caught him. I wouldn't say they were well armed."

"Good. The O'Kelly knows what's best for him, I'll grant him that. He's a sly bastard, though. You never know what to expect." Bran took off his gloves and folded them into his belt. He didn't like Fellbrigg. Fellbrigg always treated him courteously, but Bran knew that he looked down on him because he wasn't a knight. One of the Gascons had heard Fellbrigg tell Arlen that he thought it strange to have an unbelted Welshman in charge of his men.

They went into the tower. Because it was such a gray drizzling day, it was very dark inside. Fellbrigg called one of his servants down to light a torch. When the torch was flaring nicely, Fellbrigg lifted the trapdoor to the storeroom and started down the ladder. Bran followed him down, half blinded by the bright torchlight.

A thick stench of blood and urine clogged his nostrils. In a sudden flash of thought, Bran saw himself miss one of the ladder rungs and break his neck in the sickening, torchlit hell below. What a place to die, he thought. The reiver must be thinking that too. He stepped onto the packed clay floor behind Fellbrigg, blinking his eyes rapidly, trying to see the men that he could feel all around him.

"Captain!" Arnulf exclaimed, grinning hugely. "I see that Martin found you all right. Look at this pig!"

The reiver was stretched backward over a fat barrel with his ankles tied to his wrists. Several turns of thick hempen rope secured him fast around the waist. Arnulf gripped the man's jaw and wrenched it hard. The reiver groaned, drooling bloody spittle.

"Don't break it," Bran warned. "I don't want you to hit him in the mouth any more. In Spain I saw a man bite his tongue off that way. Then he couldn't tell them anything. God knows he wanted to!"

Arnulf laughed. "All right, all right. He's a stubborn one, though." He slammed his fist into the reiver's belly. "Doesn't know what's good for him, does he?" Arnulf said loudly in Irish.

Bran bent over the man and whispered in his ear. "I'm going to let them cut your prick off and feed it to you. You'd better start talking."

The reiver strained against the ropes, arching his back at an impossible angle. His chest was bloody where they had drawn their daggers lightly through the flesh. He wasn't too badly maimed yet, though Bran saw that two fingers were missing from his right hand.

"Did he lose those in the fight?" Bran asked, knowing better.

Arnulf shook his head. "No. I cut them off after we'd been at him for over two hours. He's trying my patience."

Bran nodded. A sick bile-taste rose in his mouth. It was bad work, but necessary. "Did you promise him anything?"

Arnulf chuckled. "Of course. I promised him everything. Said we'd give him a horse and he could go home to his loved ones and live to be an old man."

"I don't think he believed you."

"Perhaps it was the way I said it." Arnulf punched the man again, hard. His fist came away bloody.

"God crush you," the reiver gasped in Irish. "My name is Declan MacFlan, and I curse you with my dying breath!"

Bran moved a small cask closer to the reiver and sat down.

"That's wishful thinking," he told the man. "You're a long way from being dead."

"Fucking shangoll!" The reiver tried to spit at him and missed.

Bran shook his head, looking up at Arnulf. The Irish could be very brave, and very stupid too.

Arnulf squatted down beside him. Some of the Irishman's blood was smeared on his face. The reiver's blood was everywhere—spattered on the clay floor, on the armour of Arnulf's men. They sat or stood braced against the stone wall, watching. One of them, Armand, had a jug of wine.

"Give me that," Bran said, reaching for it.

"Your men lack discipline," Fellbrigg said. "My steward didn't give them any wine."

"I found it," Armand said, unconcerned. He was too old to be easily intimidated.

"Your steward lacks courtesy," Bran told the knight.

Fellbrigg's face went hard. "Your lord will hear of this, sir."

Bran smiled. "The wine? I think that will not trouble him overmuch."

"Your insolence," Fellbrigg said.

"Ah," said Bran. "That." He tilted the jug to his lips and drank, splashing wine onto his breastplate.

Fellbrigg nodded curtly and started up the ladder, stopping when he met Bowyer coming down. They edged past each other awkwardly in their armour. Bowyer came over to Bran and Arnulf.

"He doesn't look very happy," Bowyer said with a questioning look.

"Sir Robert?" Arnulf said. "Our captain here has pricked him full sure, haven't you?" He pushed Bran's shoulder.

Wine lapped out of the mouth of the jug, splashing onto the packed clay.

"Careful," Bran told him. He raised himself half off the cask and held the jug to the reiver's lips. "Go on. Drink it."

Wild, bloodshot eyes glared at him. The Irishman shook his head violently, cracking his teeth on the rim of the jug.

Bran sighed. "Look. I'll tell you how it is. Just say where he's hiding. When we've found him we'll hang you. Quick. No more pain. I promise you. You're going to die, you know that don't you."

The man closed his eyes. He knew.

"Tell me," Bran said. "There's no point in taking any more of this. I'll have them do what I said, if you don't talk now. I've seen it done. It's pitiful . . . "

"Stop. Please," the reiver said quietly.

"All right," Bran said. "But you must tell me now. Where is Conor? Where do you hide?"

"God forgive me," Declan whispered. Tears streamed across his battered cheeks.

"Tell me, Declan," Bran said, as if he were speaking to a child. "Where is Conor?"

Bowyer retched and turned away. "Sweet Jesus. Sweet Jesus Christ."

Bran jerked his head back over his shoulder. "Shut up!" he barked. Arnulf got up and spoke quietly to Bowyer.

"But sweet Jesus . . . " Bowyer was saying. He looked pale.

Bran turned back to the prisoner. "You'll tell me now, won't you?" he asked gently.

Declan made a slight movement with his chin. "I will," he said in a cracked voice. "God forgive me, I will."

"Faster . . . faster!" Bran told the boy working the grindstone's crank-handle. The boy complied as best he could, his red face shining with sweat.

"That's better," Bran said. "Good." The stone wheel spun smoothly, wobbling slightly on its axis. Bran dipped a cup of water out of the barrel beside him and poured it slowly over the wheel's grinding surface. He held his swordblade at an angle to the blurring rim of the wheel. Wet stone rasped fine steel. Tiny droplets of water started up and stung his face like needlepoints of rain. Bran moved the blade evenly across, careful not to grind too much or too little. He allowed his mind to flow into the work, thinking of nothing. The sword edge grew brighter and keener. It gave him pleasure.

"I hear you're hunting Irishmen today," Matty said, suddenly beside him.

Bran cursed as the grindstone lifted a notch in the edge of his blade.

"You should have an expert do that," Matty observed dryly.

"Yes, I'm hunting your friend Conor. What of it?" Bran laid the sword across his knees. "All right," he told the boy, "you can stop now."

The boy released the handle and stepped back, puffing. Matty whispered to him in Irish and slipped a penny into his hand. The boy grinned and ran off toward the stables.

"I wasn't finished with him!" Bran exclaimed. "God's death, harper!" Then more calmly, he asked, "What's Conor to you anyway?"

"Nothing to me," Matty replied, "but much to his father."

Bran snorted doubtfully. "And are you his keeper?"

Matty shook his head, annoyed. "Nor yours either. But you may have a war on your hands if you kill Conor O'Kelly. I don't think your lord will appreciate that overmuch."

Bran motioned at the grindstone's handle. "Turn that," he said. "I need to finish this."

As Matty set the grindstone spinning faster and faster, unwelcome thoughts crowded into Bran's mind. The harper's interest in Conor had been suspect since they had nearly drawn steel over it in the Bird In Hand. It was something that Bran preferred not to think about. But now he had to know.

Bran dipped the cup into the barrel and poured water over the wheel. "That's good," he told Matty. "Almost too fast. That's better." The stone threw off a sparkling mist as the blade touched it.

"I'll ask you again, Welshman," Bran began carefully, "what's Conor-In-Iron to you? You said that you helped him. What kind of help?"

Matty's mouth twisted into a half-smile. "The best kind. I saved his life."

"Ho!" Bran whistled sharply, impressed. "I'm sure many would thank you for it. Unfortunately, they're all enemies of the Crown."

"*Your* enemies—" Matty bridled.

"I know, I know!" Bran interrupted, holding up his hand. "Let's not get into that again. Just tell me why."

Matty cranked the grindstone furiously. "I was staying with one of the Burkes in northern Connacht—not Alysoun's father. One of their relations."

"When was this?" Bran asked quietly.

The harper stopped turning the handle and looked up at him. "About a year and a half ago. Almost two years, I guess. Anyway, Conor was raiding in the north then—a stupid thing for him to do. He was in force—he had maybe a score of men with him, all well horsed and armed. So, being a hot-headed fool, he got over-bold . . . "

"And then Burke took him," Bran finished.

Matty nodded. "That's right. They'd burned out a village and killed three or four of this lord's serfs." The harper laughed bitterly. "Conor reckons that the Burkes are still Normans, you see—shangoll. I doubt the serfs he killed thought so . . . "

"Go on," Bran murmured.

"So ordinarily Conor would have outrun the Burke's men . . his horses were small and fast and his men weren't wearing armour, of course . . . "

Bran snorted. "Of course."

"But the men chasing him knew the territory and he didn't— it was that simple. He'd fled into strange country. We took a shortcut and hit them broadside—"

"*We?*" Bran asked, raising an eyebrow.

Matty pursed his lips and blew through them hard. "That's right. I was riding with the Burke lord. Why not? We were hunting when we spotted the smoke. It was Conor's bad luck that we were anywhere near."

"Umm," said Bran, "I'll say. So Conor was taken."

Matty ran his fingers over the grindstone's slick rim. "So Conor was taken. We had a running fight—which I managed not to take part in—killed three or four of Conor's men, and took Conor alive. He'd been grazed by a mace and knocked off his horse. They were going to hang him. I remembered his face from a few years back—when I'd spent Christmas with the O'Kelly."

"Oh?" Bran said. It was a small world indeed.

Matty laughed. "He mentioned you—the O'Kelly. And Arlen. I never thought we'd meet."

"Who could have imagined such good fortune," Bran said, grinning in spite of himself. "I take it that you asked for Conor's life. Why the Burke gave it to you I'll never know."

"Well," Matty said, "I did, and he did. He knew of the O'Kelly by reputation, and he didn't want to make an enemy of him. Besides, he enjoyed my music."

They looked at each other and laughed.

"I chose the wrong profession," Bran said. "I see that more and more every day. So Conor went free and now he's your dearest friend."

"Not exactly," Matty said. "But he thinks of me as his friend. Some day that might do me some good."

Bran inspected the edge of his sword. "I don't think Conor will live long enough to do you some good. With any luck at all."

Matty looked sad. "Perhaps not. Anyway, now you know."

"Thank you," Bran said. "Now turn that wheel. This sword is a long way from being sharp."

"I'll call the boy back," said Matty, turning away.

"What did you find?" Matty shouted as Bran came riding into the bawn at Ballinasloe. The harper held the horse's bridle as Bran dismounted.

"Nothing," Bran sighed heavily. He was tired and hungry and vaguely disgusted. "But they were there all right." He drew in a deep breath and let it out slowly. "They hadn't been gone long. The turf in the fire was still glowing."

Arnulf swept past them and reined his horse to a halt. He looked down at Bran, his face frozen in a tight grin. "Well, Captain?"

A twinge of nausea stirred Bran's stomach. He nodded at Arnulf. "Hang him. Make it quick, as I promised."

Arnulf saluted. "As promised, Captain." He prodded his horse toward the tower, shouting orders to the other men riding in.

"Turf fires can go for days," Matty said.

Bran gave his horse to one of the Irish grooms. He took off his gloves and folded them into his belt. "That's right," he said. He needed a drink badly.

"They may have expected Declan to break," Matty said. They walked together across the bawn. A man shouted something to Bran from the wall. Bran ignored him.

"Yes," Bran said slowly, "That's true."

"Do you think they were warned?" Matty finally asked.

Bran did not look at him. "It's possible."

The condemned man was brought up from the dungeon and dragged across the bawn to the gate. Armand slung a rope over one of the projecting timbers. At the sight of the swinging noose, Declan gave a muffled shriek and collapsed onto his knees. The two Gascons holding him hauled him upright.

"There's no need to be so rough," Armand told them in French.

Arnulf came striding cheerfully across the bawn. "Ho! Here's a pretty one for hanging. Who's bringing the ladder?"

Bran shook his head and cursed. He shouted at Arnulf, "No! Not here, you bastard! Take him outside."

Arnulf looked disappointed. "Where, then?"

The sick bile-taste rose in Bran's mouth. "Use your imagination," he growled.

Arnulf called for his horse, and turned back to Bran. "How about one of the big oaks along the river road?"

"I don't care," Bran said too softly for Arnulf to hear.

Arnulf cupped his ear. "What's that, Captain?"

Matty walked toward him. "That's all right," he said loudly. "Conor and his friends will be sure to see it."

Arnulf grinned widely. "That's what I was thinking." A groom brought his horse and held it for him to mount. Bran heard Matty mutter under his breath in Welsh. Matty smiled at Arnulf and waved his hand. Arnulf mounted his foam-flecked horse and rode over to the gate. The Gascons were tying Declan across the back of a packhorse.

Bran decided that he would get very drunk. "Come on," he said to Matty.

"Don't you want to come, Captain?" Arnulf shouted.

Bran shook his head.

"He's only a murdering reiver," Matty told him. "Don't you want to see that justice is done?"

Bran's face twisted. "Don't provoke me, harper. Hanging a man doesn't give me any particular pleasure."

Matty put his hand on Bran's shoulder. "I know. I'm sorry." They started up the wooden steps into the tower. "I didn't warn them," Matty said.

Bran stopped and looked at him. "I didn't think you did," he lied. "Let's get something to drink."

The Last Month

The Bird In Hand
March 1382

"I don't know," Fionna said wearily. "Am I supposed to run this place by myself for two days?"

"Ple-ease, mither!" Sean implored, looking back over his shoulder at Bran.

Bran shrugged. "Don't look at me. She's your mother, not mine." He laughed. Fionna gave him a dirty look.

"I'll have everything ready," Sean said, excited. "I'll scrub out the brewing tubs and kill the spotted pig—and hang her up—and I'll bring in enough turf to keep Hell burning for a week!"

"Sean!" Fionna scowled at Bran. "You'll ruin this boy."

"He's a boy," Bran countered. "He could stand a bit of ruining."

"Ple-ease, mither!"

Fionna sighed. "All right. All right. Two days, that's all." She looked at Bran. "Right?"

Bran nodded. "Right. We'll be back. I had thought of selling him to the gypsies, but since you've made me promise—"

"Oh, get away!" said Fionna, trying not to laugh.

"What are gypsies?" Sean asked.

Bran chuckled. "What's for supper? Something smells good—I know it isn't me."

A strange look came over Fionna's face. She shook her head. "Sometimes . . . never mind." She retied her apron, unnecessarily. Bran leaned the stool back against the wall, watching her.

"Well?"

"Tripes," she said.

"I don't believe you."

"Better than you deserve!" She turned on him suddenly, her face twisted with anger. "Eating up all my best provisions, never paying a penny—"

"You never asked me," he protested. "I've tried—"

"I'm a fool for not asking," she said hotly, sloshing ale from the flagon into his mug. Sean watched them, open-mouthed. Bran unlaced the purse from his belt and threw it onto the table. The coins chinked coldly together. Fionna turned her head and started to walk away. Bran stood up and took her arm.

"No." She was crying. "I'm a fool."

"No, you're not," Bran said, stroking her hair. He caught Sean's eye and looked meaningfully at the curtained doorway into the common room. Sean left quietly.

Fionna laid her head against Bran's shoulder. Her hair tickled his nose. He patted her back, feeling helpless. Maybe she was a fool, he thought. She wept without making noise. He felt her warm tears on his neck. Bran put his arms around her and hugged her tightly. His tongue felt thick, as if it filled up his mouth entirely.

"Fionna . . . " he whispered thickly. He couldn't think of anything to say.

Fionna straightened. "I'm all right," she sniffed. "Sit down and I'll get your supper."

"I'm not hungry."

She smiled faintly. "Liar. Go and sit down." She wiped her eyes with a corner of her apron. Bran sat down and watched her move about the kitchen preparing the meal. There was no wasted motion in her movements. He was reminded of the slow, sweeping dances of the Spanish slave women.

Suddenly the ale displeased him and he wanted to drink

wine. Strong red wine, thick as bull's blood. He finished the
ale, trying to pretend that it was wine.

After they made love Bran tried to go to sleep, but Fionna
kept talking to him. He felt as if he were about to fall into a
deep soft hole, with mindless nothing at the bottom, and each
time he started to fall she nudged him and said something.
Bran was almost irritated enough to say something about it,
but he didn't want to wake himself up. It was so soothing and
pleasant lying beside her warm body. She'd been nice enough
about the trip to Galway, and he didn't want to say anything to
set her off.

"You're not listening," she said, nudging him.

"Mmm. I am." Falling, falling.

"You're not. Look after him. Galway's a big town; he's never
been in a town before."

Bran yawned, stretching. "It's not so big." He wished that
she would go to sleep. Still, it was better to let her talk.

"Big enough," Fionna said. "You will look after him . . . "

"Hush." He patted her hip. "Go to sleep."

"Easy enough for you to say. He's not your son, is he?"

Bran groaned. "Fionna—" She settled her head into the
pillow. Bran put his arm around her.

"All right," Fionna sighed. "He'll be all right, I know that.
It's just . . . it's just . . . I don't know."

Bran felt her fingers brushing his cheek. He didn't think
she would say any more. He pulled her closer, resting his chin
in the little hollow between her neck and shoulder. The hole
opened again and this time he fell all the way.

Fionna watched him for a long time. She liked to watch him sleep. His face softened as he slept, getting younger, less forbidding. He was like a little boy almost. MacTieg had been like that too.

Bran was snoring a little, very softly, like a cat purring. She touched her fingertips to his cheek. He smiled. He is dreaming of a woman, she thought. Some ghost of a woman. In his sleep he looked so happy; he was never this happy awake, even drunk. She wanted to kiss him, but was afraid she might wake him. She kissed him anyway. He stirred.

There was no good reason for it, but she loved him. He probably did not know. Fionna couldn't decide if she was glad about that or not. Perhaps he would tire of her and things would go on as before. Maybe that would be best. Then again . . .

Fionna stared at the ceiling, listening to the mice rustling in the thatch.

Fionna shook him gently. "Are you awake?"

Bran felt himself cut loose from the tendrils of blissful sleep and rose grumpily to wakefulness. "I am now. What time is it?" He had to be back at the castle before the priest sang Tierce. Arlen wanted to see him.

Fionna played with his chest hairs. "Mmm. About Prime, I'd guess. The cock hasn't crowed yet." Her other hand rested lightly on his thigh, caressing him.

Bran chuckled raspily. "It will if you keep that up."

Her fingers tightened around the base of his cock. It started to swell, almost against his will. He was too thirsty to fuck. His mouth tasted like a dog had shit in it.

"What's this?" Fionna asked, playing the innocent.

"Mmm. I don't have time for this. I've got to leave."

Fionna giggled like a little girl. "What? Are you going to miss Morning Mass? I'd better go with you then; I think the priest will be interested to hear my confession."

"He'd have us whipped through the village in our shirts, barefoot."

Fionna cupped his cheek, turning his head to face her. She looked cross. "He wouldn't! Well, would he?"

Bran laughed. "No, I'd kill him."

"Good. I mean— I'm glad he wouldn't."

"He's not that kind of priest, thank God," Bran said. "Nobody pays any attention to him."

"I take it Lord Arlen is not known for his piety."

Bran laughed. His throat felt rough. "Oh, he's pious enough, I guess. As lords go." Talking made him thirstier.

"What about Lady Arlen?"

Bran shifted a little. He started to lose his erection.

"What about her?" he asked. He should leave immediately, before she could ask any more questions. Damn her! He realized suddenly that he wasn't quite sure who he was damning, Fionna or Alysoun.

Fionna smacked his shoulder. "You know what I mean. Doesn't she make everyone go to Mass? I thought ladies were strong on that kind of thing." She gave his softening cock a gentle squeeze.

Bran shook his head. "Ah, careful now. Mmm. What were you saying?"

Fionna bit his shoulder. Bran yelped and tried to roll away, but Fionna still had hold of his prick.

"Jesus, woman, you'll kill me!"

She laughed. "Hardly. You're impossible, do you know that?"

Bran pried her fingers away from his painfully swollen organ. "Yes, I know it well."

"As long as you do."

Bran rolled over onto her, spreading her legs. Fionna gasped and gripped his hips firmly. "Little bitch," he said. He could feel the heat pouring out of her. He penetrated her almost brutally, like a rape. She cried out, holding him tighter. Bran buried his face in her hair. "Little bitch," he groaned, hammering her with his prick and hips. "Ah, sweet lady . . . "

"Shoo . . . Stop that!"

The black horse bent his neck and tried to bite Bran's knee. Bran pushed the horse's head back with the toe of his boot, laughing. The horse wanted a mare. It fretted constantly and fought against the reins whenever they passed a field with mares in it. Most of the castle horses were stallions or geldings.

"I ought to geld you," Bran said, patting the horse's neck. He could not blame the horse for wanting a mate. He remembered the way Fionna's face looked when he left. Her eyes were crinkled a little at the edges, like the track of a small bird on powder snow. It meant she was getting old, but he liked it anyway. He liked her eyes too, her witchy eyes, always changing, sometimes green, sometimes blue, sometimes the slate gray of the sea. She was a redhead too, and apt to be fiery, but he had decided that he liked fiery women. Well, almost decided. She still puzzled him a great deal.

Did she love him? It had been such a long time since anyone loved him that he could not remember what the signs were.

He did not love her. If he did, he was not aware of it. It was safer to be loved and not to love in return. Otherwise plague or war could rob you of everything. He was leery of anything he could not touch or easily understand. When he thought of the women he had known, and the few friends he had been close to, there was only a cold emptiness.

Thinking like this was like probing an open wound where the nerves had been cut. He was irritated with himself. He wanted to fill up the hole with wine. Fill it up and haze everything over with wine. *In vino veritas.* But wine could hold lies too, and sometimes the lies were better.

He liked Sean and liked to think about him, but sometimes it hurt to think about him. He could not really understand why. When he was riding alone or sitting on the parapet drinking wine, he would sometimes pretend that Sean was his son. He would show him how to hawk and hunt deer and use a sword. Sometimes in these fantasies Arlen would grant him a fief; then he would be a landed knight and Sean would be his heir. A gentleman. And Sean's son would be a baron, and there would be an engraved brass slab in the church the baron had built, and the fine Latin inscription would read: Here lies Sir Bran ap Howell, Knight. Rest in Peace.

Bran patted the horse's neck. His face felt tight. He felt the muscles pulling his mouth into a frown. A single tear ran down one cheek. He wiped it away with his palm. He looked at the wetness on his palm, amazed.

The horse snorted and pulled against the bit. Bran decided to think about fighting. He still remembered all of his good fights. All the close calls. It made him feel good to think about how he had survived and his opponents had died. It was nothing personal. Fighting men understood that. It was all right to feel good about it.

An ox-cart struggled through the muddy ruts, coming toward him. The farmer cursed from under his broad leather hat. Cursing the ox for being too weak, cursing God for having made it rain so much that the road was not fit to travel on. Not fit for God-fearing men of the soil to travel on in pursuit of their daily business. The man was not cursing very hotly. Bran had the feeling that he and God were old friends. He laughed, remembering the hawk-nosed priest in the Burke's chapel. He would not approve.

"Well met, Goodman," Bran said in Irish.

The farmer touched his hat brim respectfully. There was a patch sewn into the crown. "Good day, knight," the man replied in bad French.

Bran's eyebrows rose. He laughed. "The road is very bad, isn't it?" he said in French.

The farmer shook his head. "I don't know any more French."

"Good," Bran said, laughing. He switched to Irish, "I don't think I could take any more."

The farmer frowned. He beat on the ox's back with his long goad. "Get up there! Godforsaken mindless beast . . . " He mumbled a stream of incomprehensible obscenities.

Bran leaned back in his saddle, watching the man. The face under the wide brim was baked brown by the sun; hard winds had scoured deep ruts into it. He looked old, but Bran could see that there was bunched muscle under the worn leather tunic. The man was still very strong. He might have done some fighting in his youth. Perhaps he had learned his bad French in the wars with old King Edward. More likely he had just picked up a word or two from some passing merchant, or one of the shire reeves. They all made it a point to speak some French in this wild land they were still trying to claim after two hundred years—this outpost of the great Plantagenet empire.

Bran snorted. Ten years ago he would never have dreamed that it would all end here. He accepted that now. Throughout his first few years in Ireland he had told himself that he could leave whenever he liked, that something would come up, some opportunity would grab hold of him and suddenly he would be somewhere else, doing something else. He knew now that he would die in Ireland. It only remained for him to carve out a cozy place in which to die. No good teasing himself any more about *maybe someday* and *next year I'll go,* that kind of hoping could only bring him pain. He would stand by Arlen and Arlen would reward him with a fief. Not the kingdom he'd dreamed about so stupidly in his youth, but a good, solid fief. He couldn't get that in France or Wales. Ireland was not so bad. He was lucky, really.

The cart moved past him, rattling and creaking. Bran raised his hand and shouted farewell to the old man. The old man pretended not to hear. Bran spurred his horse alongside the cart. The cart moved on slowly; the old man's fist was tight around the handle of the goad. He hid his face under the wide brim, pretending not to notice Bran's looming presence.

"Goodman," said Bran.

The cart jolted and swayed, but the old farmer hardly moved at all, he was as stiff as wood. Bran brought his horse around in front of the ox. The patient, labouring beast stopped immediately. The farmer raised his eyes slowly from under the hat brim. His face was tight with fear. The ruts in his cheeks looked like old battle scars.

"How old are you?" Bran asked, trying to make his voice sound gentle.

The old man shook his head. He did not understand.

"How *old* are you?" Bran repeated, drawing out the Irish words very distinctly.

The farmer squinted sideways at him. He thought that Bran was mad.

"I don't know," he said slowly. "Forty winters, maybe."

Bran let out a long breath, slumping his shoulders. Forty. This man was only two or three years younger than he was. He wondered what the farmer had looked like two years earlier.

He turned his horse out of the cart's path and waved the farmer on. The man whipped the poor ox's back ferociously, but the beast would move no faster than before. The farmer's shoulders shook with the strain. Bran felt sorry for him. He had not meant to intimidate him. There was nothing he could say, at least nothing that the man would understand. Bran touched his spurs to the horse's flanks. The horse jumped ahead, moving away from the cart. Bran kept the horse on the grassy side of the road, away from the ruts.

His meeting with Arlen was routine. They talked about the usual things: How the men were shaping up, the condition of the horses, whether or not the curtain wall was strong enough. The men were fine, Bran told him, the horses were less so, and the wall, while not strong enough, would do.

He had the feeling that Arlen just wanted to remind him who was boss. Well, that was all right, Bran decided, it was his money.

They were in Arlen's bedchamber, sitting at a small table under the window. Bran looked over at the heavily curtained bed that rose like a monument from the center of the room. Lady Alysoun was still inside asleep, or pretending to be.

A serving man came in and set a flagon of red wine and a platter of hot rolls on the table. Arlen motioned him to go and poured the wine himself.

"By your leave, my lord." Bran picked up his goblet and tasted the wine. "This is good."

"It's the last," Arlen said. "There's about half a pipe left. Did Sir Hugh give you the list?"

Bran nodded. "He did. Twenty pipes of Spanish red, three of sack, and forty gallons of white, if they've got it, which I doubt. The rest of the list is in Latin; I hope Master Wainwright is a learned man."

"He is," Arlen said drolly, "after his fashion."

Bran grinned at that. "At least his grandfather could make wagons. I figure we'll need three to carry this lot at least. And guards."

"Tell him we'll send guards as quick as he sends his messenger. I don't want that cargo sitting in his warehouse too long."

"Am I to take money with me?"

"If he asks you for a deposit, tell him to go to Hell. The money will be here for him. If he doesn't trust me that far, I don't want to do business with him." Arlen made a face into his winecup, annoyed.

"All right." Bran finished the wine in his goblet. He had not known that Arlen had so much left. Half a pipe was still fifty or sixty gallons. The sly devil. Where was he keeping it?

"Here," said Arlen, reading his thoughts, "Drink up." He pushed the flagon toward him. Bran refilled both their cups and sat down. "Arnulf tells me you're pretty intent on this MacTieg woman—what's her name?"

Bran frowned. "Fionna. Arnulf talks too much."

"No, no," Arlen said. "I think it's a good thing. A man needs a woman. Especially at our age. When you're young, you don't care as much, I think. You don't get . . . lonely." Bran thought he saw pain in Arlen's eyes. "Do you know what I mean?"

He did. "Aye, my lord. Thank you."

"Yes, I think it's a very good thing. When will you be married?"

Bran laughed. "I haven't asked her yet. I'm taking Sean— her son—to Galway with me. Maybe I'll ask her when we get back, I don't know."

"Don't wait too long," Arlen said.

You didn't, Bran thought, looking at the curtained bed. Perhaps you should have.

"No, my lord."

"How old is the boy?" Arlen asked. He seemed genuinely interested.

Bran felt embarrassed. "Ten, or thereabouts. I've never been much on judging the ages of children." He decided to take a chance. "Would my lord mind if I brought him to the castle now and again. He's very interested in—" Bran struggled to find words, "in how we do things here. Our life."

"Of course, of course." Arlen was smiling. "Do you think he wants to be a soldier?"

This was it. "He wants very much to meet you, my lord."

Arlen's eyebrows rose. "He does? Why is that?"

"You're a knight. He wants to be a knight too, someday."

"Ah," Arlen said. He picked up his goblet and set it down again carefully, without drinking. "Ah. Well, we have two knights here at Ballinasloe."

"You're a real knight. I've told him about you, and the Black Prince . . . Sir John Chandos . . . all about those days."

"Those old days . . . " Arlen looked out the window, drifting into a brief reverie. Bran smiled inwardly. He had appealed to Arlen's vanity. No one was around to tell the silly bastard what a valiant, noble fellow he was. Not his wife, surely. Bran felt sorry for him. Still . . .

"Perhaps you can find some use for him," Bran said. "As some sort of page, perhaps. Keep your gear cleaned up, serve you at table . . . He's very eager to learn manners—things I can't teach him."

Arlen smiled. "You do yourself wrong, Captain. Well, I could use another page. Alysoun will like that, I think. She was expecting our life here to be a little more, well, courtly. Bring your young lad to meet me, Captain. I'm sure I can find a use for him."

Bran inclined his head. "Thank you, my lord. I'll see if I can tear him away from his mother once in a while."

"Do that. It'll be good for him." Pretty soon Arlen would think that it was his idea.

"I heard my name," Alysoun said. She stood outside the bed wrapped in a heavy cloak.

Bran expected Arlen to stand. When he didn't, Bran decided not to either.

"I was telling the Captain here that you would like having a new page. Someone to teach good manners to and help you with little things."

She raised her chin. "You said that Sir Robert will be sending his son to us next year." So, Bran thought, she's heard everything.

"That's next year," Arlen said. "Besides, what's wrong with another page, or two—or three? You're the one who complains about not being well enough attended. I've told Sir Bran that the boy will come and he shall."

"I do not complain, my lord," she said stiffly.

Arlen looked away. "Well . . . I'm sorry. I thought that you would welcome a page. Those maids of yours must get pretty tiresome."

"They do, my lord," she said evenly. "I thank you for your concern."

Bran felt ashamed for him.

"You are my—" the words strangled in Arlen's throat, "dearest concern, lady. Would that you would so concern yourself with me."

Alysoun's face reddened. "I . . . I will not be upbraided in front of one of your common soldiers—a gallowglass! Imagine the tales he will tell to his fellows in that sty of a guardroom—"

"I do not tell tales, lady," Bran said coldly. He wanted to kill her.

"That will be enough, Alys!" Arlen snapped, standing. "Apologize to Sir Bran!"

She stepped back toward the bed. "I will do no such thing." She climbed inside and pulled the curtain shut.

Arlen seemed to grow smaller. He sat down at the table, staring blankly at his hands folded in front of him. Bran saw that his fingers were trembling.

"I'll take my leave, my lord."

"Yes," Arlen said, not looking up. "Yes, go now."

"As you will, my lord." Bran moved toward the door.

"Farewell," said Arlen. "On your journey."

"Thank you, my lord." Bran bowed and left.

Early the next morning Bran got up and packed a few things into his saddlebag for Galway. He went down to the kitchens. The ovens were lit and they were making bread for the day. Bran broke open a hot loaf and ate half of it on the spot. He tucked the other half in his jerkin for the ride to the Bird In Hand. He picked two small dried apples out of the bin and went to the stables.

The other horses nosed toward him as he walked past the stalls to where the black horse was kept. They wanted the apples that he carried in his hand. He lifted the bar to the black horse's stall. He patted the horse's glossy head, feeding him the apples, speaking softly to him in Welsh.

Four of the horseboys were huddled together in the hay, pretending to be asleep. He decided against rousing them and saddled the horse himself. He did not really trust anyone else to saddle him properly anyway. Bran whistled as he fitted the various straps through their buckles and rings. It was a good fresh morning. The black horse balked at taking the cold bit into his mouth.

"Come on, don't be a bastard." One of the horseboys giggled. Bran fitted the bit between the horse's clicking teeth.

"There now."

He led the horse outside into the bawn. As he put his foot into the stirrup, preparing to mount, he saw someone walking toward him from the tower. Lady Alysoun. He took his foot out of the stirrup and stood beside the horse, waiting for her to cross the bawn.

"Good morrow, my lady," he said as she got close.

"Good morrow, Captain." The early morning light made her look very pale, like a newly made corpse.

Such a pretty corpse though, he thought. He waited for her to speak again.

Alysoun raised her head and looked directly into his eyes. "I'm sorry I called you a common soldier."

"I am a common soldier."

"No—" she sighed, "you're not. I don't like you, but you're much more than that. You know about us and you haven't told my husband. I appreciate that."

"Matty Groves is my friend," Bran said. Somehow it sounded stupid coming out that way.

"And I am not." Alysoun smiled. "Still, I appreciate it, Captain. I promise to be kind to your— To the boy from the inn. That's the least I can do, isn't it?"

"You owe me nothing, my lady. He's a good lad, he won't give you any trouble." The black horse nudged Bran's shoulder. Bran pushed him away. He stood there awkwardly, looking at her, trying to think of something friendly to say. He had not expected this.

Alysoun took a scrap of paper out of her sleeve and handed it to him. "Another list, I'm afraid. Do you mind? Just a few things I need. Cloth, thread, pins—that sort of thing."

Bran put the paper into his purse. "Of course, my lady."

"Thank you, Captain." She smiled at him. "Fare thee well."

He bowed to her and mounted the horse.

"Good-bye, lady."

"Good-bye, Captain."

The weather stayed fine all the way to Galway. The sun was bright, but it was still cold. Bran and Sean were wearing the new cloaks that Fionna had made for them. Bran taught Sean a marching song from the French wars, cleaning it up as he went along. Sean countered with a ditty he'd learned from a Kerry packman on his way to Athlone, which turned out to be one of the lewdest ballads Bran had ever heard. Half of it was in dialect, which neither he nor Sean could understand, but enough came through to give them the general gist. Something about a one-eyed, one-legged whore with one finger. They laughed so much that Bran never did learn it.

The land had colour in it again, a relief after the washed-out drear of winter. The air was so fresh it made their heads spin. Even the black horse was in a good mood, and only bit Sean's pony once. They kept to the main road, which was tolerably dry. Twice they met small groups of travellers coming from Galway. Everyone was armed, even the lowest servants, but these were not the clanking, bristling convoys that Bran remembered seeing when he first came to Ireland. From each one Bran got bits of news about what was going on in the town. The horse fair was the best ever, they said.

In the second group there was a churchman in white robes with a black satin cope covering them. Bran recognized him. He was the Abbot of Clonmacnois; Bran had gone there once with Arlen. Arlen wanted to be the official protector of the monastery, but the Abbot had very politely and very firmly turned him down. He all but suggested that Arlen might want to become *his* vassal. The monastery had its own castle and gallowglasses. They didn't need Arlen's protection.

Bran nodded at him. The Abbot nodded back, his eyes smiling faintly with recognition. Sean took off his leather cap. The good Abbot had five men with him that looked distinctly unholy, none of them monks. Each wore some sort of body armour, a jack or brigandine, and a broad-brimmed helmet. All five had swords and daggers and extra weapons fastened at their saddlebows. The rearmost man led a fine, fat palfrey, whose mouse-gray coat had been brushed to a lustrous sheen. Obviously bought at the fair. As they passed by, the Abbot called out:

"How does your master, Lord Arlen?" He had remembered who Bran was.

"Very well, Your Grace." Bran was pleased that he had remembered.

"And his lady? I regret that I have not yet met her—I had hoped that your lord might see his way to attending the Christmas Mass at St. Ciaran's. We were much disappointed that he did not come."

"I'm sorry, Your Grace." Bran could not think of a palatable explanation for why Arlen had not gone to the Mass. One of the younger monks had come with a beautifully illuminated invitation from the Abbot. Arlen did not go because his pride was hurt. But Bran could not tell the Abbot that.

"His lady," the Abbot repeated, "is well?"

"Yes, Your Grace. Very well." They were almost out of speaking range. Sean was looking wistfully at the palfrey.

"Glad to hear it!" the Abbot shouted. "God bless and keep you!"

"Thank you," Bran said automatically, but the Abbot was already too far away to hear.

"You know him?" Sean asked, eyes full of wonder.

"Yes, of course I know him."

At midday they stopped to water the horses and dug into the bag of food that Fionna had sent with them. The tart, juicy apples and crusty bread seemed like a feast. There was a roast chicken too, wrapped in waxed cloth. Bran decided to save that for the evening.

Sean finished his third apple and threw the core at a squirrel lurking nearby. He missed, but only just. The squirrel ran up the other side of the tree. Sean laughed.

"Don't eat any more of those," Bran said. "You'll get sick."

"How do you know?" Sean asked. The squirrel was looking down at them from the top of the tree.

"I know."

"When do you think we'll get to Galway?" Sean asked, reaching for another apple.

"We'll be there before dark." Bran reached for the leather bottle of wine. Leather ruined the taste of good wine; but after all these years he was used to it, it didn't bother him. He lay back against his saddle, breathing in the crisp air. They were not staying long enough to build a fire, but that would have completed it. Wood smoke, dry branches crackling with bright flame, the fresh colours all around them.

Sean bit into his fourth apple. Bran smiled. It was good to be riding with Sean. He had never felt anything like it. They would be in the town before nightfall. In a way it was a shame; he knew the riding together would be the best part. Bran did not like towns. He knew Sean would. Towns were exciting, full of different kinds of people, activity everywhere. Towns made him nervous. It was unnatural for so many folk to be crowded together in one place. Worse than a castle. In a castle there was a kind of order, every man knew his place. Towns were too chancy, more risky than any battlefield. Sean would enjoy it though. He would only see what he wanted to see.

"Do you think the horses are rested enough?" Sean asked. He was looking west, toward Galway.

Bran sighed, resting his head against the saddle. He did not feel like moving. If he fell asleep now and never woke up, that would be all right. "Why don't you ask them?" He took a hard pull from the leather bottle and stoppered it tightly. More than half left. Fodder for the road. He rose gingerly, joints cracking and popping. Sean leapt up and started gathering up all their things. The black horse noticed the activity and clicked his teeth. He wasn't ready to go either.

"Shush," said Bran, slapping the black horse's nose. He lifted up the heavy saddle and set it on the horse's back. "Stand still, damn you." He cinched the girth tightly, shoving his knee up under the horse's barrel to deflate the lungs. The horse was cunning and would dump him with a loosened girth otherwise.

Sean handed him the bag of food and the rolled up blankets. "How long before nightfall?" he asked.

Bran pulled the strapping tight on the bedrolls. "Long enough to get there," he snapped. Sean's face fell. "Not long," Bran said more gently. Grinning, he reached out and tousled Sean's hair.

"Don't be in such a hurry. There's time for everything."

"Is there?"

Bran's smile hardened on his face. "Get that pony saddled. Make sure the girth is tight."

"I know."

"Then do it." Bran took the bottle from the bag. He shook it; there wasn't that much left after all.

An hour later Bran pointed out a tall, narrow tower on a hill in the distance. "That is Sir Robert Fellbrigg's castle," he said. "Lord Arlen's vassal."

"Does Lord Arlen have many vassals?"

"Four altogether." Bran squinted up at the tower; the sun was in his eyes. The bawn was surrounded by a circular palisade of logs. There were half a dozen huts scattered on the hillside below the gate. Something like that, he thought. Nothing grand, but a good start.

"Ach, sure," Sean exclaimed, "you could fit three of those inside Kilconnell!"

Bran said nothing.

They arrived in front of the walls of the town well before dark, as Bran had promised. He had deliberately made it into a long ride.

Hundreds of tents and cruder shelters were set up along the road outside the wall. Some of the tents were framed with wood, obviously meant to be there for some time. There were people everywhere, mostly on foot, some riding shaggy ponies. Behind the tents were carts and fenced-in livestock. The noise and stink was incredible. Near the main gate lay a flourishing alehouse, built onto the outside wall with a skeleton framework of boards and flapping canvas.

"Who are those people?" Sean asked. "Why aren't they inside the town?"

"They're Irish. They don't like towns—which is just as well."

"Why is that?"

Bran let out a short, harsh laugh. "Irishmen are not welcome in Galway, or any other town that I know of. They're too wild, they don't know how to behave themselves like civilized people."

Sean nodded. "The people in the towns are afraid of them, then." It was not a question.

"Aye," Bran answered. "That's the meat of it."

"Why do they come here, then?"

"God, you ask a lot of questions." Bran smiled at him. "They come to trade. And to get drunk. The same reasons that bring any countryman to a town." Bran decided not to mention the other, which had popped suddenly into his head. Ah now, he told himself, you're soon to be a married man.

They passed through the gate without any trouble. It would not be closed until the sun was well and truly down. They left their horses at the north end of Market Street. Bran instructed the hostler on the proper amount of oats to feed the black horse and Sean's pony. The hostler, a man of many years' experience in the care and feeding of four-legged conveyances, listened patiently, wiping his sweating bald head with a rag. Knights, he was thinking. They were all the bloody same. Sean was outside in the street, gawking at the strange sights. He had never been in a town before. Galway must be to him like Granada was to me, Bran thought. He asked the hostler where they could get a bed for the night.

"Not easy," the man said, stuffing the rag behind his leather apron. "Everyone's in town for the horse fair, your honour. You might try The Shippe a few doors down. Or The Broom and Barley over by the church." He glanced outside at Sean. "Rough country there, if you know what I mean, sir. Whores, panders, cutpurses, that kind of thing—begging your pardon."

Bran nodded. "What if we can't find a place?"

The hostler scratched his shiny pate. "Werl . . . you could stay here, I suppose. Lots of good clean hay—it's warm." His eyes flickered away. "Only, uh, an extra penny a night," he said hopefully. "Apiece."

"One," Bran said, hardening his eyes. "For both of us."

The hostler coughed. "Right you are, sir. One it is then."

The black horse neighed from its stall. Bran hissed at it. He adjusted his swordbelt and went out into the street.

Sean stood shaking his head, fully amazed. "It's wonderful," he said. "I've never seen so many people. Who is their lord?"

Bran laughed. "They don't have one, most of them. They're burghers. They've got charters that say they can elect their own leaders and govern themselves. The guilds run the town."

Sean frowned. "What are guilds?"

Bran took a deep breath and let it out slowly. "You're asking the wrong man. Soldiers don't have guilds. Guilds are when the men of one trade, like weavers or dyers, get together and make up laws to protect themselves against loss and outside competition. If you're a sword-maker, say, and you'd just come to this town, you'd have to join the Armourers' Guild before you could work here or sell any of your blades."

"What if they don't let me join the guild?"

Bran hooked his thumbs into his swordbelt. "Well, you're out of luck then. You'll have to go somewhere else. Or starve."

Sean shook his head. "That doesn't seem right. What if I tried to sell my swords anyway?"

Bran laughed and put his arm around the boy's shoulders. "Come on, let's get something to eat. Aren't you hungry?"

They bought hot meat pasties at a stall, and walked along eating them, burning their fingers. Sean's chin was smeared with gravy. Bran looked at him and laughed. He felt good. He set his shoulders and forced a way through the crowd, Sean following behind him. A fishwife waved a flopping salmon in Bran's face.

"Fresh fish, my lord. Caught this morning, my lord."

Bran waved her aside, wrinkling his nose. Sean plucked at his sleeve. "Look!"

"Look at what?"

"Over there," Sean pointed. "Next to the painted wagon. You promised you'd get me one!"

Bran strained to see. "Get you what? You'll get a clout in a minute." He could see it now, a cutler's stall. Several swords hung from a bar across the top. Oh Jesus, Bran thought, I did promise.

Sean slipped into the jostling throng and disappeared. Bran drew a bead on the stall and bulled his way toward it.

Sean was already talking with the cutler, his initial shyness completely evaporated. He pointed to a shiny bastard sword nearly as long as himself. "That one," he said. "I like that one."

The cutler smiled at Bran.

"Perhaps your son would like something smaller," he said

with a thick Flemish accent. He produced a foot-long poniard, the kind that slipped so handily between the joints in plate armour. Steel hilted, plain, a soldier's weapon.

My son, Bran thought. "Let me see it."

"No!" Sean whined. "You said a sword!"

Bran cuffed him on the ear. "When you're older. Not for a while yet." He weighed the dagger in his hand; it felt right. The blade of grainy blue steel, marked with the running wolf.

"This is German," Bran said.

The cutler nodded emphatically. "*Ja. Ja.* The best. From Passau."

"Yes." Bran shaved a sliver of wood from the counter. "How much?"

Sean was trying hard to sulk, looking at the dagger out of the corner of his eye.

The Fleming pursed his lips and regarded the weapon with a critical eye. "For you, sir— Two shillings."

"One."

The Fleming grinned. "Sold." He took the dagger from Bran and fitted it with a simple leather sheath. Bran would take it to a man in the village and have a proper scabbard made for it. He counted out three silver groats into the Fleming's hand.

Sean stuck the poniard through his belt, looking very pleased with himself. He took out his little belt knife.

"What should I do with this? Throw it away?"

"Keep it. You'll use it for the things you've always used it for." He tapped the pommel of the new dagger in Sean's belt. "This is for killing men with, not for cleaning your boots or cutting up chickens."

Sean nodded, closing his fingers over the long grip. His hand will grow into it, Bran thought. He heard music coming from farther down the street, bagpipes and drums, clashing cymbals.

"Come on," he said. "Have you ever seen mummers?"

209

Fellbrigg's tiny castle jutted from the rounded hilltop, stark and black against the luminescent moon. A raider's moon, stretched wide and lit up the whole sky. Conor knew that the watchman huddled in his cloak on top of the narrow stone tower would be able to see well too. If he was awake.

Conor motioned to Ulick, crouched nearby with an armload of torches. Ulick came up beside him. "Stay in the trees until I give the signal," Conor said. "We'll have to be damned quick. He's got horses in there."

Ulick nodded. "Do you think he'll come out to fight?"

"He's no man if he doesn't," Conor said. "But he might not. He won't know how many of us there are."

Ulick hiked up the torches for a better grip. "Not many, Conor. Not many at all."

Conor grinned at him. "He won't know that. Besides, we'll be back into the woods too fast for him to catch us. I only wish we had more men."

"For an ambush, you mean?" Ulick snorted. "We'd need more than men. A few swords and axes would be grand—and bows."

"We'll have those again," Conor told him. "Meanwhile we do what we can."

Shane moved between them and took two of the torches from Ulick. His eyes gleamed red in the moonlight, like a cat's. A thin, scraggly beard completed the likeness.

"Padraig has lost the flints," Shane told Ulick, ignoring Conor.

"Mother of Christ!" Conor hissed. "That sniveling . . . "

"He has not," said Ulick. "They're in the pouch at my belt."

"Thank God for that," said Conor. He hunched down and fumbled the pouch's thong fastening loose with cold-stiffened fingers. "So." The horseshoe-shaped striking steel came into his hand, like ice against his palm. He took out the sharp flint chips and cupped them in his hand with the steel. His hands were numb with the cold and he was afraid he might drop the lot.

"Do we light them all now?" Shane asked. His unholy cat's eyes locked into Conor's. Neither man blinked for a moment.

Conor sucked cold air into his lungs. "If we light them now," he said, holding back a sneer, "then our man up there—" He jerked his head at the tower. "—will know something's wrong, won't he? He might even decide to tell someone about it."

"I suppose so," Shane agreed in a dead voice.

Conor nodded vigorously. "I suppose so," he said mockingly. "If he's not frozen to death he'll do just that. Now tell your brother to wait for my signal."

Shane went away without a word.

"Where's Padraig?" Conor growled. He was angry at Shane, because the younger man no longer respected him. And he was angry at himself for the same reason.

"He'll be along," Ulick said, expressionless.

"You think I'm too hard, don't you?" Conor said.

Ulick moved toward the tower, shifting the torches onto his shoulder. They walked up the hill together in silence. The winter-dead trees all around them made ghostly, silver-gray shapes in the moonlight. Conor shuddered violently and pulled the thin cloak closer around him.

"I do," Ulick said finally.

"Shane blames me for Declan's death," Conor said. He felt better for saying it.

Ulick shrugged. "He blames you for his empty belly. And there he's right."

Conor's face twisted in surprise. "He's right, is he? And I should have gone into my father's house on bended knee and demanded food for us all, is that it?"

"You know it is," Ulick told him flatly.

"If he won't give it for love of me, without my asking, I don't want it. And I've told you that a hundred times."

"So you have," Ulick said. "So you have, that."

"I won't beg from him," Conor said, more for his own benefit.

Lately he had thought that it might not be so bad to ask his father's help. He felt sure the old man would give it. The blood bond was stronger than any parchment agreement he had with the Norman lord. But Conor's pride could not stand it. So he would stay in his father's lands, and cause trouble with his shangoll neighbours. He kept hoping the young men would follow him again as they used to, eager for booty and shangoll blood. All winter he waited and prayed to the Virgin, as his few remaining followers slunk off home. And with each one who left, his reputation as a cunning war leader faded. No one troubled to remember his earlier successes, only the failures of the last year. They did not have his passion to rid the land of the shangoll. They could not see the danger as clearly as he saw it.

Conor and Ulick had reached the end of the trees, just below the bald crest of the hill where the castle stood within its rough wooden palisade. A few huts were scattered about, with a smithy and a small byre for cattle. The huts belonged to servants who worked in the castle. Most of Fellbrigg's tenants and cottars were spread out in the partially cleared land to the west of the castle.

The white turf smoke drifting up from the huts made him ravenous. Hunger gnawed at his shrunken belly like an aching wound. He had managed to ignore it in the excitement of planning the raid, but now it struck full force. Conor sank to his knees behind a tree, digging his fingers into the bark. Ulick hunkered down beside him and set down his remaining torches.

"We'll light one now and the rest when we reach the huts?" Ulick asked.

Conor nodded. He reached under the icy chain mail into

his tunic for the wad of tinder wedged behind his belt. The cold air prickled the hairs on his chest. Spreading the tinder out carefully between two tree roots, he struck at the largest flint without success. His fingers were too numb to hold both the flint and steel at the proper angles. He cursed under his breath.

"Here, let me do it," Ulick offered, holding out his hand.

Conor moved aside. In a few moments, Ulick had fired the tinder, a shower of sparks leaping from the flint with each stroke.

"Good," Conor grunted, irritated at his own clumsiness.

Ulick lit a torch and handed it to Conor.

"Now," Conor said, springing from his crouch into a dead run at the huts. Ulick was beside him and slightly behind; the big man's powerful breathing sounded loud in the still night air. Conor looked around for the others, saw their pale ghost-like faces floating up the slope behind him, dark cloaks and clothes nearly invisible in the moon shadow. The torch in his hand seemed as bright as a beacon. His ears were tensed for the warning shout from the sentry on the tower.

As he and Ulick reached the huts, dogs began to bark. The packed cattle in their byre shuffled together nervously, straining the thin cross-boarded walls. Conor broke his run against the side of a hut, breathless, and stretched out his torch for his men to light theirs. Ulick lit four or five and handed one to Shane.

The shout came. Conor pushed himself off the wall of the hut and stood up straight, trying to breathe. His heart pounded painfully. He wondered if he would be able to run back into the trees after all.

A man came out of the hut with a cudgel in his hand. Conor shifted the torch to his left hand and jerked out his dagger. The man yelled something and charged. Ulick was suddenly there between them, holding a lit torch two-handed above his head. The man swung and missed. Ulick stepped in close and brained him, setting the man's hair on fire. As he dropped, Ulick wrenched the cudgel from him and flung the shattered, smoldering stub of the torch through the open doorway. Someone inside screamed—a woman. Conor fired the thatch with his own torch, then spun away to pick up two that Ulick had dropped. The other huts were already blazing.

"All right, let's go!" he shouted to Ulick.

They heard the palisade gate open. Over at the byre, Shane had broken down part of the wall. The cattle burst out, panicked by the fire, taking the rest of the wall with them.

"Sweet Jesus, will you look at them?" Conor said to himself, drooling at the sight of so much beef on the hoof.

Ulick grabbed his arm and they started back down the slope. They heard the clink and jingle of armoured men close behind. Conor tripped and rolled twice. As he came up from the ground, an old man ran at him with a wooden pitchfork. Conor sidestepped the thrust and ripped his blade up under the man's breastbone. The blade stuck. Conor side-kicked him away, holding on tight to the hilt of his dagger. The weight of the falling body pulled it free. Steam rose from the hot blood on his hand. The thrill of killing rippled through the muscles along his back, making him warm all over. Two half-armoured soldiers with boar spears would be on him in seconds. Part of him thought he could kill them.

Suddenly Ulick was there, shouting in his ear. "For God's sake, Conor! Run, man! Run!"

Before he could think about it, his legs were already taking him towards the trees. Ulick's massive hand was planted in the middle of his back, pushing him through the brittle, dead bushes like a battering ram. Conor rammed his shoulder into a tree and bounced off into a running girl. They both went down. The girl leapt to her feet immediately. She was carrying a small bundle—a baby, he realized. They stared at each other for what seemed like a long time. Conor heard Ulick crashing off in another direction, leading the soldiers away from him. The girl looked down at the bloody dagger in his hand, then up into his eyes again. He saw that she was too frightened to run away. The baby wasn't crying; that was strange. He wondered if it was all right. Perhaps she had fallen on it . . .

Torches bobbed among the trees behind him. More soldiers were coming. Men shouted to each other in the dark—he couldn't understand what they were saying. His shoulder hurt, and his knees wobbled dangerously. He really didn't feel like running any more. The girl's eyes were frozen open in a wide, unblinking stare. For an instant he wanted to kill her, to stop her looking at him so.

Then he was running again, in what he hoped was the right direction. The girl's eyes haunted him. He jumped a small stream without breaking stride. The shouting of the soldiers grew fainter. They were giving up. It might be a trap, they were thinking. Well, he wished it was. Remembering the way the girl looked at him made him angry; he almost turned back for her. And then what? he thought. He had no real intention of killing her, and still less of rape. His legs carried him on, farther and farther from the burning huts and stampeding cattle. It was quiet again. He didn't know exactly where he was, but he wasn't worried; he'd find his way all right. The cold air had congealed the blood on his hand, gluing the dagger hilt to his fingers. He ran on without sheathing it. The dagger seemed a natural extension of his hand.

They rose early, brushing the hay from their clothes. Sean was hopping with excitement, eager to get going, while Bran dragged himself about like a man trying to walk underwater. Sean's early morning chatter irritated him, but he bore with it as best he could, reminding himself that he liked the boy.

A barrel of rainwater stood just outside the stable door. Bran stumbled to it and thrust his head under the water. The icy water cleared his head instantly, as he knew it would. He pulled his head out of the barrel, slopping water over his boots.

"Brrrr!" He shook his head vigorously, like a dog, spraying water all around.

Sean laughed, holding his hands in front of his mouth. Bran started to scowl at him and then began laughing himself. He was glad that he'd left the ivory mirror at Ballinasloe. I must look like thirty kinds of hell, he thought, grinning wryly. He pushed the wet heavy hair out of his face. Many times he had thought of cutting it; it was old-fashioned and inconvenient. But he disliked the new bowl cuts, and never followed fashion except by accident. He rummaged in the leather bag that held their clothes and took out the boxwood comb, with coarse teeth on one side and fine on the other. Half of the fine teeth were broken out. He would have to remember to buy a new one before they left the town.

Bran handed the comb to Sean. "Here, make yourself useful."

He sat on an overturned tub while the boy combed his hair. He particularly liked it when Fionna combed his hair for him. He felt like a hound must feel with someone scratching behind its ears. The boy was careful; he'd obviously combed his mother's hair often, and he was good at currying horses too. Bran closed his eyes, breathing in the comfortable horse and leather smells of the stable, thinking of nothing.

They had their breakfast in a chophouse, cold beef and bread washed down with ale. The ale put Bran in a better mood and he started to look forward to the day. He felt like buying Sean a new saddle—the one he had was a broken-down courier's rig from the Old King's time—but Arlen had not gotten around to paying his arrears in pay, and Bran didn't feel like pressing him for it just yet. Then he remembered that his own saddle was about done. Ah well, he thought. He ordered another mug of ale to keep his mood up. Sean was impatient to be going. He didn't like sitting around chophouses. He'd rather be in the muddy streets, jostling with beggars and cutpurses. Bran finished his ale.

"All right, we're going," Bran said. He flicked a penny to the fat man behind the counter who deftly snatched it out of the air. They pushed through the leather curtains and went out into the street. Almost immediately Sean started to wander toward a narrow alleyway, attracted by the sounds of a one-sided scuffle—several meaty thunks followed closely by moans. Bran grabbed Sean's belt and steered him back into the street.

"Don't go looking for trouble," Bran said.

"Why don't we rescue him?" Sean said eagerly, drawing his sharp new dagger.

"Put that away," Bran told him. "You'd need rescuing in a moment."

Sean replaced the blade in his belt, pouting. "A real knight would go to his aid."

Bran raised his hand; Sean jumped back, stumbling in a rut.

"Don't try me, boy," Bran said, breathing hard.

"I've killed more knights than I have fingers and toes . . ." He paused for breath. "And I ought to know something about them. They'll tell you the same thing—don't go looking for trouble. It will find you fast enough, take my word on it." Bran forced himself to breathe through his nose, fighting down the black rage that threatened to spill out of him.

Sean looked disappointed. "But you said knights—"

"Never mind what I said! There is chivalry and there is the real world. All the knights I know live in the real world. There were others, but they're dead. Does that tell you something?"

Sean said nothing, looking down at his boots as they walked along.

"Well?" Bran felt thick and ugly. He did not want the day to start off so badly. Still, he was right. The boy had to learn sometime. The world was no place for dreamers. A man had enough to do looking after himself and what was his. He had a sudden flash of memory: A French knight had charged him on foot, screaming something about his lady's honour and the glory of France. Bran dropped his heavy poleaxe through the knight's breastplate and ducked under a blow to snatch the gleaming gold collar inside. A blue silk favour was tied to the knight's elegant helm. He stepped over the knight's body and killed another man with the poleaxe.

If I had that collar now, Bran thought. The wealth that had passed through his hands, all gone. He thought of the little crocks of gold coins hidden in the walls of his house in Granada. Had anyone found them? Probably. Probably tore the house down looking. The old pain started up again and he tried to think of something else. Horses. How many horses had he owned altogether? A score at least. Most of them without names, just poor dumb beasts. That wasn't true either, he thought. Some were mean, others were clever, and one or two could fight better than he could. Those were the best, but they were hard to come by. There was a place in Normandy where they trained war-horses to break through a shield wall. They made the horses ride over dummies packed with straw. The horses weren't hurt, so they didn't mind doing it. Day after day they would make the horses trample the straw figures. Each time the horse did it just right, they gave it some hot mash and a good currying. The horses got pretty good at it. You could use them just once to break a shield wall. If the horse survived, it would never charge a wall again.

Sean walked sullenly beside him. Bran decided it was best

to let him be for a while. It would blow over. Boys had short memories. Until they got older, then they remembered every slight and injustice, every wasted opportunity. Jesus, I'm in a foul humour, he thought.

He remembered riding away from Dinas Emrys, hating his father, glad to be gone. Rhodri's face haunted him like a ghost. If he had pleaded harder, maybe Bran would have taken him along. Maybe.

He tried to picture his father's face and couldn't. Howell was big and dark, that was all he could remember. Yes, and he had a beard too. A black, bushy beard. He looked like the Devil. Bran chuckled to himself. I remember him all right, he thought. The poxy bastard.

He suddenly wanted Sean to like him. He wanted to tell him that he'd said those hard things to him for his own good. Bran couldn't treat him like a baby; his mother did that too much already. It was natural for women to do that.

"Sean . . . " he began, searching for words.

"What?"

The boy wasn't even looking at him. Damn you, Bran thought. Damn you. "Nothing. Watch out for that cart."

Near midday they walked down toward the harbour. A shopkeeper gave them directions to Master Wainwright's warehouse, which was supposed to be one of the largest in the town.

The harbour was of a respectable size for Ireland, but nothing grand, Bran thought. Not like Calais or Harfleur. He had passed through a few good-sized ports in his time. Still, this is where the Spanish ships came to trade, and it was fortunate that Arlen's lands were within reasonable distance of it.

Sean jumped up onto the low seawall and spun around

delightedly, taking it all in: Round-bellied cogs and narrow sleek galleys moored side by side, gently bobbing up and down in the swell. The wide, flat strand stretched away from the harbour mouth on both sides. Beyond it, the sea, sparkling in shifting rainbow colours, like cut glass from Venice.

Some of the ships were being loaded, others unloaded, with great swinging cranes and ropes and pulleys. The shore-men called out encouragements to each other, back and arm muscles rippling from the strain of hauling, pushing, and lifting up of their various cargoes.

Sean jumped down from the wall.

"It's wonderful!" he said. "I'd like to live here some day."

"Would you, now? Knights don't live in towns." Which was not exactly true. Still, he didn't think Sean was likely to find this out, for a while anyway.

"Oh." Sean went inside himself to ponder this briefly. "Well!" he said brightly, "I can always visit, can't I? On my lord's business."

Bran laughed. "Aye. I guess that's true. Let's see if we can find this Master Wainwright."

All manner of cargo was stacked up on the quay, waiting to go into the warehouses. Huge bolts of cloth piled like logs. Long, shapely firkins of sack from Jerez alongside squat, wide barrels of strong red wine from Rioja and Galicia. Masses of clay amphorae, three and four feet tall, containing the specialty wines. And elsewhere—boxes, bundles, and baskets of every size and shape. A king's ransom on the docks of a fourth-rate harbour on the rough western coast of an island the Romans hadn't even bothered with. Bran shook his head. The wonders and ironies of modern life.

A terrific squawking and cackling erupted from a stack of small wicker crates nearby. Sean jumped back, startled.

"God's love," Bran shouted. "Look at them—they're beautiful!"

Sean gathered his courage and knelt to look.

"What are they . . . chickens?"

Bran snorted. "Not just chickens, boy. Fighting cocks. The Spaniards breed the best fighting cocks in the whole world. Jesus, look at the colours!"

Each bird had its own closed off section of the crate. Sean poked his fingers through the openings in the wicker, pulling them back quickly when the birds struck.

"Careful!" Bran warned. "They'll call you Sean Nine-fingers."

Sean looked up at him, laughing. Suddenly they both remembered the chicken Fionna had sent with them, lying neglected at the bottom of the food sack. In their excitement they had forgotten it entirely.

"Ah, no . . . " Bran shook his head. They looked at each other and burst out laughing.

"Well, I suppose it's no good now," Sean said, not caring very much.

"We won't tell her," Bran said. "If she asks—it was delicious."

"The best we've ever eaten."

"That's right, boy. You're catching on."

Sean led the way, strutting like a soldier until they found the tall stone and timber warehouse with Master Wainwright's mark above the door.

Bran looked up appraisingly, eyeing the massive block and tackle hanging from a braced beam four stories above them. Considering that this was Ireland, the building was very impressive indeed. It was obviously built to last. The wagon-maker's grandson had done all right for himself.

They went inside and were met almost immediately by

Master Wainwright's chief clerk, who led them up a stout ladder to the shipping office on the second floor.

Bran ducked under a low door lintel, which looked as if it has been constructed from old ship's timbers. In fact, many of the interior struts and crossbeams looked that way, some with the twisted iron spikes left in them, supporting cages filled with exotic birds, leather bottles, and miscellaneous nautical paraphernalia.

Master Wainwright stood in the midst of a clutter of unrolled maps, brass-bound ledgers, inkpots, and a felled forest of quill pens. He had been writing something at a richly carved, slanted desk, something like a monk's scripting bench, when they entered the room. He slipped off the high, built-in stool and came toward them, holding out his hands in what Bran thought was an over-enthusiastic greeting:

"Good Sir Bran—I'm so pleased to see you! And how is your fine master, Lord Arlen? Well, I trust?"

"Well enough, Master Wain—"

"Good, good! I'm glad to hear it! Who is this lad you've brought with you? A fine-looking fellow, I must say!"

Bran thought a moment. "Lord Arlen's page," he answered.

"Very good!" Master Wainwright clapped his hands. "Dickon! Bring wine for these gentlemen—the good wine."

Bran decided that he looked every inch a wagon-maker's grandson: a lumpy, squarish head, broad fat hands with nimble smallish fingers, and a beer-barrel girth that looked as solid as they came. He wore a velvet cap with a silver pilgrim's badge on it. Bran squinted at it as it caught the light. Compostela.

"You're looking well, Master Wainwright," Bran said. "And very prosperous too, I might add."

"Ah . . . " Master Wainwright was pleasantly embarrassed. "Ah . . . Well, trade has been good, Sir Bran, very good."

"I'm glad to hear it."

Bran turned as the clerk came in with the wine. Sean was

staring at him, astonished. Ah yes, Bran thought, Lord Arlen's page. He'd forgotten to mention it, thinking to save it for a better time which never seemed to arrive.

"Your mother will have to agree," he told the boy privately.

"Ach, she will! I know she will."

Bran grinned tightly. "I'm not so sure, sirrah. We shall see."

Master Wainwright looked puzzled. "Here is your wine, good gentlemen—please, drink up!"

Bran drank his wine, which was excellent. He rolled it over his back teeth, holding it on his tongue for a moment before he swallowed. Very, very good. Being a merchant has its compensations all right.

"I have a list here," Bran said, snapping the roll of paper from his purse with a flourish. He showed his teeth, laughing silently at himself. So it's come to this, he thought. The great Bran ap Howell, celebrated slayer of frog-eaters and Saracens, going over another man's shopping list with a jumped-up peasant of a shopkeeper.

"Ah . . . " said Master Wainwright. He took the list to the open window where he could read it. "Ah . . . Mmm . . . Yes. Well, I see no problems here, except the white wine of course."

"I told him that," Bran said.

The clerk poured more wine into his cup.

"No," Master Wainwright repeated, "I don't see any problems. The usual arrangements?"

"Yes," Bran said, swirling the wine thoughtfully in his cup. "Send a messenger to my lord. We'll send an escort in to pick up the cargo. Hire as many wagons as you think you'll need—but not more than three. You'll be paid upon delivery at Ballinasloe."

"Ah." Master Wainwright looked pained. "I had hoped—well, never mind! Lord Arlen is an honourable man."

"He is that," Bran agreed. He raised his cup. "Lord Arlen."

"To Lord Arlen." Master Wainwright lifted his cup. "And his good lady."

"Hmmm. I'd almost forgot." Bran fumbled in the purse for the smaller scrap of paper. "Here it is. Lady Arlen requires a few things."

Master Wainwright scrutinized the tiny script. "Yes. I have all these things now, if you want to take them with you."

Bran remembered that he had practically no money with him. "That's all right. I don't think there's any great urgency—just pack them along with the rest of the order."

"Very well then." Master Wainwright held out his hand. "I wish you good day and Godspeed. Tell your lord that I will send a man as soon as I have everything in hand. That should be very soon—in two or three weeks, perhaps."

Bran shook his hand. "Thank you. God be with you."

"And you, Sir Bran."

They went back to the stable on Market Street. Sean fretted all the way. He did not want to leave Galway.

"I haven't seen everything," he cried, as Bran paid off the patient hostler.

"We'll be back again within the month," Bran said. "If your mother will let you come."

"She will—"

"And your new lord. Don't be forgetting him."

Sean's face fell. "Ach!" He had forgotten. "He'll let me come, won't he?" the boy pleaded.

Bran laughed at him. "You'll have to ask him. You'll do whatever he tells you, he's your lord now. You have . . . obligations."

Sean's face twisted into a puzzled frown. "What're those?"

"By God, boy—you'll find out!"

Bran started to saddle the black horse, chuckling to himself. Obligations. In a way, he had fettered the boy. Still, there were rewards to be had from bending one's neck to the yoke. And he had seen to it that it was a mighty loose yoke at that.

When they passed Fellbrigg's castle, Bran craned his neck for a better look. His right eye was very cloudy today. Yes, something had changed, something was wrong. Three of the huts on the steep slope below the gate were burnt-out shells. Reivers, then. Rebel bandits. He thought instantly of Conor-In-Iron. There was still a faint haze of smoke hanging over the burned huts. It must have happened after they had passed on their way to the town, probably that very night. What if the rebels had caught him on the road, alone with Sean? His heart pounded. He felt sick. Stupid to travel without an escort. Times had been too easy, making everyone—making him too slack.

He wondered if he should ride up to the castle and see how things were. No, he thought. Fellbrigg's bound to have sent a messenger to Arlen already.

"What's wrong?" Sean asked.

"Nothing. Nothing at all."

Arlen was standing at the window looking out when Bran came in. Bran glanced quickly over at the massive bed. The curtains were drawn open. There was no sign of Lady Alysoun.

"My lord," Bran said.

Arlen turned. "I'm glad you're back, Captain. Very glad."

Bran nodded. "I'm glad to hear it."

Arlen smiled briefly. "Well—" he sighed, resuming his worried look, "I had a messenger from Sir Robert Fellbrigg yesterday. His demesne was attacked by a small band of rebels, right outside the castle walls. Nothing too serious—a couple of huts burned, some cattle driven off, two of his English serfs killed—thank God it wasn't worse. Still, we've all got reason enough to worry . . . " he paused, looking away.

"Yes?" Bran felt distinctly uncomfortable.

"His Irish serfs say it was Conor-In-Iron."

"Ah," Bran said. He looked meaningfully at the flagon of wine on the table. Arlen winced impatiently and motioned for Bran to help himself. He did.

"Yes," Arlen was saying, "Young Conor again—bloody damn fool! His father, the O'Kelly, is such a reasonable man, a peaceful man—"

Bran laughed. He swirled the wine in his cup. "His father, the O'Kelly, is getting old. He's already killed his full share of Englishmen, Irish too. I hear he was a devil on horseback when he was Conor's age. Like father, like son."

"Well . . . " Arlen frowned. "That may be so. What do you recommend I do?"

Bran took a deep breath and thought for a moment.

"Send word to the O'Kelly. He'll raise your black rent, but maybe it will do some good. On the other hand, maybe it won't. Conor hasn't got enough men with him to attack the castle, or even the village, but he'll probably try for a couple of the farms. He'll want to stir up just enough trouble to recruit some of his father's people—youngbloods spoiling for a fight—and maybe some of the O'Flahertys too."

"I'll leave it up to you," Arlen said. "Whatever you think best."

"Very well, my lord."

Bran went to his chamber and sat down on the hard bed. Weak morning sunlight showed through the long slit in the wall. He put his head in his hands and massaged his temples. Fionna. He wanted to be back at the Bird In Hand, lying in bed with her, feeling her warmth next to his body.

She had not wanted him to go so soon, had practically begged him to stay, and that was not like her. But it was enough that he had stayed the night. He and Sean had arrived at the tavern very late. Sean had been asleep, nodding over his saddle the past couple of hours. Bran lifted the sleeping boy from his saddle and carried him past Fionna into the kitchen. He squatted down painfully, stiff from the long ride, and laid Sean on his pallet near the bread ovens.

The boy stirred. "Wh-what is it?" he asked grumpily, rubbing the sleep from his eyes.

"Go to sleep," Bran said, settling the blankets over him. The boy closed his eyes again.

Bran straightened up slowly. "God, he's heavy."

She came up and put her arms around him.

"I was worried," she said, her voice muffled against his chest. She had heard about the raid. Clonmacnois had sent a monk to tell her about it. Bran said that was very Christian of them. He stroked her hair. She clung to him like a child. He had decided to wait until morning to go to Ballinasloe. There was nothing he could do before then, anyway. They had gone to bed and fallen asleep in each other's arms without making love.

The light in the window slit was getting brighter. Bran stood up and arched his back, hearing the pop and crackle with grim satisfaction. It was not going to be a good day; there was nothing much he could do about that. He felt very lonely.

There was a knaggin of whiskey in the chest at the foot of his bed. He held the little wooden bottle to his ear and shook it. About half full. He shut the chest lid and sat on it, popping the knaggin's stopper free with his thumb.

An hour later he was feeling merry enough. The whiskey

glow in his head and chest helped give him a brighter perspective on things.

He started down the cramped, cold stairwell with the thought of taking a walk around the top of the bawn wall. There would be a fair bit of sun in the sky, and the sight of it would do him good.

A delicate, melodious tinkling reverberated up through the stairwell from the floor below. Matty's harp. He followed the sound down the steps and across the shallow landing to the soldiers' common room. He thrust back the leather curtains.

The music stopped.

Matty looked up from his harp, a surprised smile on his face. Bowyer and three more of the younger troopers sat on stools and rough benches nearby. Bran's whiskey elation started to dissipate. He felt like an intruder. Bowyer and the others nodded at him, murmuring polite greetings under their breath.

"Well met, friend," Matty said in Welsh. "How goes life in the wicked town?" He laughed.

"Wickedly," Bran said. "Don't stop playing."

"As you command, honoured sir. What shall I play?"

"The one about the two sisters. You know."

Matty stroked his beard. "Mmm. The older, dark-haired sister kills the fair, younger one, to get her out of the way so she can marry the handsome knight who's been mooning around their castle. A charming tale. Shall I sing it in Welsh?"

"Yes. Is there any wine?"

Bowyer set a cup of wine into his hand. Bran grunted at him. He shoved one of the benches closer to the wall and sat down. Matty sang the song beautifully in Welsh, which was better suited to the music than French. Bran relaxed against the wall, drinking steadily from the cup. The others could not understand the Welsh, still they were rapt. The words sounded almost strange to Bran. He thought in French most of the time. It made him feel young to hear the lilting, familiar words— but strange too. He tilted up the cup and let the last bitter drops run into his mouth.

He held out his cup. "More wine."

Something about the old man's overly pleasant manner made Arlen nervous. The O'Kelly sat across the table from him drinking excellent mead and making amusing conversation on many different subjects. None of them concerned his son Conor. Arlen was beginning to feel irritated, but he had gone through this before with the O'Kelly. It was a ritual of sorts, very Irish.

The O'Kelly would never come to Arlen's castle, and the day was too wet to meet in the open, so now he sat in the O'Kelly's hall with the Welsh captain standing behind his chair. Arlen felt safe enough. Six more of his men stood around the hearth, mingling warily with some of the O'Kelly's household kernes. No armour was worn, but everyone had weapons. Arlen did not think there would be any trouble. Still, the old man made him nervous.

"It's a filthy day," the O'Kelly said for the third or fourth time. He smiled at Arlen.

"It is such," Arlen agreed in his bad Irish.

The O'Kelly gestured to his servant to refill Arlen's cup. While the O'Kelly discussed the relative merits of stallions over mares, Arlen covered his growing irritation behind the fresh cup of mead. It was strong stuff, thick but not overly sweet like the meads he'd had in England as a boy. He realized that he was getting a little drunk. No doubt the O'Kelly had planned that too. The Welsh captain was uncharacteristically sober though. His men weren't drinking much either. They were ready to fight their way out if they had to.

As the O'Kelly talked, Arlen nodded and mumbled at polite

intervals, barely understanding anything. He hadn't picked up much Irish in four years. His lips were sticky from the mead. The O'Kelly asked after the health of the English king.

Bran tapped Arlen's shoulder. "He says how is the young king, my lord."

"Yes. Yes, I understood that," Arlen said in French. "Tell him that King Richard is well and very powerful and that sort of thing. Richard is my name too, tell him that."

"That will impress him," Bran said. He relayed what Arlen had said to the O'Kelly.

The O'Kelly expressed his delight at the young king's health and hoped that ruling such a powerful nation was not proving to be too much of a strain.

"Not at all," Arlen lied. "He's his father's son all right." It was a pity that the Black Prince had died so young, worn out by disease. The news from England was not very good. The O'Kelly would be unlikely to know that.

"Ask him about Conor," Bran said.

"All right," Arlen said, relieved. "You ask him. Courteously."

Bran chuckled grimly. "Of course, my good lord." He asked.

The O'Kelly stopped smiling. Picked up his cup and fingered the rim. He looked at Bran, then at Arlen, stroking his beard like a sage.

"It is very difficult," he told Arlen.

"I understand," said Arlen. He did not seriously expect the O'Kelly to betray his own son.

"Ask him for hostages," Bran said in French.

"No," said Arlen. They had discussed this before. He did not think the O'Kelly would give him hostages. "He won't do it. I don't want to anger him."

Bran shook his head. "Ask him anyway. My lord."

"All right," Arlen agreed, feeling heavy and defeated. "Ask him then." He drained the potent mead in his cup, welcoming the thought-numbing solace it offered.

Bran asked the O'Kelly for hostages. Arlen watched the O'Kelly's face. The broken veins in the old man's cheeks became livid. Arlen thought that the O'Kelly would explode. He reached under the table for the comforting grip of his swordhilt, wishing he had not drunk so much. But the O'Kelly did not explode. He did not wish to give up any hostages either, he told Arlen politely through Bran. The O'Kelly made an effort to relax back into his throne-like chair, placing his hands carefully on the ends of the armrests. Arlen looked at the old man's hands. They were wide and scarred and he could see that the knuckles had been broken many times. He clenched his own hands in his lap, knowing them to be smooth and soft, well protected by glove and gauntlet all his life.

"I see," said Arlen, searching for something to say. It was the Welshman's fault that he was in this position now, and he resented it very much.

"Still, something must be done . . . " Bran said to him in French, prompting Arlen as if he were some shave-pate priestling fumbling through his catechism.

Arlen sighed heavily. "All right, Captain. Tell him . . . tell him I want Conor gone from these lands. That's what I pay him for— peace. With Conor, there is no peace, and without peace, I won't pay his black rent. Tell him that."

Bran moved beside him and rested his hand on the back of Arlen's chair. "I will, my lord," he said with increased respect.

Arlen felt stronger, more alert. "Yes, tell him that, Sir Bran."

Bran told the O'Kelly what Arlen had said, and it was clear that the old man did not like it very much. He frowned and plucked his beard, mumbling half-understood phrases about "hospitality taken advantage of" and "agreements in good faith." Arlen was surprised that the O'Kelly was not so angry as he had expected him to be. In fact, he seemed to be rather embarrassed by it all. He *had* made an agreement with Arlen in good faith, and he wasn't living up to it very well. Arlen was relieved to find that the O'Kelly took his end of their dirty little pact so seriously.

With much throat clearing and placatory reassurances, the O'Kelly concluded their interview, looking very uncomfortable. Behind the serious face he wore, Arlen was smiling. He was beginning to enjoy himself, but it would be dangerous to linger.

Bran wound up their side of it by thanking the O'Kelly for his hospitality and help— which he hoped would be soon forthcoming. The O'Kelly assured him that it would be. Something would be done. Arlen believed him, although exactly *what* would be done was left unspecified. When he stood up to leave, Arlen was a little unsteady from the mead, but he covered this by swaggering to the door, with the Welsh captain close behind.

Outside it was not raining very hard. A "soft" rain, the Irish called it, a gentle misting that was more refreshing than wet. Arlen climbed onto his horse's back, glad to be going. A black-haired girl watched him from the doorway of a round hut near the hall. He smiled at her. She smiled back uncertainly, looking around to see if anyone had noticed. Such a lovely young girl, Arlen thought. She did not really look like Alysoun at all, but he began to feel very sad all the same. He wanted to hold the girl and be loved by her. After so many years alone, it was ridiculous that he needed love so much now that he was married. It was unmanly. He preferred the life he had led in France, where it did not matter at all. There he had made it a point to buy a woman at least once every month, for his health. So many women, but none of them had mattered very much, even the two or three he had seen fairly regularly. Like any young knight he had fallen madly in love with the wives of his superiors, and other unattainable noblewomen, but that was something different. A clean love, untainted by lust. Well, almost. He *had* burned for a certain Aquitanian baroness . . . Philippa. Philippa de . . . the surname eluded him. Husband newly dead, a large estate . . . it was no wonder he was interested, but he loved her. In the end he had been ashamed to do more than mildly flirt with her, having no prospects of his own.

"My lord," Bran said suddenly. "The men are ready. We should leave now."

The black-haired girl disappeared into the hut. "Yes. Yes, of course," Arlen said, sick at heart. He wondered what kind of husband Philippa had found for herself.

As they rode toward the gate, Arlen said, "What do you think, Sir Bran? Will he pull Conor's teeth?"

"I hope we find him first," Bran replied. "I'd like to pull them myself. Permanently."

Arlen frowned. "That we don't need. It would mean open war with the O'Kelly."

"I'm not so sure," said Bran, reining back his horse to let Arlen through the gate first.

Arlen ducked under the low timber arch and looked back over his shoulder. A young kerne stood on the thick stone wall, looking down at him. Impulsively, Arlen raised his hand in a salute. The kerne nodded slightly, leaning with both hands on his long spear.

Bran had pulled alongside him again. He was looking at the kerne too, with a hard face. "They're undisciplined bastards, the Irish," he said. "Plenty of courage, but no discipline."

"Do they make bad soldiers?" Arlen asked, not really interested.

"No," Bran said carefully. "They're good soldiers. Don't ask me why."

"Ah," Arlen said, thinking about the black-haired girl. She couldn't have been more than sixteen. So lovely . . .

Fionna banked the hearth fire and said good night to them. Bran tipped the dregs of the second flagon into Matty's cup and pulled the third one across to fill his own. They drank passionately but without joy. Bran gulped down half of the fresh cup and set it down carefully. "Just how long do you think it can go on?" he said flatly. There was an edge of bitterness in his voice.

Matty looked up, blinking stupidly. "What?" He wiped his mouth on his sleeve and looked down at his cup. "Oh," he said, "that again— Why don't you leave it alone?"

"He'll come out of this spell your pretty witch has cast over him and he'll kill you!"

"I know." Matty sighed, hiding his face in the winecup.

Bran slammed his cup down. Wine jumped from the cup, wetting the back of his hand. "Damn it, man! If you know, do something about it!" Bran's voice dropped almost to a whisper. "I need Arlen. He relies on me to keep his men and his castle and his lands in order . . . And I rely on him . . . " Bran coughed. "And I rely on him to reward me for this good service I'm doing him. I've got nothing to sell, Minstrel, no pretty songs or flattering stories or sweet music to send the lords off to sleep while you're preparing to swive their ladies. Do you understand?"

Matty nodded grimly. "Yes."

Bran refilled his cup from the flagon and held it tightly in his hand, swirling the wine close to the edge. He watched the wine swirling in his cup. He did not want to look at Matty Groves. "You can't keep tupping his ewe forever," Bran said. "He'll find out and he'll have your ballocks boiled and fed back to you." He flicked the wine from the back of his hand. His sleeve was sodden with the spilt wine. He was breathing hard, like he'd been fighting. It was the wine.

"I'm sorry," Matty had said. His eyes were sad. Merry Matty Groves. Bran looked away, felt the wine stain spreading in his sleeve.

Conor snatched a burning stick from the fire and held it up to the cave mouth, his dagger out and ready.

"It's only me," said Ulick, staggering with fatigue. The big man hunched down to avoid the sharp rocks that hung from the low ceiling. He sat down by the fire and slumped against the wall, his eyes shut.

"Did you find them at all?" Conor asked, fearing the answer.

"I did," Ulick said. "Shane and his brother both. They say they won't come back."

"Damn them," Conor said grimly. "Damn them both to hell."

Ulick opened his eyes and looked up at him. "Don't say that. They're our friends. It's not right to curse them so."

"Not my friends. Nor yours. They'd be better off dead than going home with their tails between their legs, crying of their empty bellies."

Ulick sighed. "They're young, both of them. They've had enough of hardship in the time they've been with you, Conor."

Conor raised his eyebrows. "So? Is it youth that makes them forget their comrades, to forsake all we've been fighting for?"

"More starving than fighting, lately," Ulick said. "They're young, that's all."

Conor laughed, a short, bitter bark. "We were young too. It wasn't that long ago, Ulick." He turned to look at his friend. Ulick was asleep, chin sunk forward onto his great chest.

A blanket-wrapped bundle stirred on the other side of the fire. Conor walked over and prodded it with the tip of his boot.

"Eh, Padraig?" Conor said.

A low groan came from the bundle. "Is the sun up, now?"

Conor chuckled. "It is not. Are you so anxious to get up and gather more firewood?"

A hand appeared in the opening at one end of the bundle and pulled the edge of the blanket down. Padraig's pale, sunken face peered out, blinking at the firelight.

"I am not," Padraig said. "It's just that I'm too hungry to sleep." The last more an accusation than a statement.

Conor, sighed, shaking his head slowly. "Can you think of nothing but your belly? Can you *speak* of nothing but your belly?"

Padraig pulled the blanket back over his face. "I'm hungry," he whined. "Soon I'll be famished altogether, Conor."

Conor turned and faced the fire. "I'm hungry too," he said to himself, too softly for Padraig to hear.

He sat down by Ulick, with his boots almost touching the fire. Ulick slept soundlessly, completely still, as if he were dead. They all did, all the old fighters. All gone now. Conor hugged his knees, staring into the fire. Gone to hell or gone home, it did not matter. In the spring he would go farther south, raise more men. No one wanted to join him during such a hard winter. They were all too soft, content to take Norman gold instead of Norman blood. It was a game to most of them, and when things got hard, they went home. It was that simple.

Sean could hardly believe his good fortune. Lord Arlen was the kindest, most noble man he had ever met. Even Sir Bran paled a bit by comparison. He still liked Sir Bran very much, but Lord Arlen was a real knight, with his own castle, and the Black Prince had been his friend. And now Sean MacTieg was page to Lord Arlen of Ballinasloe. His work at the tavern—drawing ale, fetching out food from the kitchen, cleaning up—seemed pretty paltry to him now. If only he could live at the castle full time ... but his mother would never agree. Even Sir Bran was no help there. She would never agree—

He threw down the rag he'd been using to polish Lord Arlen's breastplate. Damn! Damn! It was enough to make a man weep! Perhaps in a year or two she would come around, change her mind. Except for Sir Bran's pleading his case so strongly, he would not be here at all. Sir Bran was on his side, he knew what was best.

Sean picked up the rag and continued rubbing away on the tiny rust spots on the breastplate. The rest of Lord Arlen's armour was strewn about him, waiting to be cleaned and oiled. It was a privilege to do this, he realized, a great privilege. Sad Hugh—*Sir* Hugh had told him that the complete harness had cost Lord Arlen more than thirty pounds in silver. It was almost impossible to imagine that much money. He did not think his mother's tavern, with her entire stock, was worth that much money. It was incredible. But that was the way of a true knight like Lord Arlen, no stinting where the truly important things— horses, weapons, and armour—were concerned.

Lord Arlen treated him almost like his own son. He was certainly more considerate and interested than MacTieg had ever been. Sir Bran even. Lord Arlen taught him about heraldry, and falconry, and the different names used in the hunt, about the tournaments he had been to, and the famous men that he had known and fought.

Sean poured some oil onto the cloth and spread it over the surface of the steel, buffing it with all his strength to a shiny blue gleam. He leaned it against the wall and pulled the backplate across his knees. There were scratches along the bottom where it had scraped against the studded cantle of the saddle. He rubbed furiously, but the scratches only got brighter. His arm ached. He had to remember to rub all the leather straps with the animal fat Mark Bowyer had given him. Mark was English, but he did not seem so bad. Sean liked him. He knew that Sir Bran did not, and that puzzled him. He could not see any reason for it. That was nothing new though; Sir

Bran was becoming more and more difficult to understand. Sometimes he would be very friendly and fun to be with—and then suddenly he would become like another person altogether, cold, cruel, and . . . Sean was actually afraid of him in those times.

Lady Alysoun was a strange one too. She was kind to him in an offhand, unconcerned way. Sometimes Sean felt he was invisible around her, the way she seemed to look right through him as if he weren't there. He knew that Lord Arlen loved her very much, so Sean always did his best to please her, but she hardly seemed to notice. She was very beautiful. Perhaps that was what beautiful women did.

The backplate was not rusted so badly. The scratches bothered him though. He would ask Mark Bowyer if there was some way he could get them out.

"Yes, what is it, Captain?" Arlen looked up from the stack of tally sheets that Sad Hugh was trying to explain to him.

"It can wait, my lord, if you're busy," Bran said, feeling particularly diplomatic.

Arlen made a weak smile. "No, no, Captain. Any distraction from this—" he scattered the papers with his hands "—rubbish is more than welcome." Sad Hugh took a step back, resentful of them both.

"My lord, I was wondering—"

"It's not like you to wonder, Captain," Arlen said, amused. "What would you have of me?"

"Well, my lord, I was won—" Bran could not help smiling. "May I have your leave to keep company with my . . . with my lady at the Bird In Hand for a few days? While Sean is staying here at the castle. She's not used to being without him—you know how women are, my lord."

Arlen nodded. "Indeed I do. Indeed I do. Well, since she's

been so kind as to supply me with a page, I can hardly object, can I? Go, Sir Bran. Press your suit with the lady. And take my good wishes with you."

"Thank you, my lord."

Bran bowed and left. That was easy, he thought, jouncing lightly down the stairs, as if he were fourteen instead of nearly forty. He'd known there would be no trouble. Arlen would relish a chance to be truly in command, sure to be a rare feeling since he had taken Bran into his service. Ah well, Bran thought, it will benefit us both, then. It was better that way, but not essential.

Two days after Bran left the castle, Lord Arlen found himself alone in his bedchamber, staring out the open window, as he did far too often now. Too much time on his hands. He couldn't even get Hugh to play chess with him, not that that was such a great challenge. The man was no part of a knight at all, Arlen decided. A harsh thought, yes, but true. Hugh was a good enough clerk all right, a master clerk, but he had nothing of the knight in him.

Arlen felt very alone. It had always been his dream to be landed and have a title, like his brother, like the great men he admired, but at times—like now—he felt like giving it all up, taking to the road with armour and weapons and a few good men—back to France. Back to freedom.

"Phaugh!" Arlen slammed his fist into the wall. The sudden violence of his action startled him. He held up the injured hand—the knuckles were split, bleeding. He looked around, feeling foolish. Alysoun was in the solar with the harper. She spent far too much time with that man . . . still, Arlen thought, I should be grateful. Otherwise there is nothing here for her. Nothing. The harper would be leaving soon. He did not know what he was going to do when the harper was gone. He knew he had no great skills at courtly phrases and pretty speeches of love. The Black Prince had, he was a master in the bower as well as in the field. Those things came naturally to him, as did everything, seemingly. But Arlen knew he was not like that.

She slipped up behind him as he cradled his bleeding fist in his other hand, hissing air through his clenched teeth, trying not to weep.

"My lord? Is something the matter?"

"Ah, my lady," he said, struggling to compose himself. It was enough that he had not the art to please her, he must not appear to be weak as well. "I didn't hear you come in."

"I have a light tread, my lord. You've remarked on it yourself."

"So I have."

"You've hurt yourself!" Alysoun took hold of his hand and raised it up to the light.

He pulled it out of her gentle grasp, ashamed.

"I fell," he lied.

"You should be more careful, my love."

She does care for me, he thought, absurdly happy. Impulsively he tilted her face up and kissed her.

"I do love you, Alys."

She pulled away, giggling nervously. "Of course you do, silly. I'm your wife!"

"To my great, good fortune," Arlen said, meaning it.

"I know what you need," she said huskily, stepping closer.

She swept her arm dramatically, taking in the room, the entire castle. "To get out of here for a while. It would do you so much good. You haven't been hunting for weeks."

"I know—"

"I've got an idea! Why don't you go and see Sir Robert? You've said yourself that he's got some of the finest hunting in Galway—and one of the finest packs too!"

"Yes, but—"

"But nothing, my lord!" Her eyes flew open wide, as if an idiot could see the truth of what she was saying. "Didn't Sir Bran say it was best to make a show of force in the area, with all these rebels about? I'm sure Sir Robert would appreciate a visit from his overlord, especially now. You could go hunting together and talk about his son coming here next year—talk about all sorts of things."

"You've become very bold, my lady," Arlen said fondly. "Not quite the shy maid I married."

Alysoun laughed. "No longer a maid, sir, in any case!"

He felt himself blushing. "Very well, my lady. But what about Sir Bran? I'll have to call him back to take command of the castle . . . "

"Not at all. Sir Bran is less than an hour's ride away, where he can be easily reached if necessary. Besides, Arnulf will keep the men together in his absence, you know that. Stop trying to think of reasons not to go. You have a duty to Sir Robert Fellbrigg—you may think me young, but I know that much."

Arlen knelt before her. "My duty is to you, my lady."

He felt her cool hands on his forehead.

"You're very sweet, sir," she said soothingly. "But you know that is not entirely true. Go to Sir Robert. Your vassals look to your strong support and guidance in these perilous times. Go to him."

The wind's cold fingers ruffled through Sean's hair as he rode behind Arlen, spurring the fat pony mercilessly in a desperate attempt to keep up with Arlen's sleek Arab-bred hunter. A wall of thicket rose up before them—Arlen's horse took it effortlessly, flying lightly over and shooting away with an added burst of speed when it touched ground on the other side.

Sean prayed out loud, "Please God, please God, please . . . "
The fat pony made a terrific, impossible leap—the thicket sailed
past below them. The impact was incredible; Sean was flung
forward, hanging onto the pony's neck for dear life. In the next
instant, his bottom slammed down onto the hard spine of the
saddle. He howled, but held on grimly, keeping the pony's head
aimed at the waving tail of Arlen's horse far ahead of them.

Other horsemen crashed through the woods alongside of
Sean, blowing their curved hunting horns, yelling
encouragements to the loudly belling hounds. His blood felt as
if it were on fire; he had never been so excited, so wildly alive.

He kept his face pressed to the pony's sweating mane.
Branches raked his back; he felt his tunic rip and he didn't
care. The man riding off to his right caught a branch in the
chest and was plucked neatly off his horse. The hounds were
baying more loudly now, and he could hear individual barking
and snarling and high-pitched yelps. This was his third day of
hunting and already he knew what that sound meant—the
hounds had brought the wolf to ground. It would fight now,
having nothing to lose, and a man would have to kill it before it
injured too many of the hounds.

The pony tried to veer off to avoid the milling confusion of
horsemen and snapping hounds forming around the wolf. Sean
whipped him brutally with the reins, forcing the pony between
two taller horses. He wanted to see the wolf. It was the second
they had killed that day. The first was a she-wolf. She'd made
a very clever attempt to lead them miles away from her cubs,
but after Sir Robert had finished her, they had returned and
found the cubs anyway. Sean thought it poor sport to kill them,
but Lord Arlen had explained that they would grow up and take
sheep otherwise, and calves too. There seemed no limit to Lord
Arlen's store of wisdom and good advice.

One of the horsemen he was wedged between pushed his arm
against Sean's chest. It was Mark Bowyer. "I wouldn't go any

closer," he said, a wry half-grin on his face. There was a long scratch across his cheek from a branch.

"I want to see," Sean said stubbornly.

"You can see well enough from here. It's almost finished now."

Lord Arlen was on foot with a heavy boar spear in his hands, balanced to strike. The wolf shook off the last of the hounds and sprang at him, spraying bloody foam from its jaws. Arlen thrust the lugged spearhead into the wolf's throat and twisted it to the ground.

"Well struck, sir!" shouted Sir Robert. The huntsmen cheered, blowing their horns in a deafening cacophony that made Sean's head reel.

The dying wolf writhed pitifully, stuck fast to the ground by Arlen's spear, working its jaws weakly as the hounds moved in to tear it apart. Sean looked away. This was the mate of the she-wolf they had killed earlier in the day. It was better this way, Sean reasoned. Wouldn't he be lonely without her? The pony trembled against his knees. Sean reached down and patted its neck. He would kill the poor beast, running it so hard. He needed a proper horse for hunting. Maybe Lord Arlen would get him one.

Sir Robert's houndmasters had caught up and were beating the hounds back into a pack. Sir Robert himself dismounted and cut off the wolf's ears, presenting them to Lord Arlen on a clean napkin. "For your lady, my lord."

"God's blood, my lord, I think not!" Lord Arlen shouted above the din. Both knights laughed.

"Do you know, sir," Sir Robert said, smiling, "I believe we are in your demesne now. Isn't that your keep showing through yonder break in the trees? There—to the left . . . "

Arlen clapped the other on the shoulder. "By God, sir, it is! You're my guest now— Sean! Come here, boy!"

Sean flung himself off the pony's back and ran over to Arlen. Arlen grinned at him, looking faintly foolish, Sean thought. It shocked him to think such a thing of his lord. "Yes, my lord?"

"Do you see the castle? Over there . . . it's about three or four miles off. Go and tell my lady to make everything ready for my honoured guest, Sir Robert Fellbrigg—"

"My lord," Sir Robert interrupted, "I must protest! If I brought a guest to my wife so close to dark, so completely unexpected, I would fear for his life—and mine too!"

Arlen nodded, looking relieved. "I take your meaning, sir. We'll camp here tonight and go on to Ballinasloe tomorrow morning. Sean, go and tell my lady to expect us on the morrow, and give her my . . . give her my compliments."

"Yes, my lord!" Sean started to go.

"Sean!" Arlen said sharply.

Sean turned, puzzled, afraid he'd done something wrong. Perhaps he should have bowed before taking his leave. "Yes, my lord," he said, expecting a rebuke.

Arlen's face was kind. "It's almost dark. Perhaps you should have someone along with you."

"Oh no, my lord!" Sean cried, insulted. Really, he wasn't a baby!

"There may be rebels about. Maybe even another wolf or two," Arlen said playfully.

"I'm not afraid of them." Sean drew the dagger Sir Bran had given him.

"Plucky lad," said Sir Robert approvingly. "He'll make a fine squire."

"Yes," Arlen agreed. "All right, be off!"

Sean leapt back onto the pony's back. The sun was already setting, colouring the sky with vivid bloody streaks. The full moon was rising, a pale ghost now, but it would make a fine lantern to light his way to the castle in the dark. He was not afraid, he told himself; it was only four miles cross-country. He would be snug and safe in an hour or less.

"Get up, now!" he told the pony, digging in his heels.

Bran was dozing over his mug of ale like an old man when Fionna came to wake him.

"Let's go to bed," she said. He got up and leaned on her shoulder.

"Aye, let's do that," said Bran. He was so sleepy he kept walking into things. Once inside the bedchamber he felt safe enough, even in the dark, but Fionna had moved the blanket chest earlier in the day so he managed to bark his shin against it. Bran staggered to the wall, holding his knee up in exaggerated pain, laughing helplessly. He was more than a little drunk, and if he wasn't so damned sleepy he'd drink more.

"Shush now, you'll wake Sean," Fionna said. "Ach, no," she caught herself, "he's not here, is he?"

Bran could feel her frowning in the dark. "It would take the Last Trump to wake him," Bran said, trying to pull off one of his boots. He hopped over to the bed with the boot half off and sat down hard enough to rattle the frame.

"So much talk in you," Fionna clucked. "You never talk when you're sober; why do you plague me when you're drunk?" She knelt before him and pulled the boot all the way off. He lay back lazily on the bed, lifting his other leg in the air. She yanked that boot off, then started to undress. Bran's eyes had adjusted a little to the dark, so he could see her as well as he wanted to, the moonlight gleaming on her skin.

The shutter was open all the way, letting in the cold night air, but he liked that. He liked snuggling up against her under the heaped blankets, sharing their warmth like children. The night air was supposed to be bad for you, but he had slept in the open more often than under a roof, and so far had taken little harm from it. He reasoned that an open shutter for the night probably would not kill him, though he knew she would get up and close it later when he was asleep.

Fionna slipped in beside him. Bran threw his arm across her, idly stroking a nipple. They were both too sleepy to make love. She wriggled against him and laid her head in the crook of his arm. He started to say something to her but she was already asleep.

As Sean raced back to Lord Arlen's camp, his heart near to bursting with excitement and terror, the awful scene he had witnessed in Lady Alysoun's bedchamber kept repeating itself over and over in his mind's eye.

The massive curtained bed standing like a tomb in the midst of flickering candle-shadow . . . But this was no tomb, for he could hear the muffled moans and rustlings of the creatures within, who were very much alive.

Pulling back the curtain a little he saw . . . a man and woman in seeming torment, hopelessly intertwined.

In that brief shocked glimpse he had been unable to see where one began and the other left off—a hideously deformed monster with too many arms and legs. The sounds that it made froze his blood.

The creature groaned loudly, mumbling obscenities and endearments with the same rasping breath—it seemed that the Devil himself was in that bed. But in his half-comprehension he'd realized that the monster was human enough. The woman was Lady Alysoun. The man's face he could not see. He had stood for a moment, trembling, feeling very much the small boy he was, the manly dagger in his belt quite forgotten.

He turned and ran then, having decided that his lady was not being attacked by some ravening beast of a madman.

Without grasping the full import of what he had seen, he knew that something was wrong, horribly wrong, and he had to tell Lord Arlen about it. Lord Arlen would know what to do.

Sean's mind snapped back into the present. Ahead he could see tents shining in the moonlight through the black web of trees.

He burst through into the clearing. Men ran at him shouting, waving swords. One of them grabbed at the pony's reins. A flaring torch was thrust up in front of his face—

"It's MacTieg's brat!"

Rough hands hauled him out of the saddle. Lord Arlen was there suddenly, looming over him.

"What's the matter, boy? Is it the rebels, are they attacking?"

As Sean looked reluctantly into Arlen's face, somehow he knew that Arlen knew that it wasn't the rebels at all.

"Faster, faster!" Lord Arlen shouted back at them.

Sean's pony was close to foundering. He was falling steadily behind. Sean flogged his neck with the reins; the pony shuddered. It occurred to Sean that they might never be friends again. Still, he could not afford to lag behind. He felt that something terrible was about to happen, and he was compelled to see whatever it might be.

They were near the castle now, the black hulk of the keep showing faintly against the lighter blue of the moonlit sky.

The pony seemed to be catching up to Mark Bowyer's horse, but Sean realized that Mark was dropping back. Before he could wonder about this, Mark drew his hunting horn and blew a tremendous blast in the direction of the castle.

Lord Arlen threw his horse about and rode back to them. He clubbed Bowyer from the saddle.

Everyone had reined up, their horses bunched together on

the narrow path between the trees. Except for the clink of bits and jingling spurs, it was deadly quiet. The men were grim faced. Sean thought that his heart would burst out of his chest.

"Take his horse," Arlen growled. They left Bowyer sitting dazed upon the ground, a bright ribbon of blood streaming from a corner of his mouth.

Alysoun woke with a start from a disturbing dream. She could not remember anything about it, but the bad feeling remained with her. She parted the curtains a little and peeked out into the pitch-dark chamber. Cock-crow was hours away, she realized. Matty stirred beside her. She spread her fingers in the silky patch of fur on his chest. He mumbled something and rolled over onto his side.

"I love you," she whispered, kissing his shoulder. Alysoun snuggled up against his back and was quickly asleep.

It was a dream, it had to be. Alysoun peered through slitted eyelids and saw— the curtains pulled back, someone holding a blazing torch as bright as a hundred suns. Arlen's white ghost-face looking down at them.

It was no dream. She pretended to be asleep—what else could she do? It was up to Arlen to make the first move. She was terrified, but oddly resigned.

She felt Matty's body stiffen. He was awake.

"How do you like my fine soft bed, Minstrel?" Arlen asked in a cold, even voice.

Matty pulled himself into a sitting position, his back braced against the headboard.

"I like it just fine," Matty replied.

"Do you now?" Arlen said, his voice thick with rage. "Do you indeed? And how do you like my pretty bride—does she suit you as well?"

"Very well," Matty said. Alysoun held her breath.

"Well," Arlen said, "she's yours then. But custom demands that we fight first. You'll indulge me in this small matter, surely?"

Alysoun opened her eyes. "No," she said, flinging her thin arm across Matty's chest. "He's unarmed, as you can see!"

Arlen smiled horribly. "Never let it be said that I killed an unarmed man." He drew his broadsword and threw it onto the bed beside them.

A man moved behind Arlen. It was Sir Robert Fellbrigg, Alysoun realized with a shock. She struggled to draw the sheet up over her nakedness.

"Don't do this, my lord," Sir Robert said.

"This does not concern you, sir," Arlen snapped. He handed Sir Robert the torch. As Fellbrigg reached for it, Arlen jerked the knight's sword from its scabbard.

"My lord!" Sir Robert protested.

"I'll return this in just a moment," Arlen said, checking the borrowed blade for balance.

Sir Robert stepped back, shaking his head. Alysoun saw that there were other men in the room—Arlen's hunting party. They stood in a knot near the door, stirring uneasily, unsure of what to do.

"Now, sirrah," Arlen said. "Get out of that bed that you like so well."

"No!" Alysoun shouted.

Matty threw his legs over the side and stood up, naked, holding the sword.

Arlen stepped forward and swung at Matty's head. Matty ducked—Arlen's sword chunked harmlessly into a bedpost. As he wrenched it free. Matty thrust into his side. Arlen spun away, clutching the wound. Alysoun saw blood seeping through his fingers. She hoped he would die.

Arlen bared his teeth at them. "You'll have to do better than that, sirrah," he told Matty. "Just a scrape along the ribs. Let me show you how it's done."

Arlen came closer, torchlight gleaming on his swordblade. Alysoun's eyes blurred with sudden tears. *NoGodpleasehelp.*

Matty stepped back. Arlen's sword shot straight at him with impossible speed. There was a sickening thud. Matty turned to her, already falling . . . Alysoun screamed. Matty fell across the bed like a split sack, bright blood jetting from the gaping slash in his throat. His head struck her knee. She screamed again, afraid that it would come off. Hot blood soaked into the sheets. Alsyoun knelt over him, trying to close the wound with her hands, to hold in the spurting life. His eyes were wide open, staring through her. She knew he was dead.

"You bastard!" she hissed at Arlen.

"How do you like him now?" Arlen asked, standing over her, holding the bloody sword above her shoulder as if he were preparing to knight her.

She looked up at him, not caring any more.

"One kiss from his dead lips is worth ten thousand of yours, my noble, honourable lord." She spat out the last words as if they were vile curses. Then kissed her poor dead Matty full on the mouth. She knew Arlen would kill her now. She wanted him to kill her.

Arlen raised the sword.

Alysoun closed her eyes. She began to say the Hail Mary— "Hail Mary, full of grace—"

But it was too late.

Bran heard a horse come to a skittering halt outside the tavern. He was awake instantly, grabbing for his trews in the dark. Sean's hound yapped wildly and rattled his chain.

"What is it?" Fionna mumbled sleepily.

"Someone's outside. I'll go and have a look."

She sat up in the bed. "I'm going with you."

"No. You stay here." He laced up the trews and headed for the door.

"I'm going anyway," she said. He heard the rustle of her smock as she pulled it over her head.

Sean was outside the main door, with the blown pony shaking and snorting behind him. Bran stuck his sword in the dirt and walked out to him. "What is it?" Bran felt sick inside.

Sean stood rooted to the spot, afraid to come any nearer. His mouth moved without words, as if his tongue had been cut out.

"Well, boy?" Bran shouted, fearful of the answer. He grabbed the frightened boy by the shoulders and shook him hard.

"Stop it! You're hurting him!" Fionna came running up behind him, the loose smock whipping about her legs.

Bran knelt down and stared into the boy's face, still gripping his shoulders. "Damn it, Sean, tell me what's the matter!"

Sean looked away, refusing to meet his eyes.

Bran pushed him back and ran into the tavern to hurry on his clothes.

Since his return from Ballinasloe just before dawn, Bran had sat with his back to the warm hearth, drinking steadily. So far he had vomited twice, but he kept drinking to dull the terrible ache that filled up his entire being.

Getting more whiskey from the stone pitcher, he reminded

himself that all of this anguish was not for his dead friend alone, but mostly for himself. Everything he'd hoped for was lost now, everything. There would be no fief, no brass slab with his name inscribed in Latin inside the little stone chapel that his never-to-be grandson would never build. Those dreams were gone forever, blown away like smoke.

Oh, he'd seen Arlen, and Arlen had been reasonable enough under the circumstances. Bran had thought he might kill Arlen, but when the actual moment came, he'd felt nothing of his original rage and vengeful bloodlust—just a deep, aching emptiness that he still felt, which no amount of alcohol would cure.

Arlen was sorry about killing Bran's friend, but surely Bran could see that he had no choice. Bran agreed that he had none. And it was true, he hadn't. So what point was there in Bran killing Arlen?

He'd seen the bodies laid out on a table top in the main hall, bundled together in the bloody sheets they'd been killed in. Arnulf told him that they were to be buried in the same grave, by Lord Arlen's order— beyond the north wall, near the Old German and Planchard the crossbowman, where their marker would be stolen for firewood, and there would be nothing at all to show that they had ever existed.

And that was how it would be for Bran ap Howell. No brass slab to hold down his bones. Nothing left behind but a pitted suit of plate armour and a dented sword. Not even his name.

He pressed his hand over his face and wept.

In the early afternoon, some soldiers from Ballinasloe came into the tavern. Arnulf was with them. He told Bran that Bowyer had come into the castle on foot, collected his things, and left with hardly a word to anyone.

"On foot?" Bran asked.

"Oh, aye," Arnulf said. "His horse wasn't paid for yet. Arlen offered him one of the packhorses but he said he wouldn't take charity."

"That was well done." Bran nodded his approval. "Did he have any money?"

"I don't know," Arnulf said. "He wouldn't take any of mine."

They drank together in silence. The other men sat far from them, afraid of Bran's black looks.

At sunset, Fionna came up and tried to press food upon them, but Bran refused, as he had done all day. He had no stomach for it. Even the whiskey tasted like ashes in his mouth, but he kept drinking it anyway. When that ran out, he started on wine and threw up again.

When he staggered back inside, there was a meat pie steaming on his table. Arnulf had already eaten part of it, a smear of gravy on his chin, matting the whiskers below.

"It's good, Captain. You should eat something. All this drink on an empty belly will kill you."

"No, it won't," Bran said.

A few hours past midnight Arnulf got up and stretched, and said he was going back to the castle.

"I'll be along in a little while," Bran told him.

Arnulf put his hand on Bran's shoulder. "Now, Captain. Why don't you stay here with your good woman and let her take care of you. There's no point in going back there tonight, no point at all."

Bran shrugged his hand away. He was very drunk, and he had to concentrate to make his words come out right.

"I'm in command here, you whoreson, and I'll decide where I'm going to spend the night, and who I'll spend it with. Now get out of here and leave me alone."

After Arnulf and the other troopers left, there was no one in the tavern. Good, Bran thought, resting his head on the cold table top. He was incredibly thirsty, for water rather than wine, but he did not feel like shouting for Fionna to bring him some. He would probably just throw it up anyway.

He had not seen Sean all day. Fionna had not said where

the boy was, and Bran hadn't asked. Well, that was best all around.

Bran stood up, swaying against the table, banging his knee on the edge of the stool. He hardly felt it. He adjusted the swordbelt over his hips and started for the door, half tripping over one of the benches. It was time to go home.

Fionna came out of the kitchen. "Don't go," she said, pleading with her eyes.

He made a clumsy bow to her, almost falling over. "Thank you for your kind hospitality, Mistress MacTieg. I'll be on my way now."

"Please, Bran . . . "

He stumbled out into the cold night air, to where the black horse had been standing all day, fully saddled.

"Let's go home," he told the horse.

Conor-In-Iron stood at the top of the ravine with his two remaining men. The men were cold and hungry, and daring to grumble about it, particularly Padraig. Padraig was always the troublemaker. The bloodless sack of shit. Conor spat into the ravine to emphasize the thought.

An hour earlier, eight of Arlen's gallowglasses had ridden through in full armour on their way to Ballinasloe. Conor had itched to take them, to kill at least one, or two, but his natural prudence held him back. Perhaps there would be a straggler, but he was beginning to lose hope of that. They would have to be back at their caves in the old hill fort in another hour or so. It would not do to get caught in the open by one of Arlen's patrols in broad daylight, not that this infernal moonlight wasn't bad enough.

"How much longer, Conor?" Padraig whined. "I'm about to fall down dead with hunger—I'm famished to the bone."

"Oh, shut up yourself!" said Ulick, smacking Padraig on

the back of the head. "Do you think you're the only one who's suffering?"

Conor sighed. "We'll go in an hour. Just one hour more." Conor was determined to avenge the death of his friend Matty Groves while his outrage was still fresh. That bastard Arlen, killing a guest in his own house. Well, there'd be at least one shangoll bastard in his grave for that. He would show them, by God . . .

"What's that?" said Ulick, straining forward to hear.

"Quiet!" Conor hissed. "Sounds like a horse," he whispered. Sounds carried far at night.

"Just one, d'you think?" Ulick asked, licking his lips. His broad face gleamed like silver in the moonlight.

"Sweet Jesus," Padraig said in a small voice.

Conor glared at him. He turned to Ulick. "It's just the one, I think. Stay behind the trees as best you can, there's not much cover up here."

"All right," Ulick grunted, trying to angle his massive bulk behind the narrow tree.

"There he is . . . " Conor breathed. "He's not wearing armour."

The lone rider faded in and out of the tree-shadows, moonlight glinting off the weapons in his belt. The black horse brought him steadily closer. It hadn't smelled them yet.

"He's got a sword," Padraig whispered fearfully.

Ulick lifted his cudgel, as thick as a man's arm. "And I've got this."

Conor drew his long dagger. "All right," he said quietly. "Wait for it. Wait for it. Now!"

The black horse reared; Bran felt something slam into his back, blasting the air from his lungs. Another tremendous blow crashed into his ribs, splintering them like dry sticks. He opened his mouth to scream but no sound came out. A sharp length of steel scraped along his hip bone, shredding and spilling his sweetbreads.

His drunkenness was blown away by the sudden intense pain. There were three of them, he noted with his soldier's eye through the red haze of his agony. One of them was trying to pull him off his horse. With a single motion he drew his dagger and ripped across the man's face. The man screamed and fell away.

Bran felt another dagger thrust in his back. And another. He tried to whirl the black horse about to trample that man, but the heavy cudgel whooshed out of nowhere and broke his forearm. The dagger dropped from his nerveless fingers. The cudgel struck again and again—smashing into his chest and shoulder, clipping the bottom edge of his jaw—

He tumbled from the saddle, landing on his back. A man knelt over him and pushed his knee into Bran's chest. He felt another sharp thrust as the dagger struck home.

The pressure on his chest was suddenly gone. He turned his head and saw two men running away, supporting a third between them.

"My eye!" the wounded man screamed in a high-pitched shrill. "My eye! The bastard's taken my eye!"

They dragged the wounded man to the end of the ravine and disappeared into the trees by the side of the road. The man's screams became fainter and fainter until finally Bran could hear nothing at all.

He lay on his back, staring straight up at the dim morning stars. His legs were cold and heavy. He did not think he could move them. If he moved he might fall apart.

The bastards had cut him up pretty badly. He was glad the black horse had gotten away. Probably run back to the tavern. The castle or the tavern—he could not guess which the black horse would run to. If he stayed very still and kept awake, maybe someone would come along the road and find him. His eyelids were heavy. He was afraid to close them, afraid even to blink. He imagined the black horse galloping wildly down the road with the empty saddle on its back.

The cold had reached up into his chest; the pain was not so bad now. They would see the horse and come looking for him. Bran wanted the pain back to help him keep awake.

The sky was lighter. He could not see the stars. Birds sang. The red sun lifted above the trees, shining in his face, blinding him. He closed his eyes.

DAVID WINSTON EGGLESTON
1954 - 1990

David Winston Eggleston was a true Renaissance Man. It is a characterization he would have objected to—*his* primary interest was in the medieval period. A creative writer, in all the best meanings of the term, he wrote not only fiction, but also for magazine features, newspaper, and advertising. As a student of history (especially medieval), he could seldom be faulted for any pronouncement he might make on historical matters. He was a member of the Society for Creative Anachronism (SCA) since university days, and loved participation in medieval fighting tournaments and in historical event reenactments. In his beloved Ireland where he was working as a founding partner in a Dublin advertising agency, David Winston Eggleston died in an accident. He is buried in Galway, a locale of which he was especially fond, and in the area where most of the action of this book takes place.